Also by Maxime de La Falaise (McKendry)

THE SEVEN CENTURIES COOKBOOK

FOOD IN VOGUE

FOOD IN VOGUE

Maxime de La Falaise

illustrated by the author

Doubleday & Company Inc., Garden City, New York

1980

For Loulou and Alexis

Designed by LAURENCE ALEXANDER

Library of Congress Cataloging in Publication Data
Main entry under title:
FOOD IN VOGUE
1. Cookbook   I. Maxime de La Falaise

Copyright © *1942, 1946, 1948, 1950, 1955, 1958, 1960, 1963, 1968, 1969, 1970, 1971,*
1972, 1973, 1974, 1975, 1976 and 1981 by The Condé Nast Publications Inc.
ISBN: *0-385-09220-2*
Library of Congress Catalog Card Number 79-8920

CONTENTS

SECTION II
CELEBRITY RECIPES

Part I

Breakfast / Brunch

CONTENTS   vii

Part III

Dinner

FISH 190

POULTRY AND GAME 198

MEAT 208

VEGETABLE ACCOMPANIMENTS 224

PASTA 231

SALADS AND SALAD DRESSINGS 236

DESSERTS 241

SAUCES 256

Part IV

Supper

SECTION III
VOGUE TWISTS

Culinary Tips for the Busy Cook and Hostess

SECTION IV
MENU IDEAS

Foreword

For the better part of a century (if a century, like valor, can be said to have a better part) *Vogue* has been offering its readers a unique selection of culinary suggestions contributed by artists (Fernand Léger, Louise Nevelson, Andy Warhol, Max Ernst), writers (Truman Capote, Norman Mailer, Colette, George Plimpton), designers (Mary McFadden, Valentino, Ralph Lauren, Bill Blass), actors (Bing Crosby, Katharine Cornell, Bob Hope, Liza Minnelli), and professional cooks (Maurice Moore-Betty, Marion Becker, Julia Child, Craig Claiborne) from about the globe. While this long effort has had the effect of helping to make dining a more pleasant interlude, it has, on reflection, also reinforced the belief that eating habits, like fashion, are willfully subject to social influence. For our idea of a proper menu has gone from Lucullan feasts featuring nine courses to *cuisine minceur,* with a pause for macrobiotic foods, in about the same time it took us to transfer from bloomers to bikinis. Together with this adjustment in intake and outlook (along with gradual relaxation of formality and the withdrawal of servants), a more health-oriented society has drastically changed our whole approach to food. These trends are interesting to monitor in the pages of *Vogue.* When the magazine was founded back in 1892 and formality was in full flower, it was often felt necessary to address that portion of the public who, while not having been born with silver spoons in their mouths, had nevertheless redressed this grievance by amassing through their own wit and cunning not only a lode of silver service, but enough crystal, china and glass to satisfy Louis XIV: "Mr. John C. Furman has recently made a handsome fortune which he apparently proposes to share with his friends" (*Vogue,* December 31, 1892). Unfortunately, unlike vacuum cleaners and chain saws, the directions for proper use by Mrs. Furman of a 180-piece place setting of Spode along with the accompanying 540 Waterford red wine, white wine, and champagne glasses were not included in the package. That information must be "got" elsewhere and so *Vogue* took up the cudgel.

Early on we offered not only hints as to what M'Lady's chef might tackle for the evening banquet, but also the proper method of getting his triumph into M'Lady's mouth: "Soup must be taken from the side of the spoon." Then there was advice on how to set a table: "An oyster fork is placed to the right of any knives and the soup spoon parallel to them"; dress a butler: "Note that a butler always wears white shirts, dull black low shoes and black socks *without clocks*"; how to seat a bishop "softly," along with other sage advice about the arts and mysteries of etiquette as well as insights on entertaining: "Have a Bohemian or two" (*Vogue,* 1893). Still it must have been unsettling work to give a dinner in those days of unrestrained Diamond Jim Brady appetites together with Emily Post's demand for an almost Ming Dynasty refinement in manner. Then Americans began to travel, and the subtlety of the French cuisine, the joy of Italian cuisine, the bravado of the Spanish cuisine (known in *Vogue* as the "Paella Period"), and the robust nature of the German cuisine began to influence our palate. If all goes according to plan we should soon, I suspect, be entering a period, to use the vernacular, of "Eating Chinese."

There is, of course, no dearth of cookbooks to instruct us on the preparation of whatever ethnic cuisine that we may wish to investigate; however, the advantage that this book has stems from the fact that Maxime and *Vogue* have had an entrée to an international clientele who have culled out their favorite recipes from wide culinary experience. The hundreds of recipes in this book reflect that cross-index of lifestyles and nationalities that can come only from a periodical that is at home in five languages and on four continents, together with an author who is herself a citizen of the world. Moreover *Vogue* has been fortunate over the years to be able to tap such talents as Marion Flexner, Ninette Lyon, and Thomas Phipps, alias Joe Carter (he fancied the initials J.C. on his cigarette case), along with many others who have contributed in fact or spirit to the unique quality of this book. But perhaps even more important are the two hundred or more private individuals whose friendship for Maxime is witnessed in the thought and quality of the recipes they contributed.

WILLIAM P. RAYNER
for *Vogue*

SECTION I

VOGUE'S FOOD GAZETTE

While the essence of French gastronomy is to be appreciated in its restaurants and little bistros, the Americans and English best display their culinary skills in the seclusion of their own kitchens and barbecues.

An American's own recipe and menu book, put together by trial and error over the years, is as intimate as a diary and not dissimilar in that many conscientious hosts and hostesses have added the likes and dislikes of their friends (Pat can't stand spinach . . . remember Bill's sweet tooth, make a rich dessert . . . Rita allergic to mussels) and who was served what, when, where, in order not to duplicate the situation. A writer, centuries later, might well reconstruct fascinating patterns of social behavior, entertainment, friendships, and fallings-out by reading between the lines of these notebooks.

American recipes are different from European ones, and are especially interesting in that they are the notations of immigrants and globe-trotters. The French, Italians, Spanish, as well as many other nationalities, prepare almost exclusively their own national cuisine. American food is international and domesticated-ethnic—Brooklyn-Italian, San Francisco-Japanese, Mexico-Texan—and reads like a travelogue. The recipes may come from a Polish mother, Italian father, a Greek nanny and Jewish in-laws, with a trip around the world thrown in.

This food becomes Americanized by the great non-seasonal supply of produce to be found here, and because Americans of all ages, of either sex, of any income or social position get into the kitchen and cook up a meal themselves. They enjoy it. What gets sacrificed in classic techniques and demi-glazed stocks, which only a full-time cook or chef can undertake, gains in individuality, informality, and a pleasantly human quality. The food prepared with friends around is a gift for them, a small ritual, another form of tea ceremony, a creative gesture even where skill is sometimes lacking.

Probably more men cook non-professionally in this country than in any other. This is a guess, based on the recipes sent to me for this book. They do it well and quite imaginatively, and without unnecessary waste of food or action. They are also pretty neat and clean up as they go along. They often spoil themselves enough to have the most attractive kitchens—alchemic laboratories from which they emerge, Merlin-like, to announce the meal.

In this collection of my *Vogue* articles there is, I think, variety and at the same time there is a kind of unanimity. The cooks I interviewed came up with some pretty exotic recipes, but they were all very much alike in their affection for good food.

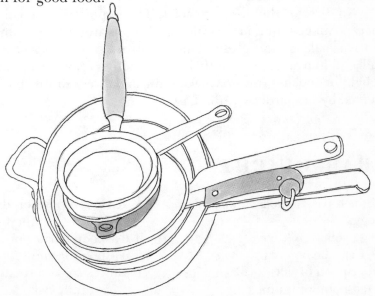

A PICNIC WITH A MOROCCAN DESSERT

Menu

*Buttered thin slices of brown bread rolled around
asparagus spears, lightly cooked and salted*
Crab Quiche☆
Raw vegetable sprigs, lightly seasoned, but no mayonnaise
Imported ham and cold meats, thinly sliced
*Cheeses, including St. Marcellin, wrapped in vine leaves;
and Boursin, either peppered or herbed*
*Moroccan Marmalade with Rose Water☆ served with ice cream
or whipped cream*
Vin rosé or iced mint tea or iced apple juice

NOTES   A happy picnic needs some privacy. Spear the ground with sharpened bamboo poles and on them drape a fragile wall of color with calico or quilts. Tie dried flowers to the poles. On the grass lay Arabian rugs or printed cloth cushions. Baskets and wine bottles can be gypsy-wrapped with cotton kerchiefs.

No dips for the raw vegetables. The imported ham, cold meats, and cheeses can be found in specialty food shops around the country. "Moroccan marmalade" was given to me by two Moroccan sprites, Colette and Stella. In Marrakech one of their grandmothers gave them the recipe. The delight of cooking this marmalade during a weekend is that the house is scented by the gardens of the East.

CRAB QUICHE   SERVES 6

2 8-inch pastry shells, unbaked
2 eggs
1 egg yolk
¾–1 cup heavy cream
¼ teaspoon of salt
⅛ teaspoon of nutmeg
Tiny pinch of cayenne

⅛ teaspoon powdered saffron,
    dissolved in the heavy cream
1 teaspoon curry powder
1 teaspoon Pernod
6 ounces cooked fresh crab meat,
    carefully flaked

Preheat oven to 400°.

Bake the pie shells blind (lined with buttered foil and weighted with dried beans) for 10 minutes, then remove from oven. Remove beans and foil. Lower oven temperature to 350°. Beat the eggs, egg yolk, and cream and saffron together. Beat in the seasonings, then add the crab meat. Pour the mixture into the pie shells and bake 20 minutes, or until the custard is just set. Serve warm.

The quiche can be made a day ahead, refrigerated, and then rewarmed in an oven preheated to 325°.

MOROCCAN MARMALADE WITH ROSE WATER

1 dozen juicy seedless oranges
3 cups sugar, preferably raw
    sugar (at health-food stores)
2 tablespoons cinnamon
1 cup ground almonds

$2\frac{1}{2}$ cups rosé wine
$1\frac{1}{4}$ cups rose water (which can
    usually be found in
    drugstores)

Slice the washed, unpeeled oranges very thin. Fill a thick earthenware casserole with layers of slices, alternating with sprinklings of sugar, cinnamon, and almonds. Add the wine and rose water to cover. Cook without stirring over very low heat (use an asbestos mat under the casserole) for 24 to 48 hours (the time will depend on your container and stove), keeping the casserole covered for at least 18 hours, and adding more mixed wine and rose water if needed to prevent sticking. The marmalade is finished when it is dark and syrupy and the fruit, keeping its form, is completely softened. More sugar may be added during cooking if you wish.

Vogue's Food Gazette, August 1, 1970

COOL IT

Cook in the early morning or in a midnight breeze. The refrigerator doesn't care. Don't plan menus. Plan good food. Who needs more than one or two superior, loved-over dishes plus the best of salads, cheeses, wine? Eat where it's cool and pretty.

Some more delicious cook-and-cool recipes:

SORREL SOUPS, RICH AND LEAN

Oseille to French cooks, *schav* to Yiddish-speaking cooks, sour grass to country kids, bitey, lemony sorrel has one of the freshest tastes in town. Both soups start this way:

Wash 2 pounds of sorrel and remove the coarse stems. Add to 3 cups boiling, salted water. Stir, wilt, cook gently 3 minutes. Drain. Save the cooking broth for diluting the soup.

HINT   Creamy sorrel soup, chilled to the thickness of mayonnaise, makes a good surprise sauce for asparagus or, mixed half-and-half with vinaigrette, it is a delectable salad dressing.

LEAN OR LOW-FAT SORREL SOUP

SERVES 4

2 pounds sorrel, cooked as described above
2 cups chicken broth
1 tablespoon lemon juice
½ cup chopped chives
1 tablespoon well-drained grated horseradish (optional), either fresh or bottled
Salt and pepper to taste
1 cup sorrel broth

Combine the sorrel, chicken broth, lemon juice, ¼ cup of the chives, and the horseradish (if included), and process in a blender until the sorrel is finely puréed. Season with salt and pepper. Dilute with sorrel broth if necessary. Reheat and serve hot, or serve cold, in either case sprinkled with the remaining chives.

RICH AND CREAMY SORREL

SERVES 6

3 small tender-skinned potatoes, unpeeled
2 cups sorrel broth (as given above)
2 cups chicken broth
2 pounds sorrel, cooked as described above
¼ cup chopped fresh dill
1 cup heavy cream
Salt and pepper to taste
4 tablespoons finely chopped prosciutto (imported or domestic)

Scrub the potatoes and cook in the sorrel and chicken broths until soft. Cool slightly. Combine with the sorrel and dill in a blender and process until creamy. Return the soup to the pan and heat gently, then add heavy cream and rewarm. Season with salt and pepper. Serve sprinkled with the chopped prosciutto.

MARIE-PIERRE DE CICCO'S CAVIAR PIE
SERVES 6 TO 8

Mexican beauty Marie-Pierre brought this marvelous pie to Diana Vreeland as a present for lunch.

Crush 8 to 10 hard-cooked eggs through a strainer until completely mashed. Mix with ¾ stick (6 tablespoons) of melted, unsalted butter. Press into a 9-inch Pyrex pie plate. Mask the eggs with a frosting-thick layer of dairy sour cream. Freeze 1 hour. Remove, spread with caviar, preferably fresh (6 to 8 ounces should do; drained red caviar is a good substitute for the costly beluga), and American caviar is delicious. Set until serving time in the fridge. Should be cold, not frozen. Cut and serve like pie.

PORTO FRUIT JELLY
SERVES 8 TO 10

1 cup seedless raisins
1½ cups white port wine
1 heaping teaspoon finely
    chopped preserved ginger
Juice and finely chopped rind (no
    pith) of 2 lemons
Juice and finely chopped rind of
    1 orange
Flesh of 1 ripe melon (musk-
    melon or cantaloupe),

    crushed or chopped
2 envelopes unflavored gelatin
½ cup water
1 cup slivered and blanched
    almonds
3½ additional melons, peeled,
    seeded, and cut into chunks
4 oranges, peeled, seeded, and
    sectioned

Soak the raisins overnight in the port. Next day, combine the ginger, lemon rind, orange rind, and crushed melon and set aside. Soak the gelatin in the water, add the port and raisins, and heat slowly, stirring to dissolve gelatin. Cook over very low flame for ½ hour. Take from heat and add the almonds. Cool to room temperature. Place the cut-up melons and oranges in a serving bowl; pour the wine-gelatin mixture over fruit. Chill until set. Before serving, cut the jelly into crystalline fragments.

BELLISSIMO BELLINI

In Venice at Harry's Bar, its owner, Arigo Cipriani, has a drink called Bellini, an angelic slurp: One to one, freshly pressed peach juice and white sparkling wine. Or champagne . . . why not?

A FROZEN BOWL OF SEASHELLS

Freeze shells into an ice bowl for summer foods. Line a big bowl with shells. Fit a small bowl inside. Pour water between bowls. Freeze. Unmold. Admire.

Vogue's Food Gazette, September 1970

A visit to Alexis de La Falaise in South Wales. Narrow lanes tumbling with honeysuckle, wild roses, foxgloves. A small farmhouse in a valley with a stream. Beyond, the bracken-covered moors. This is apple country, and elderberry; and there are a million good ways of living off the land. For instance:

ELDERBERRY-BLOSSOM PANCAKES

Cut the fresh blossoms from the elder trees. Remove their stems and whip the flowers into a standard pancake batter. Cook the pancakes and serve them with melted butter and honey warmed together.

APPLE CHUTNEY   MAKES 7 TO 8 PINTS

5 pounds tart apples, peeled and
   cored, coarsely chopped
2 pounds (about 4 cups) raw
   sugar (found at health-food
   stores)
2 quarts cider vinegar
2 pounds seedless raisins,
   chopped
1 small onion, minced
1 tablespoon coarsely ground

   black mustard seed if
   available
1 tablespoon coarsely ground
   white mustard seed (or 2
   tablespoons if the black seed
   is not included)
2 tablespoons ground ginger
1 tablespoon salt
2 or 3 pods dried hot red pepper,
   minced

Cook the apples, raw sugar, and vinegar over low heat, stirring often, until you have a smooth purée. Add the rest of the ingredients and bring to a boil. Turn off heat and let mixture stand overnight. Bring to a boil again, put up in clean, hot Mason jars, seal, and process in a boiling-water bath for 10 minutes (for pint jars).

SAVORY BAKED APPLES

Delicious with meat dishes or for luncheon, alone. Core and wash tart cooking apples and fill them with equal quantities of bread crumbs, minced mushrooms, and diced parboiled potatoes, seasoned with a little tomato purée, basil, or thyme. Place in a baking dish with a little water or veal stock; put a dab of butter on each. Bake at 350° until tender, about 45 minutes.

"A GENTLEMAN'S NIGHTCAP"

Mrs. Henry J. Heinz II

In her William Kent House near London, smaller than it seems from the exquisite blond façade—the interior devoured by huge rooms—Drue Heinz offers this treat for guests: Beside each bed a miniature decanter of scotch whisky, a tiny ice bucket—a gentleman's nightcap. The food at the Heinzes' is always a surprise. Here is one of Drue's desserts.

GINGER LOAF WITH LEMON SAUCE

SERVES 6 TO 8

2 cups flour
1 teaspoon baking soda
1 teaspoon ground ginger
½ teaspoon salt
1 stick butter
½ cup raw sugar (found at health-food stores)

2 eggs, separated
½ cup dairy sour cream
½ cup molasses (or Lyle's Golden Syrup if available)
½ cup coarsely chopped preserved ginger with its syrup

Preheat oven to 350°.

Sift the flour, baking soda, and ground ginger with the salt. In a bowl cream the butter until soft. Gradually add the raw sugar and work until the mixture is smooth and light. Beat the egg yolks well and stir them in. Combine the sour cream and molasses (or syrup) and add to creamed mixture alternately with the dry ingredients. Fold in the egg whites, beaten until they are stiff. Fold in the ginger and its syrup. Pour the batter into a well-oiled loaf pan (about 8 by 5 inches). Bake the loaf for 50 to 60 minutes, or until the center is springy when touched. Let it cool in its pan for about 10 minutes, then remove to a rack. Slice it while it is still warm and serve with Lemon Sauce (recipe follows):

LEMON SAUCE

MAKES 1 CUP

⅓ cup sugar
1 tablespoon cornstarch
Pinch of salt
1 cup water
3 tablespoons butter

½ teaspoon grated lemon rind (no pith)
1 to 1½ tablespoons lemon juice
¼ cup chopped preserved ginger

In a saucepan combine the sugar, cornstarch, and salt. Stir in the water, cook the mixture over low heat, stirring constantly, until it is almost clear and slightly thick. Remove from heat and stir in the butter, lemon rind, and lemon juice. Serve warm, sprinkled with the chopped preserved ginger, as a sauce for the ginger loaf.

THE BEAUTY OF STEAM

No added fats, no lost flavors: get a Chinese steamer: Layers of bamboo baskets nesting over a single pan of boiling water. *Slow cookers on the bottom, quickies on top.* Steam stacks of vegetables and save the cooking water in the bottom of the pan. Use it as a soup base or drink it, cooled. As refreshing as fruit juice, the collected gulp of nutrients good for the skin.

Vogue's Food Gazette, October 1970

EATING RUSSIAN AT ANNABEL'S

In London when the elegant restaurant-club Annabel's has a Russian gastronomic festival, the menus copy those used by the Czar. Here is a recipe for a Russian dessert:

RASPBERRY OR BLUEBERRY KISSEL

MAKES ABOUT 4 CUPS

Bring to a boil 1½ pounds raspberries or blueberries and 1 cup sugar in 1 cup water; rub through a fine sieve. Return the purée to the saucepan. Mix a little potato flour, cornstarch, or arrowroot with a little of the cooled purée, then stir into the pan of heated purée and cook just until thick, rather jam-like. Cool, then chill, and serve very cold.

Kissel can be made from any soft berry. It's delicious served over vanilla ice cream or with heavy cream.

Vogue's Food Gazette, November 1970

Thanksgiving is a time for caring and for presents to friends of foods that are prepared with special love. Some are delicate, to be delivered by hand in a generous rush from fridge to fridge. Others are sturdy enough to withstand time or even travel by mail. Below are four suggestions to start your cooking now, for Christmas: Honey-Nut Butter, Madeleines from Mexico, Lemon Vodka, Marron Icebox Cake.

HONEY-NUT BUTTER

Soften fresh butter and mix with an equal quantity of organic honey. Crush mixed unsalted nuts coarsely in a blender, then work into the honey butter. Pack in crocks. Give.

MADELEINES FROM MEXICO

MAKES ABOUT 20 TO 30

A French Recipe from a Mexican friend.

1 cup extra-fine sugar
2 cups sifted cake flour
4 eggs
Pinch of salt

Grated rind of 1 lemon
1 cup (2 sticks) melted butter
Dash of Cointreau

Preheat oven to 375°.

Work the sugar, flour, eggs, salt, and lemon rind together with a spatula. Add the melted butter and Cointreau. Fill buttered madeleine molds three-quarters full. Bake 15 to 20 minutes, or until golden brown; a toothpick should be dry after piercing one.

Pack the cookies in a pretty wooden box lined with white paper and tie with a deep pink ribbon—or put them in a patterned Indian basket.

LEMON VODKA

Peel the rind (no pith) from two to three lemons and drop the strips into a full bottle of vodka. Recork bottle. Steep until the liquor is pale yellow, its flavor sharp and delicious. Pour into beautiful bottles to give. At Mark's, a noted London club, the lemon-vodka cocktails are poured from bottles frozen in blocks of ice.

MARRON ICEBOX CAKE · SERVES 8 TO 10

A Parisian version of chestnut cake.

4 ounces semisweet dark
    chocolate
1 stick butter
4 egg yolks
4 teaspoons strong brewed coffee,
    or 2 tablespoons instant coffee powder

¼ cup sugar
1 pound canned chestnut purée
    (*purée de marrons*)
1 cup dark rum
½ cup heavy cream, whipped
20 whole champagne biscuits, or
    10 ladyfingers, split

GARNISH (OPTIONAL)
1 egg white, beaten
½ cup slivered, blanched almonds

In the top of a double boiler melt the chocolate, butter, and sugar over simmering water. Whisk in the egg yolks thoroughly, one at a time. Remove from heat, add the coffee or coffee powder. Fold in the chestnut purée, then ½ cup of the rum. Cool to less than lukewarm, then add the whipped cream and fold in. Line a mold with champagne biscuits or split ladyfingers sprinkled with the remaining ½ cup of rum. Fill with the chestnut mixture; refrigerate overnight. Unmold. You may brush the unmolded cake with a little slightly beaten egg white and sprinkle it with slivered almonds.

NORMANDY QUAIL, A THANKSGIVING SWITCH

SERVES 6

6 very large cooking apples
2 sticks butter
6 quails, legs removed
Salt and pepper
6 cardamom seeds, crushed

1 cup Calvados (or applejack)
Pastry dough, enough for three
    double-crust 8-inch pies
2 egg yolks, beaten slightly

Preheat oven to 350°.

Cut off the top of each apple and carefully scoop out the core and enough of the flesh of the apple to create a cavity for the quail, without piercing the skin. Melt a half stick of the butter in a skillet over medium-high heat. Sauté the quails gently for 15 minutes or until golden brown. Season with salt and pepper. Place each quail on top of a small piece of butter in the apple cavity; add a share of the crushed cardamom and a little Calvados or applejack. Cover with the top of the apple. Wrap each apple in a round of thinly rolled pastry dough, seal, and paint with beaten egg yolk. Place on a cookie sheet and bake for 35 to 40 minutes, until golden brown. Serve hot with the remaining butter, clarified and sprinkled over the apples; add more if needed.

ROAST DUCK TIP-OFF

Start a day early in order to keep the duck crisp and the gravy fatless. Calculate the roasting time for the oven temperature you prefer and divide by two. Rub the duck with salt and prick the breast thoroughly. Roast on a rack in a pan for half the total roasting time. Cool the bird in the oven with the heat off and door open, then refrigerate the whole pan. Remove it from the refrigerator and remove all congealed fat. Preheat the oven to the selected temperature. Roast the duck for the remaining time. It will be crisp and the gravy will be relatively free of fat. Baste frequently during this time.

SCOTTISH CHRISTMAS SECRETS

Brew and Age Well

North of Scotland's coastline, Orkney Islanders home-brew rich, malty beer to use in plum pudding. The Orkney pudding recipe below is from Lady Reay, sister of the Honourable Simon Fraser, the Master of Lovat. At their family's castle, Beaufort, at Beauly, Inverness-shire, flower petals are collected all summer long and aged with spices in a huge carved chest to make potpourri for Christmas presents without counting.

Readers of Agatha Christie know that a proper English Christmas dinner starts with:

OYSTER SOUP   SERVES 8

6 dozen oysters in their shells
2 quarts strained seasoned Fish
    Stock (given below)

4 tablespoons flour
½ stick butter
Juice of a half lemon

Put the oysters in a large pan, heat on top of the stove just until shells open. Remove and reserve the oysters and juice. Strain the juice into a clean saucepan and heat with the fish stock; bring just to a simmer. Thicken with blended flour and butter, simmer for 15 minutes. Add the lemon juice and oysters, allow to warm for a moment, and serve at once.

FISH STOCK

Wash and drain 3 to 4 pounds of fresh fish heads and bones, put into a large pot. Pour over a glass of white wine, bring to a boil, and boil for a moment to reduce the wine. Add to taste: carrots, parsley (stems can be used), an onion or two (each stuck with a clove), lemon juice, mushroom stalks and peelings, a strip of orange rind, a pinch of thyme. Add boiling water to cover, bring to boil, boil 20 to 30 minutes. During the last 10 minutes add salt to taste and a few peppercorns. Strain.

KASHA

Mix 2 cups of coarse kasha (buckwheat groats) with a beaten egg. Stir over high heat in a heavy skillet until the grains are dry and separated. Transfer to a preheated fireproof casserole, add 1 medium Spanish onion, quartered, and 3½ cups boiling water. Salt lightly and simmer, covered, 25 minutes. Remove lid, cook 5 minutes more. Serve hot.

Vogue's Food Gazette, February 1, 1971

STEAK: THE AMERICAN WAY

As patriotic as any apple pie, steak suits Americans . . . pioneers by habit who don't eat soufflés when there's work to be done. The French feel the same way about *biftek* and *pommes frites*. They linger through two-hour luncheons over steaks and have invented delicious sauces for grilled meat.

PANBROILED STEAK

Ask for "butcher's tenderloin." (Butchers call it a "hanger" or a "hanging tenderloin.") These are hard to find, so any favorite tender steak may be substituted.

Rub a heavy iron skillet with oil, sprinkle it with dried herbs (thyme, sage, tarragon), and heat the pan to very high heat. Sear the steak on both sides, reduce heat, add a little oil or butter, and cook gently, uncovered, to desired doneness. The steak will be more moist than when broiled. A sauce may be added to flavor the meat in the last few minutes. To keep the juices in, let the steak rest for a few minutes at room temperature before slicing. Chopped fresh parsley always makes a steak look terrific.

For plus flavor, top the steak with Béarnaise Sauce☆ or with one of these butters or sauces:

GARLIC BUTTER   MAKES A GENEROUS 1 CUP

Make this with ¼ cup peeled garlic cloves, parboiled 3 minutes and drained, blended with 2¼ sticks softened butter. Rub through a fine sieve and season with salt and pepper.

MAÎTRE D'HÔTEL BUTTER

MAKES ½ CUP

Blend 1 tablespoon chopped parsley with 1 stick softened butter, add a squeeze of lemon juice, season with salt and pepper.

SHALLOT BUTTER

MAKES A GENEROUS 1 CUP

Blend ¾ cup finely chopped shallots, parboiled 3 minutes and squeezed dry, with 1 stick softened butter.

SOLFERINO SAUCE

SERVES 8 TO 10

Put 15 very ripe medium-sized tomatoes through a food mill. Simmer the pulp and juice until syrupy and thick and reduced to 2 cups. Add salt, a pinch of cayenne, 3 tablespoons beef essence (or gravy or concentrated bouillon—be careful about salt if you use the essence or the bouillon) and the juice of a half lemon. Remove from flame and add Maître d'Hôtel Butter and Shallot Butter (recipes above), mixing everything to form a thick paste. Drained canned whole tomatoes may be substituted for fresh.

BORDELAISE SAUCE FOR RIB STEAKS

SERVES 6 TO 8

Cook the steaks only partially—just sear them well—and set them aside to keep warm while making this sauce.

½ cup beef marrow, removed
    from bones
6 shallots, peeled and chopped
2 tablespoons butter
1 cup red wine (more if needed to
    thin sauce)
¼ teaspoon ground dried bay
    leaves
2 tablespoons chopped fresh

thyme or 1 teaspoon crum-
    bled dried thyme
1 heaping tablespoon cornstarch
    mixed smoothly with ½ cup
    red wine
Juice of a half lemon
Salt and pepper to taste
4 tablespoons chopped parsley

Poach the marrow in simmering water for 1 minute. Drain, chill, chop, and set aside. Cook the shallots in the butter until golden and softened. Add the wine, bay leaves, and thyme; reduce to one-third of the original volume. Add the cornstarch and wine mixture and simmer, stirring, until

---

thickened. Add the lemon juice, salt, and pepper. Add the steaks to the skillet and warm thoroughly, turning them and spooning sauce over them (add a little more wine if the sauce is too thick). Pile the marrow on top of them, sprinkle with parsley, cover, and rewarm briefly. Serve at once.

MARCHAND DE VIN SAUCE
(Wine Merchant's Sauce)

A simpler version of Bordelaise Sauce (recipe preceding):

1 tablespoon finely chopped shallots
½ cup red wine (Bordeaux or Beaujolais)
1 tablespoon beef essence (or 1 tablespoon bouillon, salt omitted, which has been reduced by two-thirds)
Salt and pepper to taste
2 tablespoons chopped parsley
1¼ sticks butter, softened and cut into bits
Juice of ¼ lemon

Simmer the shallots in wine until reduced by half. Add the beef essence or reduced bouillon, salt and pepper, and parsley. Stir in the butter, bit by bit, then the lemon juice. Mix well and serve along with steaks, or pour over the panbroiled steaks while still in the skillet and let the sauce warm through.

Vogue's Food Gazette, February 15, 1971

FROM A TRAVELER'S FOOD DIARY

The late David Edge wandered the world, grandly, and collected a favorite recipe at every stop. *Pastilla* is from Morocco; *pasta e fagioli*, a hearty winter dish, is from Venice.

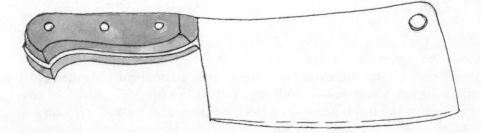

PASTILLA
(Moroccan Pigeon Pie)

SERVES 8

4 ounces frozen strudel dough
(two 2-ounce packages); or
substitute frozen filo dough
(at Middle Eastern food
shops)
2 sticks butter, melted
4 squabs, fresh Cornish game
hens, quails, or squab

chickens, halved
Salt and pepper to taste
4 teaspoons cinnamon
½ cup sugar
½ cup ground almonds
Sugar and cinnamon for sprinkling finished *pastilla*

Preheat oven to 350°.

Thaw the pastry. Butter a large round ovenproof metal platter or paella pan. Spread on it one leaf of pastry, paint with melted butter. Repeat until there are 6 layers. Cook the halved birds in some of the butter in a large skillet, turning them often to brown evenly, until almost done. Season with salt and pepper. Arrange the birds on the pastry, sprinkle liberally with the cinnamon, sugar, and almonds. Add 6 more layers of pastry, buttering each after it is laid in place. Moisten the edges and seal together, cut a few gashes in the top. Bake 25 to 30 minutes or until pastry is golden brown. Dust with additional sugar and cinnamon and serve hot.

PASTA E FAGIOLI
(Pasta and Vegetable Soup)

SERVES 8 TO 10

1 pound fat bacon, diced
2 pounds onions (8 to 10
medium), sliced
2 pounds fresh tomatoes (5 or 6
medium), skinned, halved,
and seeded
2 small cans (6 ounces) tomato
paste
2 pounds (before shelling) fresh
white beans (red-podded),
shelled

1 tablespoon chopped fresh
thyme or 1 to 1½ teaspoons
dried
1 quart chicken stock
Salt and pepper to taste
½ pound small pasta, any shape
6 ounces Parmesan cheese,
grated, and its rind
Additional chicken stock to thin
the finished soup
Additional grated Parmesan

Render the bacon in a heavy skillet until crisp, remove it, and set it aside. Cook the onions in the bacon fat until tender. Combine them with the tomatoes in a large casserole. Add the tomato paste, beans, thyme, and 1 quart chicken stock. Season well with salt and pepper. Cook slowly, covered. When the beans are tender, add the pasta and cook slowly down to a mush. Add the cheese and some of the rind cut into thin strips. Cool, then refrigerate, covered, 24 hours. The mixture will be a solid mass. At serving time reheat slowly, adding more stock to make the soup spoonable though thick. This should be served warm, not hot, in soup plates, with the bacon bits and more grated Parmesan on top.

CUMBERLAND CHICKEN SERVES 4 TO 6

To stuff a tender farm chicken as they do in the North of England, toss together the following (the mixture should be rather wet and mealy):

A chicken or capon 5 to 6 pounds

STUFFING

1½ cups fresh bread crumbs
½ cup finely minced ham
1 teaspoon dried thyme,
    crumbled
1 teaspoon chopped fresh parsley
½ teaspoon salt
½ teaspoon pepper

1 teaspoon finely chopped orange
    rind
1 teaspoon finely chopped lemon
    rind
2 eggs, lightly beaten
1 stick butter, melted

Preheat oven to 500°.

    Stuff the chicken. Roast the bird 10 minutes at 500°, basting often. Reduce heat to 350° and roast 1½ to 2 hours longer, or until done, basting frequently.

Vogue's Food Gazette, April 1, 1971

COOK LAUGHING

Le rire aide à digérer, and the laughter helps the cooking, too. In Paris, an amusing young man and woman, the late Michael Warren and Yves Larsen, have created in French a tiny, funny cookbook, *The Anti-Steak* (Paris, Editions Denoël), subtitled *A Little Treatise on Culinary Dandyism.* Here are two of their recipes.

DEVIL'S KISSES MAKES ABOUT 30

Beat the whites of 3 eggs into snow-white rigidity. Exaggeratedly season with cayenne pepper. Add salt and 2 tablespoons of grated Parmesan cheese. Mix. Drop by teaspoonfuls into boiling oil (375°). When golden brown, remove with a slotted spoon. You should obtain tiny meringues to be drained on paper and dusted with paprika. Serve hot at the cocktail hour and you will have devilish good luck!

VEAL-STUFFED LEMONS (PRECIOUS LEMONS)
SERVES 8

8 lemons
Boiling salted water
¾ pound cooked veal, finely
    chopped
2 tablespoons oil
1 egg yolk

Grated rind of 1 lemon
1 slice bread, crumbled
1 tablespoon cream
Salt and pepper to taste
2 tablespoons butter
2 to 4 tablespoons beer

Boil the lemons for 10 minutes in salted water. Remove, drain. Cut off the top ends of the lemons, reserving these "lids." With a curved grapefruit knife or sharp spoon, scoop out the flesh of the fruit, leaving only the skin. Mix the chopped veal with 1 tablespoon of oil, egg yolk, grated lemon rind, and crumbled bread softened in the cream. Season with salt and pepper, blend well. Fill the lemons with the veal stuffing, replace the lids, and secure them to the lemons with toothpicks. Place them upright in a sauté pan, add the remaining oil, the butter, and the beer. Bring to a boil then simmer on low heat, covered, for about 20 minutes or until the veal is cooked. As the cooking liquid evaporates, add more beer. Correct seasoning, Serve each lemon upright on a little mound of puréed potatoes with some of the cooking juice sprinkled over the top.

POACHED-EGG SOUFFLÉ
SERVES 4

Also in Paris . . . the Hôtel Vendôme serves this airy dish for a late, late breakfast— but only to order, wafted up by room service. Serve it accompanied by champagne.

4 eggs for poaching
2 tablespoons butter
2 tablespoons flour
1 cup milk
Dry mustard to taste

Salt and pepper to taste
¼ cup grated Swiss and ¼ cup
    grated Parmesan cheèse
4 eggs, separated

Preheat oven to 350°.

Lightly poach the 4 eggs, set aside. Melt the butter in top of a double boiler over simmering water, stir in the flour, cook gently until foamy, stirring. Slowly stir in the milk and season with dry mustard, salt, and pepper. When thickened, add the cheese, stir, and remove from heat. Cool for a few minutes, then beat the 4 egg yolks well together and mix in. Cool this mixture—the soufflé base—over cold water. Beat the 4 egg whites very stiff and fold into the soufflé base very gently with a spatula. Fill a greased 1½-quart soufflé dish half full, arrange the poached eggs on top, cover with remaining mixture. Set the dish in a shallow pan of boiling water and bake in the preheated oven until puffed and browned, about 30 minutes (do not bake for more than 5 to 10 minutes extra, and do not lower temperature). Serve immediately.

SHAD ROE WITH ORANGES

Another Paris recipe . . . this one is from Maison Prunier, the venerable fish restaurant at 9 Rue Duphot. Here is one way that Prunier serves shad roe:

Season one pair of shad roe with salt and pepper and cook gently, uncovered, in a skillet in ½ stick butter. Place on a serving dish, squeeze over a few drops of lemon juice, and scatter a little chopped parsley. Surround with orange sections and sprinkle with 2 tablespoons butter, browned in a skillet until foamy and nut-brown. Serve with endive salad.

EAST INDIA SALAD   SERVES 6 TO 8

1 anchovy fillet, drained of oil
2 tablespoons olive oil
6 tablespoons tarragon vinegar
6½ ounces cooked crab meat, fresh or canned, well picked over
1 teaspoon chili vinegar or pepper

sherry, or ½ teaspoon chili powder
Salt to taste
3 celery hearts, thinly sliced (about 2 cups)
1 head Belgian endive
¼ cup finely cut chives

Crush the anchovy with a fork and mix with the oil and vinegar, then with the crab meat. Season with the chili vinegar, pepper sherry, or chili powder and with salt. Clean and chop the salad greens. Toss all ingredients together just before serving. Good for luncheon with grilled cheese sandwiches.

APRIL FOOL

Take equal quantities of boiled rhubarb, sweetened with raw sugar and flavored with a curl of lemon peel, and yogurt. Try to get goat's-milk yogurt, which is sweeter and creamier than the commercial kinds (it is available in health-food stores). Purée the cooked rhubarb in a food mill to remove the fibrous parts. Mix with the yogurt and chill.

Vogue's Food Gazette, April 15, 1971

TO COOK: THE GOING THING

Take food . . . on the air lanes, the seaways, anywhere that travel takes you. Make it light, tempting. Go easy on carbohydrates or aromas that have too much clout.

John Stefanidis, an architect-designer, lives in London, works in Greece. He heli-hops from mainland to islands, often takes guests with him. Here are some of the packable, pick-up-able foods he takes along to serve in the air:

Slices of Swiss cheese wrapped around dill pickles

Strips of banana in curls of ham, wrapped in plastic to prevent darkening

Well-seasoned Steak Tartare☆ packed into celery stalks

Wisps of prosciutto around raw carrot sticks

Cold boiled and seasoned rice, mixed with chopped nuts, grated carrots, and a little horseradish, encased in a lettuce or vine leaf (these come brined in jars)

Raw flowerets of cauliflower, topped with American cheese and broiled just until the cheese melts and coats the vegetables; served cold, sprinkled with celery salt

Prunes filled with cottage cheese sweetened with Greek honey

Coffee, tea, or an air-fair drink

Alcohol has a stronger punch at high altitudes. Soften the blow by taking along, in vacuum bottles, beef bouillon and fresh orange juice, both laced with vodka in safe proportions.

The late **Fulco di Verdura,** who designed lavish jewels and did exquisite tiny paintings, was in demand to design food on friends' boats. This dish is refreshing in hot weather, nourishing for snorkel fiends.

SEAWORTHY PASTA

2 ripe medium tomatoes per
    person
1 medium zucchini per person,
    cubed
¼ pound pasta per person

Olive oil
Salt and pepper to taste
Coarsely chopped fresh basil and
    parsley

Peel, halve, and seed the tomatoes, cut into chunks. Combine with the zucchini in a casserole or earthenware bowl. Set in a warm (250°) oven long enough to become juicy but barely cooked. Boil the pasta until *al dente,* then drain. Dress it with oil, salt, pepper. Mix the vegetables and their juices with the pasta. Throw a huge scattering of coarsely chopped basil or parsley, or a mixture of the two, over all.

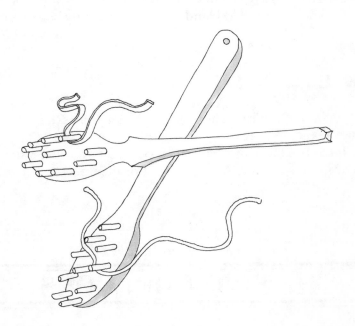

On the Greek island of Patmos, the painter **Teddy Millington-Drake** lives in a scattering of whitewashed houses. There he serves fine food, including this special baked fish with the Provençal version of *pesto:*

BASS WITH PESTO SAUCE   SERVES 8 TO 10

Bake a 4- to 5-pound bass (or other large fish) in foil. To serve, unwrap (save the juices for the sauce), split the fish, remove the spine, and douse with Pesto Sauce (below). Garnish with lightly broiled tomato halves.

PESTO SAUCE

1 cup coarsely chopped fresh
    basil, moderately packed
½ cup olive oil
Salt and pepper to taste

4 ripe tomatoes, peeled and
    seeded
¼ cup pignolias (pine nuts)
⅓ cup grated Parmesan cheese

Combine the ingredients in a blender, process until fairly smooth. Add the juices from the cooked fish and blend again. Heat gently before serving.

DRINK UP

A cool fresh-up from English writer and art dealer **John Richardson,** who lives in New York:
    Into a huge tumbler with lots of ice pour 2 parts rosé wine, 1 part bitter Campari, 1 part water. Add a twist of orange peel.

Vogue's Food Gazette, May 1971

THE SPORT OF COOKS

Cooking is a marvelous exercise if you stir up vitamin-jammed dishes that brace muscles and rouse the circulation.

OFF-WITH-A-BANG BREAKFAST SERVES 2

In a blender combine a little less than 2 breakfast cupfuls of hot coffee, 1 heaping tablespoon non-instant dried skim milk, 1 or 2 whole eggs. Sweeten with dark honey and blend. A cappuccino foam with hours of energy.

ROGNONNADE DE VEAU
(Braised Loin of Veal with Kidneys) SERVES 8

Extra protein and minerals come in the organ meats. Try this veal and kidney braise: a specialty from Burgundy.

1 loin, flank, and 4 veal kidneys (8 ribs)
4 quarts water
Salt
Veal bones, about 3 pounds
A calf's foot or pig's foot, split
2 onions
2 cloves
4 carrots

4 ribs celery
Peppercorns
3 bunches (a handful each) fresh tarragon, or 4 tablespoons dried tarragon
1⅓ cups white wine
Veal stock, made as described below
Salt and pepper to taste

From your butcher obtain a loin and flank of veal, cut in one piece stretching from the backbone to the center of the chest, with the kidneys in their natural position. Extra kidneys may be added, if you like, and the ribs almost cut apart for easier carving. Remove most of the fat.

Make a veal stock by simmering for several hours in 4 quarts of lightly salted water: the veal bones, calf's or pig's foot, onions, each stuck with a clove, the carrots, celery, a few peppercorns, and a good handful of fresh tarragon or 1½ tablespoons of dried tarragon; partly cover the pot. Strain and reserve the stock.

Pepper and salt the veal and cover the kidneys with the second bunch of fresh tarragon, or sprinkle them with 1½ tablespoons dried tarragon. Roll up the roast like a jelly roll, wrapping the flank over the ribs, and tie loosely with string. Brown the veal lightly in a large heavy stewpan, add the white wine, and boil to reduce it until the meat almost sticks to the pan. Add enough of the veal stock to cover, another bunch of tarragon (or 1 tablespoon dried), and simmer gently 1½ to 2 hours. The meat should be fork-tender but firm.

Remove the string and place the meat in a deep serving dish. Pour the juices from the pan around it. Cool, then chill. Remove any fat from the surface of the jellied stock and cut the jelly roughly into fragments. Carve the meat from the dish and serve with the jelly and a cold *macédoine* of vegetables. This dish may also be served hot.

VEGETABLE JUICE KICKERS

Carrots, celery, parsley, lettuce, radishes, watercress, all solid with health-giving good things. Combine them in your own juicer, or have them liquefied for you at a health-food shop. These juices are a delicious and vitalizing drink—cold or hot.

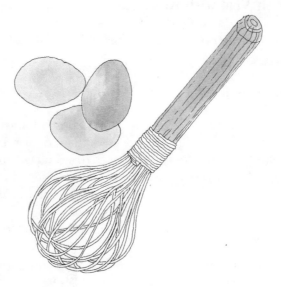

STEAK TARTARE

SERVES 8

Genghis Khan often gets the credit for the first raw beef energizer. Here's a version that can go (packed on ice) on the road:

1 2-ounce can anchovy fillets in oil, drained
3 pounds ground butcher's tenderloin (hanging tenderloin or "hanger") or ground filet, which is more expensive
4 eggs, beaten
2¼-ounce bottle of capers, drained
1½ teaspoons salt
1½ teaspoons pepper

½ cup finely ground nuts (walnuts or hazelnuts)
1½ teaspoons dry mustard, preferably English
1 cup finely chopped fresh herbs (chives, basil, or parsley, or a mixture)
Lemon juice
Olive oil
Rind of 6 lemons, minced

Crush the anchovies with a fork and mix with the meat, eggs, capers, salt, pepper, nuts, mustard, and ⅔ cup of the herbs. Add lemon juice to taste and olive oil to moisten (mixture should remain firm). Cover and chill 1 hour. Combine the remaining herbs with the lemon rind, spread on a flat surface. Form meat into walnut-sized balls and roll in herb-lemon peel mixture. Stick a toothpick in each; or (for a picnic), wrap each ball—like a candy—in a twist of waxed paper. Keep cold until serving time.

LIQUID GOLD

Aga Khan III, the grandfather of the present Aga Khan, served guests this nectar:

Purée the flesh of a ripe fresh pineapple with its juice in a blender; then combine with a cold bottle of dry champagne in a chilled earthenware pitcher.

Vogue's Food Gazette, June 1971

AMERICAN WOMEN

Really Cooking

Mrs. John Barry Ryan III, a New Englander who cooks New England dishes for her family in a New York kitchen, found on the island of Martha's Vineyard a superb local way of preparing bluefish. "D.D." Ryan (she was born Dorinda Dixon) serves a meal designed "for summer appetites—huge, like ours, but not too heavy." Here, her bluefish recipe:

NANTUCKET BLUEFISH

2 to 2½ pounds bluefish fillets
Sea salt
Freshly ground black pepper
1½ cups dairy sour cream

½ cup mayonnaise (preferably
   homemade and very yolky)
3 tablespoons chopped chives
3 tablespoons lemon juice

Preheat oven to 375°.

Wash and dry the fillets, rub with sea salt and pepper, and arrange in one layer in a buttered earthenware baking dish. Mix the sour cream, mayonnaise, chives, and lemon juice, season with salt and pepper as needed, and spread over fillets. Bake about 30 minutes or until just flaky. Put under the broiler for a minute or two to brown the top a little.

Vogue's Food Gazette, July 1971

EAT FREELY IN THE OUTDOORS

*... and cook there, too, using sea air
or alpine sunshine as seasoning!*

SALT-AIR FISH

Lady Lambton combed the beach on Children's Bay Cay, the Bahamian island that was once the home of Mr. and Mrs. Henry J. Heinz II, for the makings of her bonfire for this fish and vegetable barbecue by the sea.

Collect: 1 empty champagne crate, 4 empty beer or soda cans, lots of driftwood—logs, sticks, twigs, straw. (Don't forget to bring matches for this venture!) Set the crate on the cans, one at each corner, and fill with kindling—largest driftwood last. From beneath, light the crate.

Rub a cleaned 2-pound fish with olive oil, coarsely gound pepper, and salt. Tuck sprigs of fresh basil in the cavity and wrap the fish, along with more basil leaves, in heavy aluminum foil that has been coated with oil on the fish side. Clamp the fish in a double, fish-shaped broiling rack and, when the fire is burning low, place the rack across the crate, end to end. A 2-pound fish will need about 30 minutes on the first side, 15 to 20 minutes on the second. You can open the foil and test with a fork (flesh should be flaky and white).

ROASTED MARINATED VEGETABLES

Thread on skewers—one per person—unpeeled chunks of eggplant, zucchini, seeded green peppers; thin strips of hot red peppers; thin slices of crusty Italian bread. Marinate all in lemon juice, olive oil, pepper, salt, garlic, and thyme for at least an hour. Grill beside the Salt-Air Fish (given above), turning occasionally until tender but still crisp.

CITRUS SALAD FOR A PICNIC

Sharp contrast for the lull of the sea, bonfire reveries: peeled sections of oranges, lemons, grapefruit, ugli fruit, tangerines, all combined with their own juices. Add sugar sparingly, crushed fresh mint with abandon.

GIGOT À LA FICELLE
(Leg of Lamb Roasted on a String)

Stringing up the roast is a French cooking ploy, usable in front of a fireplace or in the field.

Tie to the end of the bone in a leg of lamb a stout string long enough to suspend the meat in front of (not inside) an open fireplace, or before an outdoor cooking fire (you'll need an improvised crosspiece supported on sticks for outdoors). Rotate the meat to wind up the string. Release, and the meat will revolve as it roasts, unwinding and winding by its own momentum, with only an occasional nudge.

Set a pan of browned potatoes and lightly cooked greens—collards, spinach, beet tops—underneath the meat to catch the juices that drip. (Or you can combine parboiled onions and carrots with the potatoes.) Baste the roast by brushing it with a branch of dry thyme dipped in olive oil flavored with lemon juice and crushed garlic.

BOEUF À LA FICELLE
(Beef Cooked on a String)

Prepare a rich beef stock by boiling bones and stew meat with seasoning vegetables; strain and chill; remove fat.

Cut sirloin steak into 2-inch cubes and remove fat, allowing 4 to 6 cubes per person. Tie each piece with string like a parcel, attach to a long string with a loop at the end. Refrigerate.

Prepare bowls of condiments for the beef: Horseradish Sauce,✩ ketchup, chopped parsley, Garlic Butter,✩ English or French mustard, chutney, pickles, coarse salt.

Prepare enough fresh vegetables—potatoes, carrots, turnips—to serve as a separate course with broth, and boil in the beef stock until just tender. Remove the vegetables and keep warm. Arrange the pot of boiling stock over a tabletop burner so that each guest can cook his or her meat by slipping a chopstick through the string loop on a piece of steak and lowering the meat into the boiling stock. Each cooks his own meat to his own taste (1 to 5 minutes), then dips it in his choice of condiments. Serve the vegetables and broth separately.

SUMMER CARROTS SERVES 4 TO 6

Sam Le Tulle, a Texan, architect-decorator, and a standout cook, makes this casserole of barely cooked organically grown carrots with Texas "rat cheese," to serve with summer cold cuts and a bottle of Bordeaux wine. It may be served hot or it may be chilled and cut in slices.

Butter	5 eggs
Sharp Cheddar cheese ("rat cheese")	2 cups half-and-half
	Salt and pepper to taste
3 cups grated carrots, lightly packed	¼ teaspoon powdered turmeric
	2 tablespoons butter
1 cup chopped parsley	

Preheat oven to 350°.

Generously butter the sides and bottom of a casserole (Sam Le Tulle uses an oven-glass loaf pan). Grate enough cheese to make 2 cups. Make three or four layers each of carrots, parsley, and cheese, in that order, ending with cheese. Do not pack down. Beat together the eggs and half-and-half, season to taste with salt, pepper, and turmeric. Pour this mixture over the layers in the casserole; liquid should come to the top. Place thin slices of Cheddar over the top and dot with butter. Bake in the lower part of the oven until the custard is almost set, then move to an upper shelf for 5 minutes to brown slightly. The carrots should be crisp and parsley still green.

LEMON CAVIAR

For each serving, cut one-third off one end of a lemon (a piece large enough for a good squeeze of juice). Scoop out the large portion of the lemon, removing most of the pulp but leaving a juicy lining of flesh. Cut a thin slice off the bottom so lemon will stand upright on a plate. Fill the lemon's cavity with caviar and top with the smaller lemon piece, which will be squeezed for juice when wanted. Arrange the filled lemon on a pretty plate and serve with a vermeil spoon and a heavy glass goblet of pink champagne.

RESANDWICH

On each slice of crusty, homemade whole-wheat bread lay a slice of baked ham or well-seasoned roast beef. Between the two slices of meat, sandwich this mixture: cream cheese with peanuts, sweet pickles, and fresh watercress or spinach, all chopped.

Vogue's Food Gazette, August 1, 1971

A forty-eight-hour feast with the host or hostess as relaxed as the guests. Good plans make good weekends. Here's a weekend food scheme for six people—noon and night menus, with recipes for starred dishes. For breakfast, add at will.

Friday Supper

Aid for tired guests
Oyster Stew☆
Pilot Crackers
Cold Cuts
Cheese and Salad
Strawberries in Orange Juice☆
Beer

OYSTER STEW

SERVES 8

2 cans frozen oyster stew
3 dozen shucked fresh oysters,
    with their liquor
3 cups milk
4 to 5 liberal dashes Worcester-

shire sauce
6 tablespoons butter
Salt and pepper to taste
Paprika

Combine all ingredients except the paprika. Heat just to a boil. Sprinkle with paprika and serve with pilot crackers.

STRAWBERRIES IN ORANGE JUICE

SERVES 6 TO 8

3 to 4 pints strawberries
2 oranges
Fine sugar

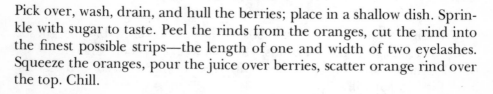

Pick over, wash, drain, and hull the berries; place in a shallow dish. Sprinkle with sugar to taste. Peel the rinds from the oranges, cut the rind into the finest possible strips—the length of one and width of two eyelashes. Squeeze the oranges, pour the juice over berries, scatter orange rind over the top. Chill.

Saturday Brunch

Whether the morning goes to sports or sleep,
the meal should be light, refreshing
Vin Blanc Cassis☆ ("Kir")
Potted Shrimp☆
Melon with Prosciutto
Fillets of Sole with Tomatoes and Pesto Sauce☆
Snow Peas
Orange and Mint Salad☆

VIN BLANC CASSIS (White Wine with Cassis)

Chilled white wine with a few drops of *crème de cassis* (black-currant liqueur) in each glass. (*Kir royal* is chilled champagne with the same quantity of *cassis*.)

POTTED SHRIMP SERVES 6 TO 8

A favorite from Britain:

3 jars tiny Danish shrimp
Butter to cover shrimp (about 1½
    to 2 sticks)

Cayenne to taste
Garlic (optional)

Drain the shrimp and pack firmly into a serving dish or dishes (a small soufflé dish is good, or individual crocks). Melt the butter with cayenne and a clove of garlic, peeled and flattened, and pour over shrimp just to cover. Chill. Remove the garlic before serving. Serve with toast.

FILLETS OF SOLE WITH TOMATOES AND PESTO SAUCE SERVES 6

6 ripe tomatoes
Butter
Salt and pepper to taste

6 fillets of sole
½ cup Pesto Sauce☆
3 tablespoons butter, cut into bits

Preheat oven to 300°.
    Peel, slice, and seed the tomatoes. Butter a shallow casserole or gratin dish and cover the bottom with half the tomato slices. Season with salt and pepper. Bake 15 minutes. Place the fillets of sole on top of the tomatoes, each fillet folded in half with a tablespoon of heated pesto sauce inside. Cover with the remaining tomato slices. Season again and dot with butter. Grill 5 to 10 minutes or until fish is pure white and flaky. Serve hot or cold.

ORANGE AND MINT SALAD SERVES 6 TO 8

12 oranges, preferably seedless
Raw sugar (at health-food stores)
    to taste

½ cup finely chopped fresh mint
Bourbon, if desired

Peel the oranges, removing all white pith. Slice crosswise directly into a serving bowl to keep the juice. Sprinkle with the sugar and mint. A little Bourbon may be added; if so, add extra sugar. Chill well before serving.

Saturday Dinner

The big, jolly relaxed meal of the weekend.
Time for pretty dresses and bare feet.
Cocktails
Tomato Salad☆
Capon with Onion and Celery Stuffing☆
Roast Potatoes
Braised Endives☆
Pecan Pie with Vanilla Ice Cream

TOMATO SALAD

SERVES 6 TO 8

12 ripe tomatoes
9 tablespoons olive oil
1 tablespoon wine vinegar
1 tablespoon Dijon-type mustard
½ teaspoon salt
1 teaspoon pepper

4 shallots, peeled and slivered
3 tablespoons finely chopped
    parsley, coarsely chopped
    basil, or snipped chives, or a
    combination of these herbs

Peel, slice, and seed the tomatoes, arrange on a shallow dish. Make enough vinaigrette sauce for two days by combining the oil, vinegar, mustard, salt, and pepper. Sauce the tomatoes and store the remainder of the vinaigrette in the refrigerator. Sprinkle the shallots over tomatoes, then add the chopped herbs.

CAPON WITH ONION AND CELERY STUFFING

SERVES 8 TO 10

2 sticks butter
2 medium onions, coarsely
    chopped
4 ribs celery, finely diced
1½ teaspoons dried thyme
1½ teaspoons dried sage

¾ teaspoon dried marjoram
¾ teaspoon dried rosemary
Salt and pepper to taste
1½ cups fresh bread crumbs
1 lemon, halved
5- to 6-pound capon

Preheat oven to 350°.

Melt 1 stick of the butter, add the onions, and cook without browning until soft. Add the celery and cook a few minutes (it should remain crisp). Stir in two-thirds of the herbs, add salt and pepper and the bread crumbs. Rub the inside of the capon with the cut lemon. Stuff the cavity of the bird and skewer or sew up the opening. Roll ½ stick of the remaining butter into two large lumps and roll them in the remaining herbs; slip these butter balls and a little lemon pulp from the lemon halves under the loosened skin of the breast and fasten the skin over the neck opening. Put the remaining ½ stick butter into a roasting pan. Roast the bird for about 2 hours, basting often. Add peeled Idaho potatoes, parboiled until three-quarters done, to the pan for the last half hour of roasting.

Sunday Brunch

Leftovers can be a bore at a weekend house. Use up the extras for brunch before you leave.

Arrange a big platter of cold cuts and sliced capon. Add a sauce of mayonnaise mixed with Pesto Sauce,☆ lemon juice, and herbs. Oranges and endives make a salad with the remaining vinaigrette sauce. Cheese, crackers, and a second pecan pie should finish off the meal and your weekend supplies.

Vogue's Food Gazette, August 15, 1971

THE COOKING GAME
WELL PLAYED

Country peace and easy food were built into the romantic barn-roofed house on Long Island that decorator Lil Groueff designed and decorated for her Bulgarian husband, Stéphane Groueff, and their son. In her house fabrics from Bali, a flowered rug from Paris, blue and white china, and fresh garden flowers keep up the color-pattern beat. The garden grows flowering herbs for cooking. Here is one of Lil's summer dinner menus with recipes. Serve her favorite Hot Fruit Salad☆ for dessert, or substitute another sweet.

Menu

Wine Cup☆
Cherry-Ripe Duck☆
Zucchini Casserole☆
Green Salad☆

WINE CUP

SERVES 6 TO 8

1 ripe peach
1 basket raspberries, rinsed
3 to 4 tablespoons sugar

1 to 2 jiggers brandy
1 to 2 bottles domestic Bordeaux-
    type wine

Peel the peach and place in the bottom of a glass pitcher. Add all other ingredients. Chill.

CHERRY-RIPE DUCK

SERVES 6 TO 8

2 5-pound ducks
Salt and pepper
2 envelopes unflavored gelatin

½ cup cold water
2 packages frozen black cherries,
    thawed

Preheat oven to 400°.

Season the ducks with salt and pepper and preroast them for about ¾ hour. Remove from the pan and pour the juices into a bowl. Place the juices in the freezer to chill. Place the ducks on a platter to cool, propping one end of each up with a wooden spoon to help the fat to drip off. Return the ducks to the oven and roast at 350° until tender, basting occasionally. Cool the ducks, then chill them.

Soak the gelatin 5 minutes in the cold water. Meanwhile, remove congealed fat from the surface of the chilled duck juices and heat juices with enough water to make 3¼ cups; dissolve the soaked gelatin in the broth. Place the mixture in the freezer until not quite set.

Drain the black cherries. Coat the ducks, on a serving platter, with the almost-jellied broth. Dip the cherries in jelly one at a time and stick all over the ducks. The ducks may be carved before adding the aspic and cherries—less dramatic but easier to serve.

ZUCCHINI CASSEROLE

SERVES 6 TO 8

4 large zucchini (about 2½
    pounds)
4 tablespoons butter

Salt and pepper to taste
2 tablespoons chopped parsley
2 tablespoons bread crumbs

Preheat oven to 325°.
    Slice thin the washed, unpeeled zucchini; arrange in a casserole with dots of butter, salt, pepper, and chopped parsley. Sprinkle with bread crumbs. Bake until tender, about 45 minutes to 1 hour.

GREEN SALAD

Make this with greens in season, tossed with French Dressing.✩ Lil Groueff likes to add herbs to green salads and often includes the flowers from the fresh herbs. Her mint flowers are a beautiful blue.

HOT FRUIT SALAD

SERVES 6 TO 8

Fruit desserts are Groueff favorites. Here is Lil's combination of canned and fresh fruit in a hot "salad."

1 large can cling peaches
1 large can pears
2 large oranges, preferably
    seedless

½ pint dairy sour cream
Brandy
Sugar

Drain the peaches and pears and boil down their juices until thick. Peel the rind from the oranges, cut it into slivers, and add to the juices. Let stand several hours on a warm stove (over the pilot light) or on an electrically heated serving tray. Drain, reserving the rind and syrup. Combine the fruits and heat in the reserved syrup. Flavor the sour cream with brandy and sugar and serve as a sauce with the hot fruit. Sprinkle orange rind over top.

Two Recipes for Chicken

These are served with ripe summer melons and Yorkshire Mint Pasties.✩

HOT CHICKEN WITH RICE AND MELON

SERVES 6 TO 8

Melon (allow half a small cantaloupe or muskmelon, or a
slice of a large one, for each
serving)
3 cups freshly boiled rice
½ cup chopped fresh parsley

Uncooked chicken pieces (allow 2
to 3 small pieces per person)
Salt and pepper to taste
1 stick butter
2 to 4 tablespoons vegetable oil

Remove the seeds and filaments from the melons and chill. Spread cooked
rice on a flat pan in a warm oven 10 minutes to dry. Stir in the chopped
parsley. Season the chicken pieces with salt and pepper and fry in butter
with a little oil added to prevent burning. Fill the melon shells with hot rice
and place the chicken pieces on top. Serve at once.

Melon is scooped out with rice and eaten with the chicken. Use the
butter and oil from the chicken to dress string beans, broccoli, or green
peas to serve with chicken and melon.

COLD CHICKEN WITH MELON IN CURRY SAUCE

FOR EACH SERVING

½ small cantaloupe or muskmelon
½ cup chopped cooked chicken
¼ cup chopped celery

Mayonnaise
Curry powder to taste
Paprika

Remove the seeds from the melon and scoop out the flesh; cut into
chunks; chill both the melon flesh and shells. Mix the chicken and celery
with mayonnaise flavored with curry powder. Chill.

Fill the shells with melon mixed with chicken, sprinkle with paprika,
and serve cold.

YORKSHIRE MINT PASTIES

SERVES 6

This recipe is adapted from *Traditional British Cooking for Pleasure*, by
Gladys Mann.

About 12 ounces short pastry
dough (double the recipe for
short pastry in Marmalade
Tart☆)
½ pound dried currants

½ cup (packed) brown sugar
½ stick butter, melted
4 tablespoons chopped fresh mint
Grated rind of a lemon
Milk

Preheat oven to 400°.

Roll out the pastry and cut into six 6-inch circles. Mix the currants, sugar, butter, mint, and lemon rind. Divide the filling on the pastry rounds and fold each into a half-moon. Dampen the edges, seal, crimp, brush with milk. Bake for about 20 minutes until golden brown.

Vogue's Food Gazette, September 15, 1971

The cooking game, English finesse: Mrs. David Mlinaric in her husband's London studio and in their country house.

Fragile, dark-eyed Martha Mlinaric looks tender enough to be a fairy princess; in fact, she takes care of her family, the large, rather nervous greyhound, Speed, and cooks all meals, including dinners for twenty.

For parties, she begins to prepare cold foods early in the morning that are always good to look at, but that appear from a kitchen as small as a closet, and are served from a sideboard formed by the tops of architect's cabinets under the skylight of a high, eggplant-colored room where guests sit at a variety of antique round tables. This is a historic room; it was the studio of the painters John Singer Sargent and Augustus John, now is the studio for David Mlinaric's interior designing. The window looks on a city surprise—a rose garden that holds also delphinium, lilac, jasmine, and a mammoth tree peony looking as though it were stuck all over with large yellow paper flowers.

Here are two of Martha Mlinaric's recipes, taken from friends and books, adapted by her own touch.

EGG MOUSSE SERVES 8

5 hard-cooked eggs, peeled
Salt and pepper to taste
1 teaspoon anchovy essence (at specialty food shops) or finely chopped anchovies
Few drops Worcestershire sauce
1 envelope unflavored gelatin
¼ cup cold water

1 chicken bouillon cube, dissolved in ¾ cup boiling water; or ¾ cup canned chicken stock
⅔ cup heavy cream, lightly whipped
4 tablespoons chopped mango chutney
Paprika

Put the egg yolks through a fine sieve and chop the whites rather fine. Season the yolks to taste with salt, pepper, anchovy, and Worcestershire sauce. Soften the gelatin in the cold water, dissolve in the hot bouillon or stock. Pour ⅓ cup of this aspic into a small shallow pan, chill until firm, set aside. Mix the remaining aspic with the sieved egg yolks and chill until somewhat thickened. Fold in the whipped cream, chopped egg whites, and chutney. Pour into a serving dish or dishes (Martha uses soufflé dishes, brown on the outside). Chill well. Garnish with the reserved aspic, chopped, and the paprika.

TOFFEE FLAN
SERVES 4 TO 6

6 tablespoons butter
7 tablespoons light brown sugar
2 eggs, separated

Baked 8-inch pie shell
Sugar

Preheat oven to 425°.

Melt the butter over low heat, stir in the sugar and slightly beaten egg yolks. Remove from heat at once and beat until thick. Pour into the pie shell in its baking pan. Beat the egg whites, gradually adding sugar, to stiff peaks. Spread this meringue on the pie, bake until it is light brown, 10 to 15 minutes. Serve hot.

Vogue's Food Gazette, October 1, 1971
Someone's in the Kitchen with Maxime

ARABELLA LACLOCHE
COOKS ITALIAN

Arabella LaCloche, a blond-maned young Roman who has chosen to live in London and the wilds of Scotland, is for the out-of-doors, whether in town or at her cottage in a Highland glen. A garden designer, she's good at devising nooks for wild flowers, quiet places to sit—like those in the garden of her house in St. John's Wood, the London district where artists lived a half century ago. There, french windows on the stone portico let gardening gear invade the house—spades, forks, pots, forcing boxes. Seed packets spill off her eighteenth-century tables. Plants and light fill the box windows, and the kitchen is aromatic with the scents of herbs she grows in the garden—in pots or troughs to give proper drainage. Arabella uses herbs lavishly and likes cooking in the classic Roman way, even when Scottish game is on the menu. A crack shot, she takes care of supplies herself, deer-stalking on the Scottish moors.

Arabella gave me her recipe for the classic Italian sweet-and-sour wild boar. This delightful dish has a chocolate-flavored sauce that resembles Mexican *mole*. Venison may be substituted for the boar; in New York and other large cities one can find venison, and sometimes boar, in season at certain fine meat markets.

SWEET-AND-SOUR WILD BOAR

SERVES 8 TO 10

MARINADE

1¼ cups dry red wine
5 tablespoons wine vinegar
2 ribs celery, sliced
1 onion, sliced
1 carrot, sliced

Parsley
4 peppercorns
3 cloves garlic
1 bay leaf

FOR COOKING THE MEAT

Leg or loin of boar, or a similar
  cut of venison
Vegetable oil
Salt and pepper
2 medium onions, chopped
1 carrot, sliced

2 cloves
½ bay leaf
2 tablespoons fat trimmed from
  prosciutto
1¼ cups dry red wine

Boil up the marinade ingredients and cool.

Skin the leg or loin and place it (or the oven-ready venison) in a glass or earthenware dish. The meat may be whole or cut into pieces. Pour the marinade over the meat, cover, and let stand in a cool place 2 to 3 days, turning the meat and stirring the marinade twice a day. Drain the meat (discard the marinade) and sear well in very hot oil in a heavy casserole. Season with salt and pepper, add the onions, carrot, celery, cloves, bay leaf, and the fat from prosciutto. Cook, stirring occasionally, until the meat and seasoning vegetables are well browned. Add the wine and deglaze the pan. When the wine boils up, cover and cook slowly, turning the meat once or twice, until it is tender, at least 20 to 30 minutes per pound (exact time will depend in part on the age of the animal). Add more wine if needed. Remove the meat, slice for serving, and transfer to a warm dish. Spoon a little of the gravy over the meat and keep the dish warm. Let the remaining gravy cool.

Make the sauce:

SAUCE FOR WILD BOAR

6 tablespoons sugar
2 cloves garlic, flattened
2 bay leaves
1 cup wine vinegar
4 squares (4 ounces) unsweetened
    baking chocolate, grated
2 cups reserved gravy from
    cooked boar
Handful each of raisins, dried
    prunes, and candied orange

peel, all soaked a half hour in
    warm water to cover
Handful of sour cherries (canned
    sour cherries can be used),
    pitted
1 cup pignolias (pine nuts)
Arrowroot or cornstarch to
    thicken sauce
Chopped parsley (garnish)

Heat the sugar with the garlic and bay leaves in top of a double boiler over boiling water until the sugar is melted and very hot. Add the vinegar and scrape down the sides of the pan as liquid foams up. Add the chocolate and stir until melted.

Remove excess fat from the reserved gravy, and stir the gravy into the chocolate sauce, strain. Add the dried fruits, drained, and cherries and pine nuts; reheat. Thicken the sauce, if necessary, with a little arrowroot or cornstarch mixed into a little water. Pour the sauce over the meat and sprinkle with chopped parsley. Serve with steamed potatoes, plain rice, or fried polenta (below).

FRIED POLENTA

SERVES 8 TO 12

Fried polenta is Arabella LaCloche's accompaniment for the wild boar. You can get polenta meal at an Italian delicatessen, or use ordinary yellow cornmeal.

Add 4 teaspoons salt to 2½ quarts rapidly boiling water; slowly dribble in 4 cups cornmeal, stirring constantly with a wooden spoon. Cook and stir about 30 minutes, until the mush leaves the sides of the pan. Season with pepper. Add 1 stick cut-up butter if you like a rich polenta. Spread the polenta about 1 inch thick on a wooden board. When cooled, cut into cookie-sized strips and deep-fry in hot (375°) oil. Drain on paper towels and serve hot.

For dessert, a light Italian ice (recipe follows).

GRANITA DI LIMONE
(Lemon Ice)

SERVES 8 OR MORE

Heat 1 cup sugar with 3 cups water until the sugar dissolves; cool. Add the strained juice and grated rind of 3 lemons. Freeze in an ice-cube tray without stirring until crystals form but a spoon still goes in. Stir before serving.

Granita should have the texture of crystallized sugar or lightly packed snow. *Granita di caffè* may be made if you prefer. Use strong coffee in place of lemon and water.

Vogue's Food Gazette, November 15, 1971
Someone's in the Kitchen with Maxime

A PRO AT THE STOVE

Maurice Moore-Betty

"My taste for cooking simmered on the side of the stove for years. Necessity finally brought it to the boil." So says Maurice Moore-Betty, a gray-haired Irishman with smiling eyes, who was born in Enniskillen in Northern Ireland, and first coped with cooks and cooking in the Thirties while tobacco farming in Southern Rhodesia and growing cotton in the Sudan. Second World War army duty took him from the Camel Corps in the Sudanese desert to Normandy, then through the Far East. Back in postwar London he found a full-time cook too great a luxury and, of necessity, became the cook himself. He started by working in the kitchen under Avignon, the renowned chef of London's Ritz Hotel, then he opened a tiny restaurant of his own—madly crowded—where he stopped cooking only when the building was torn down.

Living in New York since 1962, Mr. Moore-Betty teaches cooking in his coach-house apartment. Among his students the "small adults" (teenagers) are a treat, he says—"No hang-ups about flavors, no fears about equipment," which in his big kitchen-dining room (looking onto a terrace where he grows lemon balm, sage, and thyme) includes painter's palette knives among the slicers and choppers on a wall rack.

Here is his recipe for a Thanksgiving cranberry sauce, created especially for *Vogue,* and two uncommon vegetable preparations:

CRANBERRY CUMBERLAND SAUCE

SERVES 6 TO 8

2 oranges
½ cup red currant jelly
½ cup light port wine
1½ to 2 cups sugar

2 sticks cinnamon
¼ teaspoon whole allspice
2 cups cranberries, washed and
   picked over

Cut the rind of one orange into fine strips; simmer in water to cover for 2 to 3 minutes; drain. Combine the juice of both oranges, jelly, wine, and sugar. Add the spices, tied in a cheesecloth bag. Boil up, then simmer 5 minutes. Remove the spices, add the cranberries and drained orange rind. Bring to a full rolling boil and boil until berries pop.
   Delicious with braised ham.

TWO-SQUASH SOUP

SERVES 6 TO 8

1 large zucchini, or 2 or 3 small
   zucchini
1 large or 2 or 3 small summer
   squash, either golden or
   white (pattypan)
1 rib celery
2 tablespoons butter

½ teaspoon celery salt
1 quart chicken stock, or a little
   more if needed
2 tablespoons finely chopped
   parsley
Shredded rind of 1 orange

Peel the vegetables, cut into chunks; cook gently with butter in a tightly covered pan until just tender. Stir in the celery salt; put the vegetables in a blender with a little of the chicken stock; purée. Combine with remaining chicken stock; chill to serve cold, or reheat. Sprinkle with parsley and orange rind just before serving. (Parsley must be chopped at the last minute, or it loses its flavor.)

PANACHE

SERVES 8

1 9-ounce package frozen green
   beans, thawed
1 large Spanish onion, peeled and
   sliced
½ cup olive oil
8 ounces bottled or canned artichoke hearts or bottoms,
   drained

4 eggs
1 green pepper, stemmed,
   seeded, and diced
1 teaspoon salt
¼ teaspoon ground black pepper
Bottled pimientos
Pimiento-stuffed green olives

Preheat oven to 350°.

Boil the beans in a little salted water 5 minutes; drain. Sauté the onion in oil until transparent, combine with the beans and artichoke hearts in a blender, process until smooth. Beat the eggs to a froth; stir in the vegetable purée. Mix in the green pepper, salt, and pepper. Pour into a well-buttered shallow ovenproof dish (10 × 8 × 2 inches) and bake 50 minutes. Garnish with a lattice of pimiento strips and place pimiento-stuffed olive slices at intersections. Serve hot or at room temperature. The panache may be refrigerated and later brought to room temperature to serve.

Vogue's Food Gazette, December 1971
Someone's in the Kitchen with Maxime

LADY ARABELLA BOXER

The high wood-paneled kitchen with herb-filled windows looking onto the garden of Lady Arabella Boxer's Victorian house in Holland Park was designed for and by a professional cook—Arabella Boxer herself. At a huge old "estate management" desk there, this slender Englishwoman with a ruffle of blond hair has written two best-selling cookbooks: *First Slice Your Cookbook,* which was indeed sliced horizontally so that first-, second-, and third-course dishes could be seen together in various combinations (with recipes printed on paper in light, medium, and heavy colors so the meal is easy to balance, too), and its sequel, *Second Slice.*

Arabella Boxer believes that one should give guests the same simple food one serves the family, only more of it. She likes to make all courses equally important, often skipping potatoes so that the pudding may be enjoyed, and serving vegetables separately from the meat, perhaps in a vinaigrette or a soup. Here are some of her recipes:

CARROT SOUP

SERVES 6 TO 8

6 tablespoons butter
1 pound carrots
1 pound (about 3 medium) ripe
    tomatoes
1½ cups chicken stock

1 cup creamy milk or half-and-
    half
Salt, pepper, and sugar
Chopped parsley

Melt the butter in a heavy pan. Slice the carrots thin and cook them very gently in the butter while you peel, seed, and chop the tomatoes. Add them to the carrots, cook about 2 minutes. Heat the stock and add. Cover and simmer until the carrots are soft, about 30 minutes. Heat the milk and add to soup. Season with salt and pepper; add a pinch of sugar if the tomatoes are not sweet enough. Purée, rewarm, and serve hot, topped by whopping spoonfuls of chopped parsley. (Parsley is such a passion with Arabella Boxer that she serves alongside soups little wooden bowls of it chopped, the way Italians serve cheese.)

GRILLED CHICKEN ON WATERCRESS SALAD
SERVES 4 TO 6

1 3½-pound chicken, cut up
Dijon mustard, the smooth type
Juice of 1 lemon

Olive oil
Wine vinegar
Salt, pepper, and sugar

Paint the chicken pieces all over with mustard and lay them in a shallow fireproof dish. Pour over the lemon juice and enough olive oil to moisten. Marinate about 2 hours, turning occasionally.

Preheat the broiler. Broil chicken fiercely for 4 to 5 minutes on each side first, then lower the heat; broil slowly, turning once or twice and basting with pan juices until done. The skin side should be almost black—at least that is how Arabella likes it. During the last 5 minutes, make the following Watercress Salad:

WATERCRESS SALAD

Wash and drain 2 bunches of watercress. Dip the sprigs in the dressing (below), shake, and lay on a lightly warmed platter. Serve the chicken at once on the bed of watercress.

DRESSING
2 tablespoons salad oil
1 tablespoon wine vinegar
½ teaspoon salt

1 teaspoon pepper
¼ teaspoon sugar
½ teaspoon dry mustard

Mix thoroughly together.

MARMALADE TART

SHORT PASTRY

1 cup flour	6 tablespoons butter
Pinch of salt	1 egg yolk, beaten
Pinch of sugar	A little lemon juice

FILLING

½ pound orange marmalade	Lemon juice to taste
2 eggs, separated	

Preheat oven to 400°.

Make the pastry: sift the flour, salt, and sugar into a mixing bowl. Rub in butter with your fingers until the mixture is crumbly. Add the egg yolk and enough lemon juice to mix to a stiff paste, adding a few drops of water if necessary. Work on a pastry board until smooth. Roll out on a floured surface and line a loose-bottomed 8-inch tart pan. Prick the pastry with a fork; line with buttered foil, buttered side against pastry; partly fill with dried beans, and bake 15 minutes at 400°. Remove the beans and bake 5 minutes. Cool.

Reset oven to 350°.

Make the filling: if the marmalade is a coarse-cut one, chop the peel into small pieces. Beat the egg yolks until pale yellow. Mix with the marmalade and flavor with lemon juice. Beat the egg whites stiff and fold into the marmalade mixture. Spoon into the pastry case. Bake at 350° until the filling has risen and top is lightly colored, 25 to 30 minutes. Serve with cream.

Vogue's Food Gazette, January 15, 1972
Someone's in the Kitchen with Maxime

LADY LUCINDA HARROD

Her love affair with the past transforms two worlds for the Lady Lucinda Harrod: As Lucinda Lambton (she is the daughter of Lady Lambton), she is the professional photographer whose work centers on period architecture, old wallpapers, nostalgic portraits. As the mother of sons Barnaby and Huckleberry, she lives in one of her architectural romances—an 1880s house in the first London garden suburb built for artists.

A kind of domestic art historian, Lucie Harrod delights in surrounding her family with furniture, carpets, even potted plants and cooking utensils, reflecting her passion for details of nineteenth-century sweetness, Pre-Raphaelite kitsch. Victorian plates jostle Art Nouveau cups on the dresser of her kitchen; outside, blouses with leg-of-mutton sleeves blow on the garden clothesline. The boys love their mother's ornamental architecture in the form of glorious birthday cakes. Lucie makes her own preserves, sauces, relishes, adapting recipes from books and from those handed down in the Lambton family. Here, a pet recipe, her own invention:

VERY RICH CHOCOLATE CAKE

SERVES 10 TO 12

½ pound mild chocolate (Tobler, or a similar type)
½ pound dark sweet chocolate (Maillard, or a similar type)
4 tablespoons flour

3 tablespoons sugar
1½ sticks sweet butter, softened and cut up
4 eggs, separated

Preheat oven to 450°.

Melt chocolate in top of double boiler over barely simmering water. Stir in the flour, sugar, and butter. Beat the egg yolks well and stir into the chocolate mixture; cool. Whip the egg whites until stiff and fold into the batter. Pour into a greased, paper-lined 8-inch square cake pan and bake 15 minutes; cool in the pan, then unmold. Lucie frosts this cake with a rich chocolate-butter icing an inch thick, but the cake itself really needs no gilding. Proceed at your figure's own risk. This is a supermoist cake—almost the consistency of baked custard.

Vogue Food, February 15, 1972

Pema Thonden, whose diplomat husband, Phintso Thonden, makes dried beef (hanging it on the terrace in cold weather) and her own barley wine for the soup that is the final course of a Tibetan dinner—though she also uses champagne as a stand-in. "A very good soup to make you sleep well," Pema says. "I could make it without water, but then you would have to go to bed at once!"

TIBETAN WINE SOUP

2 cups water
1 bottle champagne (a stand-in
    for Tibetan barley wine)
2 tablespoons imported soy sauce
1 teaspoon monosodium gluta-

mate (optional)
1½ tablespoons barley flour (at
    health-food stores)
¾ cup pot cheese (uncreamed cot-
    tage cheese)

Bring to a boil the water and three quarters of the bottle of champagne; add the soy sauce and monosodium glutamate and simmer, covered, 5 minutes. Stir in the barley flour and beat with a rotary beater 4 to 5 minutes. When foamy, add the pot cheese and stir, still over the heat. Add the remaining champagne. Serve very hot.

Vogue Food, March 1, 1972
Someone's in the Kitchen with Maxime

ANDY WARHOL TURNS GOLD INTO FOOD

Andy Warhol came into my kitchen to try out some of his new cooking ideas (his own kitchen was occupied by plumbing repairers). Andy has long been interested in food; he illustrated a cookery book; and the subject matter of one of his early underground movies, *Eat,* consisted entirely of another artist, Robert Indiana, eating a mushroom.

    The first thing Andy set down on my Thirties blue-enamel kitchen table was his tape recorder; and the second thing was his Polaroid camera. He never stops watching . . . recording . . . filming . . . collecting people with his own and his mechanized memories. Andy has so much patience and is so incapable of boredom that he never tires of indulging other people, of letting them go to their limits of self-sense . . . or nonsense. A friend said, "Nothing escapes his intuition."

    Andy let his intuition lead him in the kitchen, just as he has in other arts. Stopping now and then to take a few snapshots of me (I think the tape was running, too), he created a ginseng cocktail, an entity dish (a self-reliant chicken inside a squash), and then used his reversible alchemy to turn real gold into a glittering cake. His pasta recipe came from Paris, where he had it cooked for him at the restaurant-club Sept. Its basis is black gold—caviar!

CHICKEN IN WINTER SQUASH, WARHOL STYLE

SERVES 6 TO 8

2 big winter squashes, each about 17 inches long, 10 inches high
2 3-pound chickens (may be boned)
2 chicken breasts
4 tablespoons butter

Oil and extra butter, as needed
Salt and pepper to taste
12 large mushrooms, wiped clean or rinsed quickly and dried
8 large sprigs parsley
8 large sprigs dill

Preheat oven to 350°.

Scrub and dry the squashes; cut a thin slice off the bottom of each, so they will sit firmly in the pan. Cut off the top third to form a lid. (Andy cut one squash almost straight around, with notches at each end to stabilize the lid; the other, he cut in a zigzag pattern.) Scoop out the squash seeds and furry fibers and scrape flesh from the lids quite deeply to make more room for the chickens.

Cut the legs off the chickens and put them in the freezer for some future dish. Cook the chicken breasts and the whole but legless chickens in butter and oil, seasoning with salt and pepper, until almost done. (Andy likes to add some mixed Provençal herbs, to be bought at fine food stores.) Remove the breasts and let the whole chickens braise, covered, about 30 minutes.

Slice the meat from the extra chicken breasts and arrange it in the bottom of the scooped-out squashes. Put the chickens in the squashes, breasts up. Surround them with the mushrooms and the sprigs of parsley and dill. (We tried some slices of lemon with one of the birds, too.) Replace the squash lids; you may have to do a little extra cutting or scooping to fit them over the chickens. Place the filled squashes in a roasting pan; bake for 2 hours. During the last half hour remove the lids and baste the chickens repeatedly with extra butter until brown. Replace the lids before serving. While the squashes bake, mix the sauce:

SAUCE ON THE SIDE

½ pint heavy cream, whipped
2 tablespoons tomato ketchup

1 tablespoon bottled chili sauce

Mix all ingredients and chill. Serve with the chicken-stuffed squashes.

BLACK-GOLD LINGUINE

SERVES 6

1½ to 2 pounds linguine, preferably freshly made
Oil

Butter as needed
8 to 9 tablespoons caviar

Boil the linguine in a very large pot of salted water until barely tender—*al dente*. A little oil may be added to the water to keep the strands from sticking together. Drain and return to the pan; toss with butter to taste. Serve soup plates of linquine with caviar spooned on top. Careful investors will keep the black gold in a neat mound as they eat; freethinkers will stir the caviar and pasta together.

This is the best way I know to get through a large pot of expensive caviar without caring for the cost. When finances are a consideration, this is good with red caviar, too.

GILDING THE CAKE AND EATING IT TOO

Andy brought along a huge cake, covered with white icing, and six packets of gold leaf (bought at an art-supply store). The gold is so thin that air currents and static electricity waft it about tantalizingly, even after it is on the cake. Andy let the leaves fall onto the cake in fluttering drifts, nailed them down here and there with silver spikes—shiny foil-wrapped chocolate kisses. The kisses must be unwrapped for eating, but Andy made sure—through the New York City Poison Control Center—that gold leaf in reasonable amounts is completely edible and non-injurious to health.

Dazzled by our quivering, flashing gold-drift cake, we went on to gild a gingerbread brick (2 packets of mix, baked in a bread pan) by slapping the gold leaves straight onto the cake until it looked ready for Fort Knox.

Vogue Food, March 15, 1972
Someone's in the Kitchen with Maxime

PACKING A WEEKEND BASKET

Marchesa Catherine di Montezemolo

Weekending means going home for Marchesa Catherine di Montezemolo, a cheerful blue-eyed American woman with bright white hair and a geranium's glow—a drive to a long low seashore house in Southampton, New York, built on land ("potato fields") that belonged to her mother, and surrounded by houses of a "whole mess of relations," including her sister. Cathy likes the Long Island silence after a week of city crush and blare, puts on thermal underwear for early spring walks on the beach.

Italian wines, fruits, and vegetables not in season bought in city markets, ingredients from a health-food shop—all of these go with Cathy in a big market basket, with laundry hampers holding any overflow. With her, too, goes Argia Felici, an Umbrian-born cook of enormous skill, and her long Italian rolling pin.

Argia makes all the pasta for the first courses (pasta is interchangeable with soup in an Italian menu) just before she cooks it. The rolling pin is a two-and-a-half-inch wooden dowel about thirty inches long (a lumberyard is the best source for it in this country).

Here are weekend Montezemolo dishes—Argia's recipes translated from the Italian by Cathy:

SFORMATO DI TAGLIATELLE
(Noodle Soufflé)   SERVES 6 TO 8

PASTA

2 cups flour   4 half-eggshells of water
4 eggs

Pile the flour in the center of a work surface, make a well in the center. Put the eggs and water in well and work all ingredients together with fingers until well mixed, then knead, working the dough at least 20 minutes. Sprinkle with flour, fold the circle of dough in 2-inch folds from opposite sides until the folded portions meet in the center, then fold one over the other. Cut into ½-inch slices to form strips; shake strips to unfold. Bring 8 quarts of well-salted water to a boil, add the pasta, and cook 2 minutes, testing soon and quickly; do not overcook. Drain in a colander. Have ready this sauce:

BESCIAMELLA   **(Béchamel Sauce)**

4 tablespoons butter   small pieces or grated
4 tablespoons flour   4 tablespoons grated Parmesan
1 quart milk   cheese
½ pound Gruyère cheese, cut into   4 eggs, beaten

Preheat oven to 500°.

Melt the butter in a saucepan, blend in the flour, then add the milk and cook, stirring constantly over medium heat, until thick, 3 to 5 minutes. Turn heat very low and add the cheeses, then the eggs, still stirring. When smooth (don't overcook) pour one quarter of the sauce into a buttered casserole about 10 inches across; add the cooked pasta and mix well. Pour the remaining sauce over the top, bake until well browned, about 15 to 20 minutes. Serve instantly.

TAGLIATELLE COLORATE
(Tinted Noodles with Sauce)   SERVES 8 TO 10

WHITE PASTA

1½ cups flour   3 half-eggshells of water
3 eggs

Follow the directions for making pasta in the recipe for Sformato di Tagliatelle (above).

GREEN PASTA

1½ cups flour   1 pound fresh spinach
2 eggs

Wash the spinach and boil in ample water until tender. Drain; squeeze excess water from the leaves in a towel. Rub the spinach through a sieve to make a purée the consistency of cream. Make the pasta as described in the recipe for Sformato di Tagliatelle (above), using spinach purée instead of water.

RED PASTA

1½ cups flour   3 tablespoons tomato paste
2 eggs

Follow the directions for pasta in the recipe for Sformato di Tagliatelle (above), using tomato paste in place of water.

SAUCE

15 medium mushrooms   6 slices cooked ham, diced
6 ounces Gruyère cheese, cut into   Butter as needed
   small pieces or grated   Grated Parmesan cheese to taste
3 cups milk   3 hard-cooked eggs
6 egg yolks, beaten

Wipe or rinse and dry the mushrooms, slice, and simmer in a little water until just tender. Combine the Gruyère and milk in a saucepan and let soak 15 minutes. Heat gently until the cheese is half melted; add the egg yolks, ham, and mushrooms. Stir constantly over low heat until heated to the boiling point.

TAGLIATELLE COLORATE

Cook the colored pastas separately until *al dente* according to directions for Sformato di Tagliatelle; drain. Toss each pasta with a lump of butter and arrange pastas in three mounds on a hot deep serving platter. Pour over the sauce, top with grated Parmesan cheese. Surround with slices of hard-cooked egg. If you like, you can cook all three pastas together.

Vogue Food, April 1, 1972
Someone's in the Kitchen with Maxime

COOKING HUGE MEALS TO STAY THIN

Mrs. Richard D. Kaplan

Carmen Kaplan's long, narrow figure and mystery-green eyes seem unchanged since her days as a model for fashion photographers. Only the drifting of natural frost in her dark hair is new. Carmen cooks and eats one big meal, lets her special milk shake take her through the rest of the day.

The giant soups, vast stews that Carmen serves are built on large amounts of meat or fish protein with low-calorie vegetables (beautifully cut on the slant with a Japanese cleaver) barely simmered to crisp tenderness—never allowed to boil. Precise timing in adding vegetables to the pot so that each will be cooked right and will all be done at the same time is Carmen's great skill. In her apartment, vegetables are chopped on a wood block at tall-girl height. Scraps go through a hole cut in the block to a pail in the cupboard below.

Carmen cooks by inspiration, not recipes. We translated her descriptions like this:

CARMEN'S MILK SHAKE MAKES ABOUT 3 CUPS

1 10-ounce can evaporated milk
1 cup water
2 tablespoons polyunsaturated
    vegetable oil

6 tablespoons dextrose (at health-food stores)
1 tablespoon vanilla extract, or to taste

Whip in a blender and chill. Drink at breakfast, midmorning, lunch.

CARMEN'S BEEF STEW

SERVES 8 TO 12

8 pounds stewing beef, cut into chunks 1½ inches square
Salt and pepper
Flour
½ pound bacon, cut into ½-inch pieces
1 large onion, chopped
12-ounce bottle imported light beer
4 to 6 tablespoons chopped fresh

dill
16 small new potatoes, preferably red-skinned
16 very small onions, peeled
16 carrots, scraped and cut into 1-inch chunks
2 to 3 packages frozen peas, thawed
1 tablespoon raw sugar

Salt and pepper the meat and dredge it lightly in flour. Heat the bacon slowly in a heavy 8-quart pot until fat is running; add the chopped onion and simmer, covered, until the onion is soft. Add the meat and cook gently, stirring occasionally, for 20 minutes, still covered. Add the beer and mix well. Cover and cook over very low heat for 2 hours. At the end of the first hour add the dill. The potatoes, onions, and carrots are added 45 to 20 minutes before the end, depending on their size. The defrosted peas are sprinkled with raw sugar, added 10 minutes before serving time. Correct seasonings after adding the vegetables.

EAST HAMPTON FISH STEW

SERVES 8 TO 12

1 stick butter
2 cans frozen potato soup, thawed
2 soup canfuls fat-free milk
½ pound fish fillets per person (mix textures and flavors)
Lobster (when available), raw in the shell, cut into chunks
A few herbs—thyme and oregano

plus parsley; or dill and tarragon plus parsley
12 mussels or clams in shells, when available, well scrubbed
2 raw shrimp per person, shelled
1 quart shucked scallops
Salt
Pinch of cayenne

Melt the butter with the thawed soup and milk in a huge deep skillet. Add the firmest fish and lobster along with the herbs; simmer 10 minutes. Add softer-fleshed fish and well-scrubbed shellfish in their shells. As soon as the shells open, add the scallops, simmer 5 minutes. Season with salt and cayenne. Serve in soup bowls or over boiled rice in soup plates.

Vogue Food, April 15, 1972
Someone's in the Kitchen with Maxime

TRAVEL-TRAINED IN JAPAN, A FREE-STYLE COOK

Lily Auchincloss

Travel in Japan swerved Lily Auchincloss down a new cooking route. Always an enthusiastic cook, and a tidy one ("The first thing I learned about cooking was: When you unwrap the chicken, throw away the paper"), she was delighted by the crisp shapes and firm textures of Japanese food and by the brilliance of its colors.

Colors recur in Lily's conversations about food, echoing her interest in art. She is a trustee of New York's Museum of Modern Art, and guests find over her dining room table not a chandelier but a mobile by Alexander Calder. The modern furniture and paintings, including one by Claudio Bravo of a roll of rumpled scarlet paper, in her New York apartment (where she lives with her daughter Alexandra), reflects Lily's self-possession and gentle strength.

Tall, pale-skinned, with snap-brown eyes and hair, Lily moves with almost languid poise through her ample, skillfully lighted kitchen, doing the cooking herself, with serving help only at large parties. At her house in Bermuda, overlooking a golf course (Lily says the Japanese call that "borrowed landscape"), the garden provides tomatoes, basil, and beans for *salade niçoise,* and parsley for the green soup. But in New York, Lily puts on a little Japanese apron and with ingredients bought at one of the city's many Oriental food stores cooks such Japanese-inspired dishes as these:

WATERCRESS SOUP   SERVES 2

1 tablespoon butter
3 very small onions, finely
    chopped
1½ to 2 cups chopped watercress
1 can chicken broth, defatted (or
    defatted homemade broth, or

broth made with chicken
    bouillon powder)
Extra watercress leaves
Cooked green peas or mashed
    potato (optional)
Skim milk (optional)

Melt the butter, add the onions and wilt very lightly over medium heat. Add the chopped watercress and broth, bring to a boil, and simmer only a minute or two. Cool slightly off the stove. Purée the soup in a blender with extra watercress leaves for color (include a few cooked peas or a little mashed potato as binder if needed). The soup should be thick and "chewy," not too smoothly processed. It may be held in the refrigerator and diluted slightly with skim milk or more broth before reheating.

CHICKEN BREASTS À LA AUCHINCLOSS

SERVES 2

3 cups chicken broth, defatted
1 bay leaf
1 teaspoon fennel seed
3 thin slices peeled raw ginger
    root
5 whole shallots, peeled

1 large chicken breast, cut in half
4 scallions, including tops, with
    bases peeled
2 Belgian endives, sliced
    lengthwise
A few thin carrot sticks (optional)

Combine the broth, bay leaf, fennel, ginger, and shallots, bring to a boil, reduce heat to a simmer. Add the chicken, scallions, and endives, simmer, covered, 10 minutes, or until the chicken is just tender (scallions should still be green). If carrots are used, add before the chickens, scallions, and endives, simmer about 5 minutes before proceeding. Serve the chicken in soup bowls with some of the strained broth.

    Lily sometimes replaces the chicken with rolled flounder fillets and uses dill seed instead of fennel and, for the liquid, half chicken stock, half clam broth.

LILY'S ORIENTAL SALAD

SERVES 2 TO 3

1 to 1½ cups fresh bean sprouts
½ bunch watercress
1 head Bibb lettuce, washed and

    broken into pieces
A few cooked shrimp
A handful of cooked green peas

DRESSING
2 parts lemon juice
1 part vegetable oil
A few dashes soy sauce

Slivers of pickled ginger, well
    washed to remove the brine
Pepper (no salt)

Combine the salad ingredients in a serving bowl. Mix dressing and pour over. Serve at once, tossing lightly.

SWEET CORN, SOUTHEAST ASIA STYLE

Dip roasting ears, shucked and desilked, in coconut milk (it comes in cans), salted and diluted, before putting them on a charcoal grill; redip two or three times as they cook.

Vogue Food, May 1972

SMOKE-COOKING WITH AN OUTDOOR AIR

Cheyenne Packs Lunch to Go

Cooking with smoke is the Seventies flash. If your charcoal grill has a closed hood, you already own a smoke oven. If not, there are all sorts of new ones in the shops, from shoe-box-size top-of-the-stove smokers to electric models that can handle 25 pounds of meat and are best used outdoors (or in a fireplace with the damper open).

Cheyenne—formally Cheyenne Cheyenne—a six-foot stretch of beautiful and strong-minded woman with lifty cheekbones and narrow eyes that can see for miles, had her first taste of open-fire cooking at the age of eight, visiting cousins in an Indian-reservation teepee (her mother, from Wyoming, is a Cheyenne Indian). The deer meat had first been dried on lines outdoors and had a leathery texture that may explain why Indians have strong teeth—it must be chewed.

Picnic-cooking in New York (where, after touring the country as a jazz dancer, she has paused to model, to design clothes, to write poetry), Cheyenne chooses tender smoke-roasted chicken. With it she likes a favorite cucumber salad and an Indian pudding very like the New England kind, made from her mother's recipe.

SMOKE-ROASTED CHICKEN   SERVES 6

12 serving-size pieces roasting
   chicken (5 to 6 pounds)
½ teaspoon garlic powder
¾ teaspoon paprika
3 tablespoons Worcestershire

sauce
6 tablespoons lemon juice
6 tablespoons vegetable oil
Salt and pepper to taste

Place the chicken in a shallow glass or china dish. Mix the garlic powder, paprika, Worcestershire, lemon juice, and oil, pour over chicken. Chill overnight, turning once or twice if possible. Drain the chicken pieces and season with salt and pepper.

Preheat the smoker or smoke oven. Place the chicken on the rack, roast at 325° with moderate smoke until it is tender, about 1 hour. Cool and chill before packing in an insulated container for a picnic.

NOTE   This recipe was adapted from "Brad's Chicken" in *Smoke Cooking,* by Matt Kramer and Roger Sheppard (Hawthorn Books, New York), a book that explains the hows and whys of smoke cooking.

CHEYENNE'S "INDIAN" PUDDING

SERVES 12

1 cup seedless raisins
½ cup brandy
2 cups cornmeal
4½ cups water
3½ cups (packed) dark brown
    sugar

5 cloves
1 stick cinnamon
1 tablespoon melted pork fat
½ cup chopped walnuts or pecans
Nut halves (walnuts or pecans)

Soak the raisins in brandy, the longer the better. Combine the cornmeal with 2½ cups of the cold water, let stand 10 minutes. Mix the sugar with the remaining 2 cups water, add the cloves and cinnamon, and simmer 10 minutes. Strain and return to the pot, bring to a boil, and stir in the wet cornmeal and melted pork fat. Cook 30 minutes, stirring constantly. Drain the raisins and add, along with the ½ cup chopped walnuts or pecans, cook 2 minutes. Pour into a wet loaf pan or mold. Cool, then slice. Unmold and garnish with the nut halves. Slice to serve.

Cheyenne pointed out that making "Indian" pudding is a great arm exercise. Of course, you must stir with first one hand and then the other.

CUCUMBER SALAD

SERVES 6

6 cucumbers
Salt
2 teaspoons lemon juice
½ cup coarsely chopped fresh
    mint

½ cup chopped parsley
½ pint plain yogurt
½ pint dairy sour cream
1 teaspoon freshly ground pepper
Salt

Peel and seed the cucumbers, cut them into julienne strips. Mix them with a handful of salt and chill, covered, 1 hour, then rinse and drain. Add the lemon juice and mix well. Add the mint, parsley, yogurt, sour cream, and pepper. Taste and add salt if needed. Chill and keep on ice or in insulated container until serving time.

Vogue Food, June 1972

HOW AMERICA'S INDIAN WOMEN COOK

Yeffe Kimball Explains Some Traditional Dishes

Good American food. It all started with the Indians. Yeffe Kimball—who had an English mother but identifies completely with her father's people, the Osage in Oklahoma—told me how. Twitching her Indian-style pigtails, Yeffe, a painter and wife of the nuclear scientist Dr. Harvey L. Slatin, explained the way in which many dishes considered resoundingly American (Boston baked beans, succotash) were cooked by Indian women in the five major tribal regions described in the book she wrote with Jean Anderson, *The Art of American Indian Cooking* (Doubleday), and illustrated with her own drawings.

When Yeffe's art studies took her from New York to Fernand Léger's Paris atelier in the late Thirties, the artist-designer Erté made her two Art Deco Indian dresses: one of white suede with turquoise beading; the other, with *pavé* mirrors and a small train. Yeffe's Indian-influenced paintings include "space" paintings, some of them commissioned by the National Aeronautics and Space Administration—circular acrylics looking like shields made from disks of sky for powerful, peace-loving warriors.

A sophisticated scholar of Indian affairs, Yeffe has collected recipes from every region and tribe, and cooks them in the kitchen of her Cape Cod studio. Here, a few of her findings:

From the Southwest The Indian gardeners and gatherers of the Southwest specialize in stews. This recipe comes from the Zuñi people, for whom hominy, their name for "corn without skin," is a staple:

LAMB AND GREEN CHILI STEW   SERVES 12

3 pounds boned lamb, in 1½-inch
    cubes
Flour
2 tablespoons cooking oil
¼ teaspoon freshly ground black
    pepper
6 dried juniper berries, crushed
2 yellow onions, peeled and
    chopped
5½ cups canned hominy, with its
    liquid

1 medium-sized dried chili pep-
    per, crushed
2 cloves garlic, peeled and
    crushed
2 teaspoons dried oregano
1 tablespoon salt
½ cup finely chopped fresh
    parsley
6 green chilies, quartered (include
    some seeds for more heat)
1 quart water

Dust the lamb with flour, brown in the oil in a heavy pot. Stir in the black
pepper and juniper berries. Remove the meat; drain. Cook the onions in
the same pot until golden; return the meat. Add the remaining ingredients, cover, simmer 1½ hours, stirring occasionally.

From the Northwest In the Pacific Northwest, the Indian fishermen's
staple food is the salmon; salmon roe is sun-dried to a jam and spread on
bread. Northwest Indian women wrap fruits in dough before frying them:

CRANBERRY FRITTERS   ABOUT 9 DOZEN

3 cups flour
1¼ cups sugar
2 tablespoons baking powder
½ teaspoon salt

1 cup plus 2 tablespoons milk
1 cup fresh cranberries, washed,
    well drained
Oil or shortening for deep frying

Sift the dry ingredients together, stir in the milk slowly to make a stiff
dough. Using floured hands, roll about 1 teaspoonful of dough into a ball
around each cranberry. Fry a few at a time in deep fat heated to 375°,
turning until golden brown. Drain on paper toweling. Serve hot.

From the Central Plains The Indian hunters of the Great Plains serve
their venison and rabbit in thick stews with wild rice or dumplings. They
also stuff game birds.

STUFFED GAME HENS

SERVES 6

6 Rock Cornish game hens,
    thawed if frozen
Salt and pepper
1 cup wild rice, well washed in
    cold water
1 teaspoon salt
2½ cups water
4 slices bacon, cut into narrow
    crosswise strips

Butter, about 1 stick
5 scallions, including tops, peeled
    and sliced
½ pound mushrooms, wiped and
    sliced
1 cup raw hazelnuts, halved
Game hen giblets (heart, liver,
    and gizzard), chopped

Preheat oven to 350°.

    Season the birds inside and out with salt and pepper; set aside. Combine the wild rice with cold water and 1 teaspoon salt, bring slowly to a boil, simmer until water is absorbed. Brown the bacon. Add 1 tablespoon butter and all remaining ingredients, cook, stirring, about 10 minutes. Mix with the rice, cool. Stuff the birds with the rice mixture, truss, rub each with 1 tablespoon butter. Arrange them, breasts up, on a rack in an open pan. Roast, basting frequently (add butter as needed), about 1 hour, or until done.

From the East New England's classic dishes evolved from those of the Indians who baked beans, used pumpkin and cranberries, and who invented the clambake and clam chowder. Even Boston brown bread may have begun with Indian bread using cornmeal.

INDIAN BREAD

SERVES 10

3 cups flour
1¾ cups cornmeal
1 teaspoon baking soda
¼ teaspoon nutmeg
3⅓ cups milk

1 cup molasses
Butter or shortening for greasing
    mold
Butter to accompany bread

Sift the dry ingredients together. Combine the milk and molasses, add to the dry ingredients, and beat until smooth. Grease a 2-quart mold that has a cover, using butter or shortening. Pour in the batter, cover tightly, and steam on a rack in a large covered pot containing boiling water (enough to rise about one third up the sides of the mold) for 3 hours, adding more boiling water if necessary at any point. Let the mold stand 20 minutes, uncover, and let stand 10 minutes longer. Loosen the pudding with a spatula, invert mold onto a plate, and let stand until the pudding unmolds itself. Serve, sliced, with lots of butter.

A LIGHT SUMMER MEAL BY A STRONG-MINDED COOK

Mrs. René Bouché Cooks to Suit Herself

"I do everything in my kitchen: watch telly, do my bills . . . even paint. I love cooking, but I'm dictatorial and give people what I like best. I'm an onion addict (I eat scallions for breakfast), have a passion for fish and cheese."

Denise Bouché, a small sizzly blonde, whose deep-shade voice hints of Continental ancestors (she was born in Paris) and a London childhood, brings a passionate enthusiasm to everything she does; a self-reliant optimism powers her involvement with art, with politics, with her friends. Denise was married to the painter René Bouché in 1962, just a year before his death. His New York studio on Central Park South has been torn down, but Denise's small apartment on the east side of the park still holds his old model stand (now covered by velvet and a fur throw) and his portraits of Elsa Maxwell, Igor Stravinsky, Alexander Calder, and of himself. Works by other artists, ancient and modern, are there too, in every room, including the kitchen, which overflows with paintings, sculpture, flowers, potted herbs, and a big tray of seasonings set within hand's reach on top of the stove.

"I slosh a lot of wine into the food as I cook. I like light Sancerre, enjoy champagne only when it's served with dinner. I never try to have more than six to dinner without some help with the serving; and I hop in and out of the kitchen in bare feet or tennis shoes to avoid crashing to the floor with my fish."

That fish is the main course of a delicious light summer meal that Denise devised to serve to five or six at an old Spanish table in her entrance hall. Here is her dinner menu with recipes:

Menu

Clear Tomato Soup
Striped Bass "En Bonne Bouché"
Raspberry Tart

CLEAR TOMATO SOUP

SERVES 6

6 ripe tomatoes, peeled and quartered
1 rib celery, coarsely chopped
½ bulb of knob celery (celeriac or celery root), peeled and coarsely chopped
1 white onion, peeled and coarsely chopped
Pinch of salt
1 cup water
2 to 3 cups defatted chicken broth
Hot pepper sauce
Snipped chives for garnish

Combine the vegetables, salt, and water; boil 15 minutes; cool. Purée in a blender; strain. Add enough chicken broth to make the soup clear and pink. Season with hot pepper sauce and more salt if needed. Serve hot or cold, topped with snipped chives.

STRIPED BASS "EN BONNE BOUCHÉ"

SERVES 6

4-pound striped bass, cleaned; head half severed, tail removed
1½ cups water
½ cup white wine
¼ cup pignolias (pine nuts)
3 to 4 sprigs fresh basil, chopped
3 sprigs dill
Salt and pepper
6 scallions, washed and roots cut off

SAUCE
1 stick butter
2 tablespoons dark honey, preferably organic
2 to 3 tablespoons brandy

Place the fish, cavity up, on the rack of a fish steamer. Pour in the water and wine. Fill the fish cavity with the pignolias and herbs, season with salt and pepper. Place the scallions on either side of the fish. Cover the steamer tightly, with a piece of aluminum foil under the lid. Bring to a boil, lower heat, and simmer 20 to 25 minutes, or until the fish is just done. (Remarks Denise: "I always know when the fish is cooked, as the eyes go milky white and the spine is pure white. It is very important not to overcook fish.") Slide the fish onto a serving dish. Serve with a sauce made by simmering together the butter, honey, and brandy until slightly thickened.

RASPBERRY TART

3 cups flour
1 stick butter, softened
4 hard-cooked egg yolks, sieved
½ cup sugar
Pinch of salt
Ice-cold water, about ½ cup

Extra flour and sugar
2 boxes fresh raspberries, washed and well drained (about 2 cups)
1 8-ounce jar (1 cup) red currant jelly

Preheat oven to 400°.

Blend, with fingers or pastry blender, the flour, butter, egg yolks, sugar, and a pinch of salt until you have a mealy-flaky mixture. Sprinkle in the very cold water gradually, mixing with a fork, stopping when the pastry forms a ball. Stretch the dough by stroking it about 10 times in one direction on a marble surface. Roll it out just once until quite thin. Sprinkle the bottom of a 10-inch loose-bottomed tart pan with a little mixed flour and sugar. Line the pan with dough; trim. Bake the shell for 15 minutes or until light golden brown; cool. Spread a little currant jelly in the bottom of the crust; fill with berries. Melt the remaining jelly, cool slightly, and spoon over the berries as a glaze. Remove the tart to serving dish.

Vogue Food, August 15, 1972

SUMMER TRIPPING

Start Here, Eat There

PORTABLE FETTUCCINE

This recipe is adapted from one by Beverly Pepper, an American artist who lives in Rome. Take this dish along on Friday night, start your country weekend without fuss.

½ pound ground veal
2 sticks butter
½ cup red wine
2 cups canned tomato sauce
1 package frozen peas, thawed
½ pound mushrooms, wiped or

rinsed and sliced
¼ pound ham or prosciutto, cut into small pieces
Salt and pepper to taste
1 pound fettuccine

AT HOME   Brown the veal in half the butter. Add the wine and tomato sauce, bring to a boil, simmer 30 minutes. Cook the peas, mushrooms, and ham lightly in the remaining butter, add to the sauce for the last minute of cooking, season with salt and pepper. Cool, pour into containers, cover and chill. Pack, along with uncooked fettuccine.

ON ARRIVAL   Boil 5 to 7 quarts of salted water, add the pasta, and boil until just tender. Drain. Meanwhile gently reheat the sauce and pour over the drained pasta.

PICNIC SARDINES IN VINE LEAVES

Squeeze a little lemon juice over boned skinless sardines and wrap each one in a preserved vine leaf for picnic eating. The leaves can be bought in jars or cans in Greek and Middle Eastern food shops.

TRAVELING CARROTS

8 carrots, coarsely grated
12 mushrooms, sliced
6 tablespoons finely chopped
    parsley

Salt and pepper to taste
3 tablespoons butter
1 small can vegetable cocktail juice

AT HOME   Combine the vegetables and parsley, add salt and pepper, pour into a plastic bag. Chill. Pack, with the butter and the juice, still in its can, in an insulated picnic bag for travel.

ON ARRIVAL   Melt the butter in a large skillet, add vegetables and vegetable cocktail juice. Simmer until the carrots are just tender, 10 to 15 minutes.

THE SEASON'S CHICKEN FIX

For juicy cold roast chicken: When you remove the roasted fowl from the oven, plunge it directly into a bowl of ice water for a few seconds. This instantly seals in the juices. Cool, then wrap in foil and refrigerate until needed.

Sandwich Spreads for a Picnic

ANCHOVY, CRAB MEAT, OR LOBSTER BUTTER

Pound 8 boned anchovies, drained of their oil, with 1 stick of butter; or use crab meat or the coral and dark creamy part (tomalley, or liver) of a lobster. Season with chili vinegar or with chili powder and lemon juice. Spread on slices of cracked-wheat or sprouted-wheat bread; for filling, slices of ham or chicken breast.

CURRY BUTTER

Cream 4 to 5 tablespoons butter with 1 to 2 teaspoons curry powder or dry mustard, or both. Add a little chili vinegar, lemon juice, salt, and a sprinkling of cayenne. Spread on warmed Middle Eastern bread to flavor a filling of minced cooked lamb or veal.

GREEN ANCHOVY BUTTER

Work 2 tablespoons finely minced parsley, 3 to 4 pounded boned anchovies, a little lemon juice, pepper and salt, into 4 to 5 tablespoons butter. Spread on whole-wheat bread and make sandwiches of smoked salmon, red caviar, sardines, tuna, or salmon.

HERB BUTTER

Finely chop one sprig each of fresh parsley, tarragon or basil, chervil, and one small shallot for each tablespoon of softened butter; blend. Season with salt, pepper, chopped chives, a dash of grated nutmeg. Spread on Italian or French bread, add slices of ham, roast beef or lamb.

HAM BUTTER

To a cup of very finely chopped ham add ½ teaspoon prepared mustard, 2 sticks softened butter, ⅛ teaspoon cayenne, salt if needed. Chill 4 hours. Spread on white bread and fill sandwiches with sliced turkey.

HOW TO BE A GOOD COOK

...without really slaving

Why don't good meals cook themselves, or fully laden tables rise out of the floor, as one did in a private room in Versailles for Marie Antoinette? Here's a dinner menu that cuts both time and effort down to very small dimensions.

Menu

Jellied Madrilène with Celery
Herbed Roast Chicken Legs
Tomatoes with Feta Cheese
Melon Halves Filled with Fruit Salad
Chilean White Wine

JELLIED MADRILÈNE WITH CELERY

Chill canned madrilène until it jells. Top each bowl with two tablespoons of finely chopped celery.

HERBED ROAST CHICKEN LEGS SERVES 4

1 tablespoon butter
8 chicken legs
3 to 4 tablespoons olive oil
3 tablespoons mixed dried herbs,
preferably an imported Provençal mixture
1 tablespoon ground cardamom
Salt and pepper to taste

Preheat oven to 425°.
Butter a shallow casserole, arrange the chicken legs in one layer. Brush them well with part of the oil. Sprinkle with half the herbs and

cardamom and season with salt and pepper. Immediately turn the legs over, add the remaining oil and repeat seasoning. Bake until well browned, about ½ hour, turning once.

TOMATOES WITH FETA CHEESE   SERVES 4

4 ripe tomatoes, sliced
1½ cups crumbled feta cheese
3 tablespoons olive oil

1 cup coarsely chopped fresh basil
Coarse freshly ground pepper

Arrange the tomatoes on a serving platter; cover with cheese. Dribble the oil over the cheese, grind pepper over all, and sprinkle with basil. (No salt needed with feta.)

ALSO-EATS: CHEATER'S MAYONNAISE

An emergency sauce that tastes as good as the original—even has fewer calories: Stir 2 tablespoons Dijon-type mustard and 1 teaspoon Worcestershire sauce into a carton (1 cup) of plain yogurt.

Vogue Food, October 1, 1972

WATCH A MOVIE

*... let dinner cook itself:
remote control, or how a film reviewer cooks*

Molly Haskell and her husband, Andrew Sarris, both write about movies for New York's downtown newpaper, *The Village Voice,* and Molly likes to follow up a six-o'clock movie with a dinner that's been cooking while they've been viewing.

"It happens that our favorite meat dish is also one that can cook while we're at the movies. It's roast pork basted with honey and soy sauce. A four- to six-pound loin roast can serve four comfortably, six in a pinch, with lots of extras; but we can practically polish off one between us if no one is helping (or looking)."

MOLLY MOVIEGOER'S PORK ROAST

SERVES 4 TO 6

4- to 6-pound loin of pork roast   2 tablespoons flour
2 cloves garlic

FOR BASTING
¼ cup imported soy sauce
¼ cup honey

"I rub the roast with garlic and flour, mix the soy sauce and honey. I baste before going to the movie and again upon return. I put the meat in the oven at 350°. With slow cooking, the roast retains its juices and the flavor improves; at 350° it should roast a minimum of 2 hours for a 4-pound roast, 3 hours for a 6-pound one. Incidentally, I don't cut away much of the fat initially, because the combination of the fat and the sauce gives the roast a crispy, delicious (rich and fattening) crust."

Three Leave-and-Love Dinners that cook in your oven while you relax and watch a flick. Recipes are given for starred dishes:

Menu for a One-Hour Television Movie

Potato and Leek Soup
Roast Beef with Anchovies☆
Cold Lemon Soufflé
Beaujolais or Cider

Menu for a Two-Hour First-Run Film

Hot Stuffed Artichokes☆
Molly Moviegoer's Pork Roast (recipe given above)
Apples or Pears with Cheese
Beer or Chianti

Menu for a

Four-Hour Double-Feature Old Movie

Herring in Cream, Fresh Dill Added
Flemish Beer Stew ☆
Endive Salad, Vinaigrette Dressing
Melon Purée
Beer or Alsatian White Wine

ROAST BEEF WITH ANCHOVIES   SERVES 6

4-pound eye round of beef
Olive oil
2 cans flat anchovy fillets in oil,

drained
Coarsely ground pepper

Preheat oven to 325°.

Rub the beef with olive oil. Cut shallow lengthwise slits into the sides and insert the anchovy fillets from one can. Spread the fillets from the other can over the top. Sprinkle well with pepper. Wrap loosely in foil. Roast in the oven during a one-hour television movie.

HOT STUFFED ARTICHOKES   SERVES 6

6 artichokes
⅓ cup finely chopped parsley
⅓ cup finely chopped pitted black olives
⅓ cup seasoned Italian-type bread crumbs
¼ cup finely chopped mushroom stems

2 cloves garlic, squeezed through a press
¼ cup olive oil
Salt and pepper to taste
½ can flat anchovy fillets in oil, drained and mashed
Olive oil and water in equal quantities

Preheat oven to 350°.

Trim off the stems and leaf tips of the artichokes; remove any marred outside leaves. Combine the parsley, olives, bread crumbs, mushroom stems, garlic, and olive oil; season with salt and pepper. Spread the artichoke leaves apart with your fingers. With a teaspoon, scrape out the chokes, then insert the stuffing among leaves. Put a dab of mashed anchovy in the heart of each artichoke and squeeze closed again. Set them close together in an enameled or earthenware pan; add cooking oil and water to one third their height. Cover with oiled aluminum foil (so that the leaf tips won't dehydrate), put on the lid, and bake during a two-hour movie.

FLEMISH BEER STEW
SERVES 6 TO 8

⅓ pound bacon, cut into small
    pieces
6 medium onions, peeled and
    sliced
4½ pounds stewing beef, in 1-inch
    cubes
6 medium boiling potatoes,
    peeled, cut into 1-inch cubes
6 carrots, scraped and cut in half
1 teaspoon thyme

1 bay leaf
Few sprigs Italian parsley
Salt and pepper to taste
Dark beer to cover ingredients
    (about 3 12-ounce cans)
2 tablespoons Dijon-type mustard
2 slices stale whole-wheat bread,
    crusts removed
2 tablespoons finely chopped
    combined parsley and dill

Preheat oven to 300°.

Cook the bacon slowly in a heavy pot until all its fat is rendered, remove, and reserve for garnish. Cook the onion rings in bacon fat until soft. Add the meat and brown. Add the vegetables, herbs, and salt and pepper. Pour in beer to cover, bring to a boil. Spread mustard on both sides of the bread slices: place them on top of the meat and beer. Cover the pot and put into the oven during a four-hour movie. Remove; stir the bread into the gravy. Sprinkle with parsley, dill, and bits of bacon.

Vogue Food, October 15, 1972

A SPANISH DISH
FOR ALL REASONS: BUILD ON IT

From a brownstone house in New York, Pilar Turner spreads the word, and experience through tasting, of Spanish food. Born and brought up in Spain, she learned to cook at her convent school (at the age of ten she was an expert omelette maker). Slim and vivid, with Spanish dream good looks, Pilar Turner is now married to an American and is the mother of two boys. Here, *pollo à la Chilindrón*, one of her party dishes, the better part of a good meal, plus three menus with stars indicating additional recipes to shape around it.

POLLO À LA CHILINDRÓN

SERVES 16

A Mozarab dish, this chicken with sauce is therefore Arab-influenced and dates from the period between the eighth and fifteenth centuries when the Moorish culture was ineradicably stamped on every aspect of Spanish life. As it is primarily a party piece, we give the ingredients for sixteen servings, but the quantities can easily be halved or quartered for a smaller dinner.

4 frying chickens, 3 to 3½ pounds each, cut into pieces
Salt and pepper
Paprika
2 cups olive oil
2 slices, 2¼ inches thick, of Serrano ham (if available) or prosciutto, diced
16 sweet red peppers, seeded and chopped
8 onions, sliced thin

2 whole heads (not cloves) garlic, peeled and minced
12 tomatoes, peeled, seeded, and diced
1 cup dry white wine
1½ 16-ounce cans tomato purée
10 to 12 medium potatoes, peeled and sliced
Olive oil for frying potatoes
24 pitted small green olives
24 pitted small black olives

Season the chicken pieces with salt and pepper and dust all over with paprika, fry in 1¼ cups of the olive oil until crisp and golden. Drain.

Pour the remaining oil into a large casserole (preferably earthenware) and fry in it the diced ham, peppers, onions, and garlic until the onions are transparent. Add the tomatoes, wine, and tomato purée. Cook gently, uncovered, until this sauce is reduced by half. Add the chicken, cook 30 minutes longer.

Meanwhile, deep-fry (or panfry) the potatoes in the remaining olive oil until brown and crisp. Stir them into the casserole. At the very last moment add the olives and toss all together like a salad. Serve with Italian bread to soak up the sauce.

Menu One

Seafood Salad☆
Pollo à la Chilindrón☆
Vanilla Hedgehogs (Ice-Cream Balls Rolled in Crushed Nuts)

SEAFOOD SALAD

SERVES 8 TO 10

4 cups mixed raw shellfish and
    lean, white-fleshed fish
Juice of 4 limes
1 bay leaf
½ cup chopped onions
2 cups Mayonnaise☆
3 tablespoons chopped green
    herbs (chives, green onions,
    parsley)
1 cup canned green peas, drained
1 cup cubed carrots, cooked and
    drained
Cayenne to taste
White pepper to taste

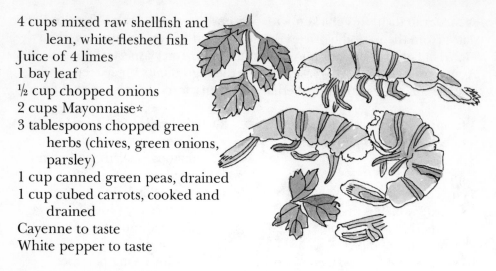

GARNISH: RADISH ROSES OR CHOPPED ENDIVES

Clean the fish and shellfish and cut any large portions into 1-inch pieces;
place in a large bowl. Pour boiling water over all and drain immediately.
Marinate in the lime juice with the bay leaf and onion in a dish, for at least
3 hours covered with plastic wrap or overnight, refrigerated. Remove the
bay leaf and mix in remaining ingredients. Season with cayenne and white
pepper and serve garnished with radish roses or chopped endives.

Menu Two

Melon and Onion Soup☆
Pollo à la Chilindrón☆
Fruit Eclairs (Sliced Fruit Added to Cream-filled Eclairs from the Bakery)

MELON AND ONION SOUP

SERVES 4 TO 6

1 medium melon (cantaloupe or
    muskmelon), or 2 packages
    frozen melon balls, thawed
1 quart water

1 medium onion, sliced
2 tablespoons sweet (unsalted)
    butter
Salt and pepper to taste

Scoop out the flesh of the melon and dice, or drain the melon balls. Boil the water, add the melon, boil 5 minutes; set aside. Fry the onion in butter until golden. Pour the melon and its cooking water over the onion and season with salt and pepper. Serve hot. With its subtle, light flavor, this is a good starter when a rich dish follows.

Menu Three

Sardines in White Wine☆
Pollo à la Chilindrón☆
Market Gardener's Salad (Mixed Vegetables in a Mustardy Vinaigrette Dressing)
Cheeses and Rye Wafers

SARDINES IN WHITE WINE   SERVES 8

16 large canned sardines, skinned and boned, the halves separated
3 medium Bermuda onions, peeled and sliced into thin rings

3 lemons, thinly sliced
White wine, heated to just below boiling point
Olive oil
Lemon juice
Salt and pepper to taste

Preheat oven to 250°.

Make a layer of the sardine halves in an ovenproof casserole; add a layer of onion and lemon slices. Repeat layering, ending with onions and lemon. Add wine just to cover. Put into the oven for 15 to 20 minutes. Remove, drain off the wine, sprinkle with olive oil and lemon juice, season with salt and pepper. Can be served hot or cold with crunchy chunks of warm buttered French bread.

BREAKFAST FLASH

DUTCH BABIES   SERVES 4

From Jack Larsen, textile designer, collector of primitive and contemporary crafts:

2 tablespoons butter	½ cup milk
3 eggs	¼ teaspoon salt
½ cup flour	

Preheat oven to 425°.

Melt the butter in a heavy 10-inch skillet in the oven. In a bowl beat the eggs vigorously 30 seconds; gradually beat in the flour. Mix in the milk and salt. Tip the preheated pan to coat with the melted butter. Pour in the batter, bake in the oven 20 minutes, lower temperature to 300°, and bake 5 minutes longer. Cut into wedges and serve hot with maple syrup, or with melted butter, lemon juice, and confectioner's sugar.

STICK TO A GOOD THING

Giorgio Sant'Angelo

"I love to concentrate on one flavor in a meal, carry it right through from soup to dessert"—that's the radical menu philosophy of Giorgio Sant'Angelo, who repeats and concentrates details and colors the same way in the clothes he designs. An Italian who lived on a ranch in Argentina as a child, Giorgio rejects not only classic menu planning (flavors and colors balanced, contrasted, no repeats) but classic foods: "I eat very lightly, nothing much before five in the afternoon, when I have a cup of spinach soup; then dinner at ten, after a nap. My favorites are vegetables, fish."

Colors are concentrated, too, in the meals Giorgio cooks. "If food is a good color, it will taste good. I hate muddy-colored food. I know by the color of the rice if it is properly cooked. Foods are like people; when people are happy and well, their hair shines, their skin glows. They get muddy-looking when they have problems or are sick. Digesting takes blood away from the brain and muscles. If you eat too much, the brain and muscles will be deprived of blood; then you can't do one thing properly.

"Presentation of food is very important to me . . . Japanese food is the most beautiful. I will eat anything in Japan because of the way it looks. I hate food all chopped up on canapés at cocktail parties; it looks like interior decoration . . . I like to look at objects all the time, but I really prefer looking at things that can be used. My grandmother said about objects: 'If it's not one of the finest quality, have a minimum of three, and then they appear to be a collection.'

"My grandmother was a fabulous cook. On our Argentine ranch, she also made her own face creams."

Here is one of Giorgio's dinner menus and the recipes for its four soup-to-sweet dishes, all with a fresh citrus taste. For good measure, Grandmother's face-cream formula follows his four recipes.

Giorgio's Lemon Menu

Cold Tomato and Lemon Soup☆
Baked Seviche☆
Zucchini in Lemon☆
Dolce al Limone (Lemon Dessert)☆
WINE
Pinot Chardonnay

COLD TOMATO AND LEMON SOUP

SERVES 8

2 medium cans tomato purée
1½ to 2 purée canfuls milk
Juice of 2 lemons
½ onion, finely minced
Salt and pepper to taste
4 drops hot pepper sauce
3 cucumbers, peeled and sliced
thin
1 lemon, cut into 8 slices
8 thin slices of peeled onion, separated into rings
8 teaspoons finely chopped parsley

Mix together in a bowl the tomato purée, milk to taste, lemon juice, onion, salt, pepper, and pepper sauce. Stir well. Salt the cucumber slices and set aside for 15 minutes, then wash, drain, and add to soup. Add a full tray of ice cubes. Chill 3 to 4 hours. Serve in chilled bowls. In each bowl float a teaspoonful of parsley. (The milk should be lightly curdled by the tomato and the lemon juice.)

BAKED SEVICHE
SERVES 8

12 flounder fillets, rinsed quickly and patted dry
Salt
Butter
Bread crumbs
1 clove garlic
1 large bunch dill, chopped (⅔ cup)
Pepper to taste

Juice of 2 to 3 lemons, or more if needed
4 tablespoons butter, cut up
1 onion, peeled and sliced into rings
1 cup plain croutons
1 lemon, thinly sliced
½ cup finely chopped parsley

Salt the fillets, lay them flat in a large shallow casserole that has been buttered and crumbed. Squeeze the garlic through a press over the fish; sprinkle with the dill and pepper. Cover the fish completely with lemon juice (the fish must be almost awash), cover the casserole with plastic wrap, leave in a cool spot 1½ hours. Uncover it, dot each fillet with about 1 teaspoon butter. Put the onion rings on top, sprinkle with croutons, then add lemon slices. Preheat oven to 500°, then bake the *seviche* for a maximum of 15 minutes. Scatter parsley on top.

ZUCCHINI IN LEMON
SERVES 8

1 onion, peeled, sliced, and cooked gently in butter until soft
1 lemon, thinly sliced
8 medium zucchini (6 inches), sliced lengthwise

Salt and pepper to taste

Juice of 1 lemon
½ cup water
½ cup dry white wine
} mixed, heated to boiling point

In a large shallow flameproof casserole that has a lid make a layer of the cooked onion. On top put half of the lemon slices. Season the zucchini with salt and pepper, lay the slices in one layer in the casserole. Cook, uncovered, on top of the stove for a few minutes. Add liquids and continue cooking until the liquid is absorbed but the zucchini is still firm.

DOLCE AL LIMONE
(Lemon Dessert)

1 9-inch round poundcake
Juice of 8 oranges
Juice of 1 lime
Juice of 1 lemon
1 jigger brandy

1 pint dairy sour cream
4 ripe peaches, peeled, or equiva-
    lent amount of other ripe
    fruit in season
1 orange, peeled and sectioned

Slice the poundcake horizontally into three layers. Mix the citrus juices with the brandy; pour three quarters of it over the cake slices. Stir the remaining juice into the sour cream. Slice the peaches (or other fruit in season, or use a mixture), add the orange sections. Starting with cake, arrange in a deep round dish alternate layers of cake, sour cream, and fruit, ending with fruit. Refrigerate 1 hour, then cut into wedges, and serve.

GIORGIO'S GRANDMOTHER'S FACE CREAM

Grind together to a smooth paste (in a mortar, or use your blender) fresh cucumber, lettuce hearts, lemon juice, and olive oil. Store in refrigerator. Giorgio Sant'Angelo says, "It kept my grandmother's skin young all her life."

Vogue Food, December 1972

DINNER IN A PIE SHELL

Margot Vonnegut

Margot Vonnegut Rivera calls herself a "pie lady." Her kitchen fills with good smells while she bakes quiches Lorraine, chicken or meat pies, all sorts of substantial main dishes in delicate pastry shells.

Daughter of the novelist Kurt Vonnegut, Jr., Margot writes, but she also paints, too, especially angels. Here is one of Margot's favorite pie recipes and the recipes for the quick-trick fig dessert she serves with it.

CHEESE PIE WITH ASPARAGUS

SERVES 4 TO 6

1 9-inch pastry shell, prebaked 5
    minutes
6 slices bacon
1 large onion, peeled and thinly
    sliced
½ cup grated Swiss cheese
2 tablespoons grated Parmesan
    cheese
1¼ cups heavy cream
2 eggs, lightly beaten
Salt and white pepper to taste
⅛ teaspoon ground nutmeg
6 asparagus tips, lightly cooked

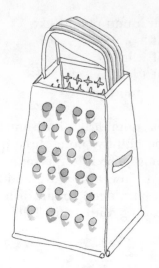

Preheat oven to 375°.

    Prepare the pie shell. Cook the bacon until crisp, then drain and crumble; reserve the bacon fat. Cook the onion gently in bacon fat until transparent; drain. Combine the bacon, onion, and cheeses, and scatter in the pastry shell. Mix the cream, eggs, salt, and pepper; pour into the pie shell. Top with the asparagus tips, arranging them in any pattern you like (they will sink a little). Bake 35 to 40 minutes or until golden brown. Serve warm, with a green salad and a nice wine.

MARGOT'S FIG DESSERT

Pour a little cognac over peeled fresh figs, perhaps 3 to a serving, and let them stand 30 minutes. Mix ⅓ cup curaçao into 1 cup dairy sour cream; serve with the figs.

Vogue Food, February 1973

NOW TRY SUMMER DISHES FOR WINTER MEALS

By February it's been winter forever and spring is nowhere. Get a head start now on summer with these Caribbean cold dishes, straight from island-goers' tables, to lighten winter meals anywhere.

    Mrs. Paul Peralta-Ramos brought this recipe for a hot-weather menu with her from her cool homeland, Sweden.

MARINATED SALMON

SERVES 8

6 pounds center-cut salmon in
    one piece
⅔ cup coarse (kosher) salt
½ cup sugar
20 white peppercorns, crushed

Pinch of saltpeter (at drugstores;
    optional)
Whole fresh dill sprigs
Chopped fresh dill

Split the salmon lengthwise into 2 halves, and remove all bones. Mix the salt, sugar, pepper, and saltpeter, spread in an even layer on half of the fish, laid skin side down on a platter. Add a generous layer of whole fresh dill. Lay the second half of the fish, flesh side down, over the dill, cover with a board, and weight this with a heavy object (canned goods or a rock). Refrigerate for 24 hours. Remove the seasonings and dill. To serve, cut the fish loose from the skin in half-inch diagonal slices. Arrange these for serving and top with chopped fresh dill. Serve with Mustard Sauce (below) as a main course with hot boiled potatoes, or serve as a first course.

MUSTARD SAUCE FOR MARINATED SALMON

SERVES 8

3 tablespoons olive oil
1½ teaspoons wine vinegar
½ teaspoon French mustard,
    Dijon type
1 teaspoon Swedish mustard, if
    available; or substitute Ger-

man mustard or another
    mustard on the sweet side
Salt and white pepper to taste
1 teaspoon sugar
Chopped dill, about 1 tablespoon

Combine the first 6 ingredients, then add the chopped dill. The mustard taste should be strong.

CURRIED RICE SALAD

SERVES 8

Marietta (Mrs. Ronald) Tree, who works in New York on hospital and health planning, planned this meal in Barbados: lightly cooked fresh string beans with a vinaigrette sauce, cold meats, and curried rice salad.

1 tablespoon curry powder, mixed
   to a paste with water
½ cup Mayonnaise☆
½ cup heavy cream
4 cups cold cooked rice
1 cup fresh pineapple chunks
1 cup sliced bananas
¼ cup pignolias (pine nuts)

¼ cup seedless raisins
Salt and pepper to taste
16 small onions, boiled until
   tender, then browned in
   butter
8 ripe small or cherry tomatoes,
   cut into wedges

Blend the curry powder into the mayonnaise and cream. Add the rice, fruits, pignolias, and raisins, season with salt and pepper. Top with the onions and tomatoes; season again; chill.

BULGUR SALAD   SERVES 6

Cracked wheat is an offshore cook's sustainer. When Mr. and Mrs. Ahmet Ertegun escape New York's cold winds on Barbados, Mica serves this version of a salad favored by Islanders.

½ cup fine bulgur (a cracked
   wheat found in health-food
   stores and delicacy
   departments)
1 cup finely chopped Italian
   parsley
½ cup finely chopped onions
½ cup chopped scallions
3 tomatoes, seeded, cut into

   wedges
1 green pepper, seeded and
   chopped
Juice of 2 lemons
2 tablespoons finely chopped
   fresh mint
1 teaspoon dried mint
Salt and pepper to taste

Soak the bulgur overnight in cool water. In the morning drain it, then squeeze it dry in a towel. Mix all ingredients together; chill until dinnertime.

Vogue Food, March 1973

MEALS THEY LIKE BEST

*Yves Saint Laurent
and His Private Five*

Yves Saint Laurent lives almost like a recluse, so seldom does he leave his Paris duplex apartment and its treasure of Art Deco objects from the Thirties and Forties. He sees only a few close friends and the people who work with him—they are his true family. What foods do Yves and his friends like best? Here, for Saint Laureed and five cronies: what they choose, typical menus, and recipes for a pair of special dishes.

Yves Saint Laurent, remote and inaccessible to the public (and, says Loulou de La Falaise, "However well you know him, you are still awed by him"), in private does funny imitations, songs, dances, wickedly pointed cartoons. A perfectionist who will throw out a marble table if it suffers one chip, he is equally selective about food. His favorite "family" meal is strangely American: canned tuna, medium-rare steak, mashed potatoes, cream cheese with sugar, apple brown Betty. Here, another meal that Yves likes:

Sole Fritters
Sautéed Veal Scallops
Rice Pilaf
Lettuce Salad
Floating Island
Evian Water

SAINT LAURENT TIP Sole fritters for this menu are made by cutting fillets in 1-inch squares. Season with salt and pepper, dust with flour, fry in ample butter until golden. Drain well.

Pierre Bergé A compact man, explosive, intensely loving and loyal to his friends, Pierre Bergé is a brilliant president for Yves Saint Laurent's business. Though a great gourmet, Bergé actually eats sparingly, likes raw sardines on toast followed by an *haute-cuisine* meat dish, then hard cheese with apples. He sips vintage wine, Saint Laurent drinks mineral water. Another Bergé menu:

Polish Vodka
Cold Poached Egg on Caviar in Aspic
Roast Saddle of Lamb
Fried Bananas
Green Peas
Passion Fruit Sherbet
WINES
Château Lafite-Rothschild, 1945
Bollinger Champagne

BERGÉ TIPS   Passion fruit juice for sherbet can be found at food specialty shops and health-food stores.

Betty Catroux   Wife of interior designer François Catroux and a long-time friend of Yves Saint Laurent, this sweet-natured languid woman has the figure that Saint Laurent thinks perfect for his clothes, which she wears exactly as he has visualized them. Here, a Catroux menu:

Sea Urchins
Green Lasagne Baked with Tomatoes, Béchamel Sauce
Roquefort Cheese with Worcestershire Sauce
Chocolate Charlotte

CATROUX TIP   Sea urchins are hard to find in the United States. If you do find them, snip off the tops with nail scissors, serve cold. Scoop out their pink roe with a silver teaspoon.

Clara Saint   A tiny, rounded girl with curious bright-green eyes, shiny red hair, and perfect legs, she is always hungry, always in a hurry, roasts baby chickens to save time, and washes them down with Coca-Cola or champagne. Clara eats enormous portions of tomato salad with vinaigrette dressing, dipping crusty French bread in the juices. Here, a favorite Saint menu:

Asparagus with Hollandaise Sauce
Fried Chicken
Lettuce Salad with Olive Oil and Lemon Juice
Sliced Fresh Peaches
Iced Tea with Lemon

SAINT TIP   In France asparagus is served lukewarm, piled on a white linen napkin to absorb extra moisture that might spoil the texture of the sauce. Hollandaise Sauce☆ is offered separately in a sauceboat.

Loulou de La Falaise   To Saint Laurent, Loulou represents the boutique style, and she is a pacesetter who is first with the next haircut or catchword. She is also his creative assistant, working with him on all aspects of design. She is Yves's idea girl, communicative, with intuition about the future in all aspects of life. She cooks vegetables in a Chinese bamboo steamer or deep-fries them in the Japanese way, adding apple slices. She likes sweet omelettes with jam, and such spicy dishes as spaghetti with curry sauce, three-pepper chicken. After the chicken Loulou serves fruit salad.

Whiskey Sour Made with Honey
Three-Pepper Chicken with Onions and Endives✩
Fruit Salad with Pineapple Sauce

LA FALAISE TIP   Purée canned pineapple chunks with their juice and half as much cream together in a blender to make sauce to top a fresh fruit salad.

THREE-PEPPER CHICKEN WITH ONIONS AND ENDIVES   SERVES 4

2 tablespoons butter
Dash of paprika
Dash of black pepper
Dash of cayenne
Salt to taste

2- to 3-pound chicken
Chicken stock
4 onions, peeled and quartered
4 whole Belgian endives

Preheat oven to 450°.

Mash together the butter, paprika, black and cayenne peppers, and salt; rub the inside and outside of the chicken. Place it in a roasting pan with a little chicken stock—enough to cover the bottom generously—and the onions and endives. Roast for 20 to 25 minutes, basting several times. The vegetables will still be a bit crisp.

Marina Schiano   Direct, passionate, and loyal, she is capable of great authority and efficiency as the director of Yves Saint Laurent's New York affairs. Marina talks and laughs without drawing breath—often on the telephone on different lines with several friends at once. Here, Marina's dinner for two:

Rigatoni with Ricotta✩
Pasticciera Cream
WINE
Château Meyney or Valpolicella

SCHIANO TIP   A good recipe for the pasticciera cream can be found in *The Talisman Italian Cookbook,* by Ada Boni (New York, Crown, 1955). It is a boiled custard, flavored with vanilla, lemon peel, and butter, then chilled.

RIGATONI WITH RICOTTA

SERVES 2 TO 3

2 tablespoons olive oil
¼ cup finely chopped celery
¼ cup finely chopped onions
1 tablespoon chopped basil
Salt
Pinch of black pepper

Pinch of cayenne
1 medium can tomatoes, drained
1 tablespoon red wine
½ pound rigatoni or a similar
    large macaroni
½ pound ricotta cheese

Heat the olive oil in a skillet and add the celery, onions, basil, salt, and black and cayenne peppers. Cook until the onions are lightly browned. Lower the heat and add the tomatoes, one at a time, crushing them into the pan with a fork. Raise the heat and cook about 7 minutes, until bubbly; lower the heat and add the wine; cook gently for 10 minutes. Taste, and adjust the seasonings if necessary. Meanwhile, cook the rigatoni in a large pot of boiling water until *al dente.* Put the ricotta in a warmed serving bowl and soften with enough water from the boiling pasta to make it creamy but not runny. Drain the pasta. Stir half the tomato sauce into the ricotta and add pasta; stir; add the remaining sauce and stir again. Serve at once.

Vogue Food, April 1973

EAT FOR ENERGY

... fast movers and the foods they choose for fuel

Adriana Jackson
Pasta for Sixty

Whirling through days at the Alex Auder Iolas Gallery in New York, where her husband, Brooks Jackson, is the director, doesn't prevent Adriana Jackson—a blond Milanese pepper—from keeping a nearly permanent party going on in their apartment, where established and far-out artists appear together—sometimes unexpected, but always welcome. Adriana stokes her energy with the Italian equivalent of Vitamin B_{12}— pasta. To give guests a chance at keeping up with her, she often serves pasta at the party, too; freezes Bolognese lasagne for sixty people, all ready to heat. Here, her recipe, divisible, if you like, for a smaller number of guests."

LASAGNE VERDE ALLA BOLOGNESE
(Green Lasagne in the Bolognese Fashion)
SERVES 60

THE PASTA

15 pounds packaged green
        lasagne noodles

TOMATO SAUCE

2 sticks butter
½ cup olive oil
6 onions, finely chopped
1½ cups finely chopped celery
7 small carrots, finely chopped
Salt and pepper to taste
6 pounds finely ground beef and
        veal, a small quantity of lean
        pork included
2 cups dry white wine
15 cups canned tomato sauce (not
        tomato paste)
10 leaves of fresh basil, chopped

BÉCHAMEL SAUCE

2½ pounds butter
4 cups flour
Salt to taste
8 quarts milk, warmed
½ teaspoon ground nutmeg

CHEESE

3 pounds imported Parmesan,
        freshly grated

TO MAKE THE TOMATO SAUCE: Melt the butter in the oil in a large heavy pot. Add the vegetables and a little salt and pepper. Stir in the meat, raise the heat, and cook, stirring, until the meat is lightly browned. Add the wine, tomato sauce, and basil, simmer, covered, for 1 hour, adding a little water if the sauce becomes too thick.

TO MAKE THE BÉCHAMEL: Melt the butter in a big heavy saucepan. Slowly stir in the flour, stir until smooth, and add salt. Add the milk slowly, stirring until smooth and creamy; cook 5 minutes after thickening. Season with nutmeg.

Cook the pasta in a large quantity of salted water until tender but not soft; drain.

TO ASSEMBLE THE LASAGNE: In shallow buttered pans, alternate tomato and béchamel sauces between layers of pasta, beginning with a little tomato sauce. Cool, cover tightly with foil, and freeze. The day of the party, defrost (allow 6 hours or more), then bake at 350° for 15 minutes or until thoroughly heated.

Anjelica Huston *Potatoes*

A young beauty who left her childhood in Ireland (where her father, film director John Huston, is a Missouri-born settler) to study in England, where she has done some fashion modeling, Anjelica Huston now lives in Hollywood. To retain her willowy model's figure, she cuts out carbohydrates that bore her and concentrates on the kind she loves: potatoes, particularly mashed.

"Potatoes aren't as fattening for me as those other starches. When I feel drained, I think they give me energy, improve my skin. In fact, I love all English food . . . Yorkshire pudding with drippings and real gravy, and all those steamed puddings with jam sauces."

Bobby Short *Beef*

To reach his top spot in the pop-music world—singing behind his piano three times a night, Tuesdays to Saturdays, usually at one of New York's best night spots, where he makes every age seem the right one for love— Bobby Short zipped through careers in California and Paris, developing the stamina of a long-distance runner. He's as careful of his diet as an athlete, eats one big meal a day, at lunchtime—and it's beef: Broiled sirloin steak with *petits pois,* or the crusty end of a beef roast. In summer, a meal of sliced cold roast beef with a vinaigrette sauce gives the same strong support. "If I still don't feel energetic," he said, "I have a steak sandwich, underdone, after my first show."

Edward Villella *Honey*

Once nude and absolutely still in the New York City Ballet's production of Jerome Robbins' *Watermill,* Edward Villella expresses more energy than other dancers project in conventionally athletic roles. To keep up the strength his dancing demands, he finds Vitamins E and B_{12} "mentally and physically reassuring," dines at four o'clock in the afternoon before performances: steak, salad, vegetables, yogurt with honey; ginger ale, coffee. While this power dancer is onstage, he keeps a honeypot in the wings, gulps a spoonful at every chance. "In the bloodstream in two minutes."

Arthur M. Schlesinger, Jr.
Soup

Always on the rush—with his bow tie seemingly permanently askew (his books include *The Age of Jackson, The Age of Roosevelt,* and *A Thousand Days*) Arthur Schlesinger has stretched his energy to edit or contribute to another half-dozen books. For fuel food he prefers a high-protein dinner of beefsteak (served with tarragon butter), string beans dressed with sour cream, and salad; ups the protein content by always starting with home-made green pea soup. Here, the recipe his wife, Alexandra, uses:

GREEN PEA SOUP
SERVES 2

1 package frozen green peas
1 cup chicken broth
1 cup milk
1 teaspoon chopped fresh dill or

½ teaspoon dried dill weed
1 tablespoon butter
Salt and pepper to taste

Cook the peas in very little water just until tender. Combine with the broth, milk, and dill. Purée in a blender, then heat, adding the butter, salt and pepper.

Vogue Food, May 1973

FREE FLOW OF FOOD

Dinner to Keep Diners Talking . . .
Soup to Sharpen Appetities and Ideas . . .
Vegetables to Brighten Eyes and Wits . . .
And the Big, Big Dessert!

For brilliant entertaining, why not try out a dinner with first a fabulous soup . . . not a consommé . . . or something unctuous, but a real soup-scoop of ambiguous and tantalizing flavor and aroma, containing just enough delectable solids to keep the slurping pace to *moderato*. Then, just as your guests are dreading the possibility of white-on-white Chicken à la King, or a beige-on-beige dish, or a brown-on-brown stew, *dazzle* them with a wide-screen color epic of perfectly cooked vegetables on long platters—a glow, a flash, a vista of orange, white, and green, as decreed by season, not by can. Don't bother about meat and fish; let them off the hook.

The conversation, which might have been a trifle earthy during the soup, will not become lighter with relief, more spiritual (a touch of melancholy from dedicated carnivores will only add depth and shading). Amusing remarks will dart around the table as the glazed carrots go one way and the braised endives go the other . . . while the asparagus with prosciutto gets hijacked en route. There is something young and artless about a slightly undercooked carrot lightly sprinkled with freshly chopped dill and chives, a hint of mint.

The cheese course must be played by ear . . . and nose. The olfactory annoyance and impetuous runniness of some of our favorites are perhaps better reserved for a lunch near an open window in spring.

That sugar craving whose satisfaction breeds such guilty good humor must be treated with brio, with dash and lashings of super-no-nos. Whatever-it-is—Viennese *torte*, English trifle or a strawberry-laden meringue layer—must puff, crunch, ooze, and explode with whipped cream or other forbidden pleasures. Its extravagance must rape the most disciplined palates. Subtle and satanic whiffs of *poire* or *framboise*, brandy or Armagnac, applejack or rum, will throw the guests into feverish talk of love, passion, and betrayal . . . wicked scraps of gossip will erupt as their expensive teeth bear down on brandied cherries . . . intriguing personal revelations will be just audible through the delicate crunch of meringue.

As for the wine, let it be copious, self-service. By the time you serve coffee, the wariest—troubled during cocktails by the social, racial, or financial status of some hitherto unknown dinner partner—will be planning trips with that person to Haiti, Persepolis, or Kashmir.

Here is a menu followed by recipes for the four vegetable dishes:

Vegetable Soup☆
Braised Endives☆
Asparagus Tips with Prosciutto☆
Glazed Herbed Carrots☆
Strawberry Meringue Layer
WINE
California Chablis

VEGETABLE SOUP

The vegetables should be in the following measures: 1 cup each cut-up onions and potatoes and 2 cups each cut-up summer squash and fresh tomatoes (peeled). Boil them in 1½ quarts water until tender; purée. Add enough beef bouillon to make a creamy consistency. Season with basil, oregano, parsley, salt, and pepper. To serve: Top each portion with sour cream, chopped chives, and a sprinkling of fried bread croutons.

BRAISED ENDIVES

16 to 24 Belgian endives, trimmed
  (number will depend on size)
20 to 24 strips bacon
½ cup finely chopped parsley
2 tablespoons crumbled dried
  thyme

2 bay leaves, crumbled
2 cloves garlic, crushed
2 onions, finely minced
2 cups (or amount needed) vegetable or chicken stock

Toss the endives into boiling water and blanch 5 minutes. Drain and pat dry. Line a large flameproof casserole with the bacon; sprinkle in the parsley, thyme, bay leaves, garlic, and onion. Arrange the endives on this aromatic bed. Barely cover them with vegetable or chicken stock, cover, and simmer until tender. Just before serving, uncover and reduce the liquid over sharp heat until it is absorbed and the bacon becomes crisp.

ASPARAGUS TIPS WITH PROSCIUTTO

36 raw asparagus tips, about 1
  inch long
2 sticks butter
½ teaspoon sugar
1 onion, peeled

1 cup hot water
Salt and pepper to taste
3 or 4 slices prosciutto (or ham),
  finely chopped (about 4
  tablespoons)

Toss the asparagus into boiling water to blanch for 2 minutes; drain. Melt 1½ sticks of the butter in a deep skillet, add the sugar, onion, asparagus, and after a few seconds ½ cup of the hot water. Cook, uncovered, very gently until the asparagus tips are fork-tender. Add a little more hot water if the moisture evaporates too quickly. Remove the onion, season the asparagus with salt and pepper. To serve: Mash the remaining half stick of butter and the prosciutto together; divide the mixture into 8 pats and arrange on top of the asparagus.

GLAZED HERBED CARROTS

SERVES 8

3 pounds carrots
4 cups chicken or veal stock
1¼ sticks butter
4 tablespoons sugar
Salt and black pepper

2 tablespoons finely chopped
   fresh mint
2 tablespoons finely chopped
   parsley
2 tablespoons finely chopped dill

Scrape the carrots, cut them into 2-inch sections, and quarter the sections. (Baby carrots need no scraping and can be left whole.) Put them into a saucepan with enough of the stock to cover. Add the butter, sugar, salt, and pepper, cook over moderate heat for 20 to 25 minutes or until just fork-tender. The liquid should be reduced almost to a glaze, so be wary of burning; carrots should be very bright and shiny. Serve with the mixed mint, parsley, and dill sprinkled on top.

Vogue Food, December 1973

KITCHEN-FREE CHRISTMAS

*... avoid that last-minute
stampede to the stove
freeze—now!*

Avoiding another Christmas like last year's is apt to be your New Year's resolution as you emerge, disheveled and cross, from a battlefield of dirty dishes, torn wrapping paper, hopelessly entangled decorations on a lop-sided tree whose needles are forever embedded in the rug.

Even where a holiday is no longer considered a Holy Day, a little leisure—a lazy morning in bed with coffee, papers, and telephone—is totally divine compared to the profanities one mutters in the kitchen while preparing early for the festive needs of others who are still sound asleep. The trick is to try to have your (Christmas) cake and eat it too: to be rested, relaxed, and looking your best even after catering to the gathering of the clan. How? As the store ads say, "Shop early"—and cook early, too—one project at a time, and refrigerate or freeze food in reasonable-sized batches that are labeled, ready to serve at a moment's notice. You can pick and choose, make your menu to suit your fancy and suit your guests. Here are some delicious things:

SAFFRON APPLES WITH ALMOND CREAM

SERVES 8

This can be prepared a day or two in advance and refrigerated under plastic wrap. It's terribly pretty, delights all ages.

8 to 10 Golden Delicious or other sweet cooking apples, peeled, cored, cut in 1-inch chunks
Enough white wine to cover bot-

tom of pan
½ cup honey
½ teaspoon saffron threads

Cook all the ingredients in a covered enameled pan over low heat until the apples are tender but not mushy; then simmer, uncovered, to evaporate the juices. Pile in the center of a flat, shallow serving dish and cool. Chill until needed. Serve with Almond Cream (recipe follows).

ALMOND CREAM

2 cups heavy cream
¼ cup sugar

½ cup ground blanched almonds
Almond extract, about 6 drops

Whip the cream until it peaks, adding sugar gradually after it begins to thicken. Stir in the ground almonds and almond extract. Just before serving, spoon the cream into a ring around the apples.

Bob Colacello, Italian-American, editor-in-chief of *Interview* magazine and man-about-many-towns, never forgets a word that's said, including his own. His mother, Mrs. John Colacello, suggests this dish as part of the traditional Italian Christmas Eve meatless dinner:

EGGPLANT STUFFED WITH ANCHOVIES

SERVES 6

6 very small eggplants, tops cut off, insides scooped out
1 clove garlic, finely chopped
Salt and freshly ground pepper to taste
1 cup packaged Italian-style bread crumbs

½ cup grated Parmesan cheese
1 can flat anchovy fillets in oil, drained and minced
3 tablespoons vegetable oil, or amount needed
1 cup meatless tomato sauce

Chop the scooped-out eggplant flesh. Mix with the garlic, salt, and pepper. Mix the bread crumbs and cheese, make a well in the center of the mixture, and add the chopped eggplant and anchovies. Mix well and stuff each eggplant. Quick-fry the eggplant cases on all sides in a pan with vegetable oil. Add the tomato sauce, cover, and simmer until tender.

For Memorable Christmas Eating—succulent corned mutton ham, a nineteenth-century surprise, updated. Try the best butcher in town for the mutton, and order in advance.

CORNED MUTTON HAM   SERVES 12

1 cup coarse salt	6 small onions, whole, peeled
1 cup light brown sugar	6 potatoes, whole, peeled
3 tablespoons saltpeter (at drugstores)	6 carrots, whole, scraped
A leg of mutton, if available, or a large leg of oldish lamb	2 tablespoons mixed minced parsley and dill
	Pepper to taste

Mix the salt, sugar, and saltpeter together and rub well into the mutton. Put it in a large enameled or stainless-steel pan in a cool place (the bottom of the refrigerator is good). In a day or two it will create its own brine. About twice a day rub the salts and sugar in the pan into the meat; turn it over every few days. If needed—if the salt and sugar have all dissolved—rub in more of the mixture in the same proportions. Leave the mutton in its pickle for at least a week (although 10 days or 2 weeks is better).

When the pickling process is finished, rinse the meat well. Then simmer it gently in water to cover, allowing about 15 to 20 minutes to the pound. During the last 30 to 45 minutes, add the onions, potatoes, carrots, parsley and dill, and pepper, but no salt, to the broth. Serve the meat hot with the vegetables. Cool leftover meat in the broth, then drain and refrigerate; the meat keeps like ham.

SAFFRON BREAD   MAKES 1 LOAF

This is a very early English and Danish bread, probably dating from the late fifteenth century. It used to be made sweet, and you can still do this by adding ½ cup sugar to the flour and kneading in ½ cup mixed seedless raisins and currants after the first punching-down. The sweet version makes a delicious tea bread and is very good toasted. The crust is shiny and golden and the crumb is a delicious yellow.

¼ teaspoon saffron threads (or
    more, if desired)
¾ cup milk
1 envelope dry yeast
4 tablespoons lukewarm water

Pinch of sugar
3½ cups flour, approximately
2 teaspoons salt
2 eggs, beaten
Flour for kneading

Add the saffron to the milk and scald. Let it cool. Dissolve the yeast in the lukewarm water with a few grains of sugar added and let it "proof": if the yeast is active, it will foam to fill a cup within about 10 minutes. Sift together 3 cups of the flour and the salt. Make a well in the flour, pour in the eggs, milk, and the yeast mixture; beat. Add more flour as necessary to prevent the dough from becoming sticky. Knead on a board, adding more flour as needed, until the dough is smooth and elastic.

    Put into a greased bowl in a warmish place (85°) and leave it to rise until it has doubled in bulk (about 45 minutes). Punch down. (For finer bread texture, let it rise again and punch down again.) Shape into a round loaf 6 to 7 inches across, put it on a greased baking sheet, and leave to rise until it has again doubled in size, *meanwhile preheating the oven to 375°.*

    Bake the bread for 25 to 30 minutes. Paint the top with ice water 10 minutes before loaf is done to make a crisp crust. Cool on a rack. Wrap and freeze it if you wish.

Vogue Food, September 1, 1946

MAURA LAVERTY

BUTTERMILK IRISH BREAD

"The secret of good cake-bread is three-day-old buttermilk, a light hand for mixing and kneading, and a brisk oven. But buttermilk is not always easy to come by," notes Maura Laverty. "In the winter when the cows go dry, some of us use a very effective substitute which we call 'winter buttermilk' or 'barm,' and this is how it is made:

    "Mix a quarter pound (1 cup) of flour to a smooth paste with 1 cupful of cold water. Put this in a large jug or crock. Add 2 grated raw potatoes and 2 mashed cooked potatoes. Now mix in 7 cups of cold water. Cover and leave on the kitchen mantelpiece or in some such warm place for at least 2 days. When you are baking, pour off carefully, and without disturbing the sediment, as much liquid as you use. This liquid may be used in the same way as buttermilk and will give you lovely, light bread. Add fresh water to make up for what you have used."

4 cups flour	1 teaspoon baking soda
1 teaspoon salt	Buttermilk or barm (see above) to
1 teaspoon sugar	mix dough

Preheat oven to 450°.

Sift the dry ingredients several times. Make a well in the center. Pour in the buttermilk or barm gradually, mixing in the flour from the sides. The amount of buttermilk needed will depend to a great extent on the quality of the flour. In any case, it's a good rule to make the dough rather wet than dry. A dry ragged dough gives a tough cake. The dough should be of such a consistency that it does *not* leave the sides of the bowl clean when turned onto a floured board.

Knead the dough lightly for a few minutes, turning the sides in toward the center, and working it round and round while doing so. Now turn it upside down so that the smooth side is on top, pat it to a round, brush it with milk, and cut a cross on it to keep it from cracking in the baking. Let the cuts go down over the sides of the cake to make sure of this. Bake for 45 minutes. Cool on a rack. Serve while very fresh.

Vogue Food, January 1974

WASTE NOT, EAT WELL

... seven-day cooking plan
to make more of less time, money, food

The message from the tube is BUY! Floored by the image of the latest mirror-bright, fairest-of-them-all, non-skid wax, we dash, drunk with desire, to the supermarket for another Impulse Tour of Disneyland . . . where the packaging blinks and beckons, where we buy, buy, buy. The crunch comes when we have to pay, pay, pay. All these goodies that no longer look so tempting (and so many of them)—did we really buy all that? Heaven knows, the well-run supermarkets try to offer us shopping advice with their special but special Specials.

Especially painful: Uncoordinated impulse buying of fool-food that always stays and stays, unused and crammed into cupboard or freezer. Totaling up the price of folly, we suddenly realize that we could have taken that trip, bought that divine feather boa . . . were it not for our own penny-wise, pound-foolishness. Below are some tips to help you run a kitchen with imaginative frugality . . . to use up every scrap of food you buy. Also, to cut down on food bills (and on time spent cooking meals), an idea: Create deliberate leftovers . . . prepare more than will actually be eaten for each meal, then use the little reserve in a new way on the following day. The unexpected guest . . . or invitation . . . fits very well into this plan, which is just a simple approach to buying and preparing food that can adapt to all your favorite recipes. The results will be unique, creative, personal.

VEGETABLE GREENS

Make a nutritious green vegetable base for soup by dumping into a heavy pot with a tight cover all your washed vegetable trimmings, including carrot, beet, and radish tops (but not potato peelings). Add water to cover, cook, covered, over high heat for 2 hours (or simmer on low for longer), then purée through a vegetable mill. If too many bitter-tasting greens have been added, run through a blender with a little sugar or creamed sweet corn. Store in a jar in the refrigerator. Add to ice-cold yogurt for a cold soup or use as a base for hot soups.

LEFTOVER BREAD AND BISCUITS

Bake on the oven shelf at a low temperature until the breads are perfectly dry, grind into crumbs in a blender. Divide the quantity in half. Mix half with mixed dried herbs, store in a jar for breading meats and chicken. Mix the other half of the crumbs with brown sugar and keep in a jar as a topping for oven-browned desserts.

LEFTOVER EGG WHITES

Make macaroons . . . meringue topping for desserts . . . or add a few whole eggs and make a low-cholesterol fluffy soufflé omelette for breakfast or lunch. Lightly whipped, egg whites also make an excellent face mask to tighten the skin.

SOURED MILK OR CREAM

Make a big batch of buttermilk biscuits, have fresh biscuits for breakfast, or freeze the dough to use later.

LEFTOVER JELLIES AND JAMS

Keep adding and stirring small leftovers into a large jar of honey. Keep as a sauce to serve, warmed, over ice cream or apple pie, or to spoon over apples before baking them. To use as a relish for pork, add vinegar to the honey-and-jam mixture.

CITRUS FRUIT

Before using the fruit, remove the peel, the thin outer part only: (1) Dry the peel thoroughly and save in jars for flavoring desserts and stews; (2) Steep the peel in vodka—for at least a month—then use the vodka as an inexpensive liqueur for flavoring desserts or even cocktails.

SEVEN-DAY PLAN FOR WASTELESS GOOD EATING

Here are a week's dinner plans, with recipes, for two people—Sunday lunch thrown in.

Monday

4 broiled fillets of flaky fish
(eat 2, reserve 2)
4 large Baked Onions☆
(eat 2, reserve 2)
Green salad

BAKED ONIONS

Preheat oven to 375°.

Without removing the outer skin, force the inner layers of onions open a little and slip inside 1 chopped anchovy for each onion. Dribble in a bit of the oil from the anchovies. Bake for about 1½ hours in a buttered dish. To serve, remove the outer skin, pour some melted butter and chopped parsley over the onions.

Tuesday

Fish Soup☆
(a meal in itself, made with Monday's fish fillets,
onions, and green salad) 10 potatoes,
boiled or steamed, unpeeled
(use 2, reserve 4 for Wednesday, 4 for Sunday)

FISH SOUP

Boil 4 cups water (or 3 cups water, 1 cup white wine) and add 4 table-spoons vegetable-bouillon powder; stir until dissolved. Cool slightly and purée in a blender with Monday's 2 baked onions (peeled), any leftover salad, and 2 boiled potatoes. Return to the saucepan. The liquid will be creamy, slightly sweet-and-sour. Season to taste. Add Monday's fish (flaked) and reheat gently. If preferred, the potatoes may be diced rather than puréed, and added to the soup along with the fish.

Wednesday

Sweet-and-Sour Poached Chicken☆
(use breasts, reserve wings and legs for Thursday,
poaching liquids for Friday)
Potatoes à la Courvey☆
(use boiled potatoes from Tuesday's batch)

SWEET-AND-SOUR POACHED CHICKEN

Loosen the skin over the breast of a 2- to 3-pound whole chicken. Peel an orange, cut into thick slices, and slip these between chicken flesh and skin. Put in a pot, add canned chicken broth to cover all but breast (which steams rather than boils). Add salt and pepper to taste. Bring to a boil, cover, and simmer about 30 minutes.

Remove and reserve the legs and wings (it does not matter if they are a bit underdone); skin and slice breasts thinly.

SAUCE

Pour ½ cup of the cooking broth into a small saucepan. Add ½ teaspoon mace and the crushed pulp of an orange, simmer 10 minutes. Add ½ cup white wine and boil gently, uncovered, 5 minutes. Remove from heat and beat in 2 egg yolks and ¼ cup sugar. Return to low heat and simmer, stirring, until thickened. Add ¼ cup tarragon vinegar, salt and pepper to taste, and stir until thick again over low heat. Pour over the skinned chicken breasts. Garnish with slices of fresh orange.

POTATOES À LA COURVEY

Peel and slice 4 cooked potatoes (from Tuesday). Sauté in 2 tablespoons butter, season with salt and white pepper. When golden, add enough chicken broth to cover by three quarters. Cook, uncovered, over medium heat until the liquid has almost evaporated. Remove from heat. Toss with 2 tablespoons butter (cut into small pieces), 2 tablespoons chopped parsley, and a good squeeze of lemon juice.

Thursday

Grilled Chicken Legs and Wings☆
stuffed with pickles and bacon-wrapped
(the reserved parts of Wednesday's bird)
Green beans
(cook 2 pounds, reserve about one third of the beans for Friday's soup)

GRILLED CHICKEN LEGS AND WINGS

Skin the wings and legs from the poached chicken. Make lengthwise slits in the flesh and fill with about 1 tablespoon drained, diced bread-and-butter pickles for each joint. Grind some black pepper over them and wrap each in 2 to 3 slices of bacon. Grill, turning once, about 15 minutes, or until the bacon is crisp.

Friday

Green Bean Soup☆
Omelettes

GREEN BEAN SOUP

Combine in a blender 3 cups chicken broth (from Wednesday, adding water if quantity is insufficient) and about ⅔ pound cooked green beans (from Thursday). Purée, then pour them through a strainer into a saucepan. Heat, add salt and pepper if needed, and top with a small pat of butter on each serving.

Saturday

Boeuf à la Mode☆, cooked with onions, carrots,
and pig's or calf's feet,
served hot (make enough for Sunday lunch, too)

BOEUF À LA MODE

Buy 2 to 3 pounds rump of beef, 2 calf's or pig's feet (have them split lengthwise by your butcher); 4 tablespoons lard, 6 strips bacon; have on hand 8 small onions, 4 carrots, 3 garlic cloves, crushed, ½ cup mixed dried herbs, ¼ bottle red wine, about 2 cups beef bouillon, and some string to tie the meat.

This cut of beef is usually larded to add flavor and succulence. Larding is time-consuming and difficult. I prefer this easier way: Make 3 deep lengthwise incisions in the meat. Into each incision lay 2 slices of bacon that have been well coated with herbs and crushed garlic. Put the meat back into its original shape and tie securely with string.

Melt the lard, brown the carrots and meat in it, then drain off all fat. Cover the meat with bouillon and wine. Add the onions and pig's or calf's feet. Season with salt and pepper. Bring to a boil, then reduce heat and simmer, covered, 2 to 2½ hours, or until fork-tender. Serve the beef, sliced crosswise, in its own gravy.

Reserve the pig's or calf's feet for Sunday.

Sunday

LUNCH
Sliced Cold Beef (from Saturday),
served with its own jelly and vegetables
Endive salad
DINNER
Grilled Pig's Feet☆ (or calf's feet), breaded and grilled
Apples and Potatoes☆ (potatoes from Tuesday)

GRILLED PIG'S FEET

Dip cold cooked feet into beaten egg and then bread crumbs. Dot with butter. Grill until crisp and golden, turning once. Sprinkle with chopped parsley or dill, serve with Dijon mustard or horseradish sauce.

APPLES AND POTATOES

Peel 4 cooked potatoes (from Tuesday). Quarter them and sauté in butter with an equal quantity of peeled, quartered apples until golden. Season with pepper and salt.

DESSERTS—A WEEK'S WORTH

Desserts for a week can be made quickly over the weekend, especially if one formula—such as cold mousse—is used with different flavorings—lemon, chocolate, coffee, and so on—employed for individual molds, covered in plastic wrap, and refrigerated until they are needed. Or consider a sumptuous compote of various fruits, or several compotes . . . and here is another possibility.

PISTACHIO CREAM

A particularly good custard cream, invented by Charles Carter, a cookbook author of the 1730s. This mousse-like cream can be served on its own or be used as a cake filling, and it is delicious in tartlets under sliced fresh peaches or other fruit or as a garnish for ice cream.

1¼ cups heavy cream
¼ cup pistachio nuts, ground in blender, measured after grinding
¼ cup sugar

Few drops orange extract
1 teaspoon grated lemon rind
2 egg yolks, beaten
2 ladyfingers, reduced to crumbs in a blender

Heat the cream and nuts to the boiling point, remove from heat. Stir in the sugar, extract, and rind; cool. Beat the egg yolks into the mixture. Reheat, stirring gently, until thickened. Do not boil. Stir in the ladyfinger crumbs, pour into a serving bowl. Decorate the top with pomegranate seeds if these are obtainable.

Vogue Food, March 1974

EASY-LIFE EGGS: FATIGUE-BEATER FOOD

And with hot bottles at our toes
We cosily in bed repose
Enjoying in a rather languid way
A little "eggy" something on a tray

NOEL COWARD

When you are tired, beset, grumpy, consider the egg. Surely one of the coziest, easiest, most soothing and nourishing foods around. In spite of the almost arrogant tensile strength of that thin shell, the inner egg is a compliant creature, a creature of good works. It slides quickly in and out of the pan with less murmur than the noisy butter, selflessly thickening, enriching, fluffing up, and solidifying its fellow edibles. Fried, the egg offers an appearance as neat as a uniform, cheerful as a child's drawing of the sun. Here, some ways with egg for March trays:

Cold Climate, Hot Eggs

The cold city shut out behind frosted windowpanes . . . dining off trays around the fire with friends, gossip, cards, television, and tapes. Or in bed with books, pets, a hot-water bottle, lots of perfume, a new face cream, the "Late Late Show," proper-sized pillows, a reading lamp that concentrates on the page, not on one's face.

NORMANDY EGGS   SERVES 6

6 eggs
4 tablespoons butter
½ pound shrimp, peeled and
    cooked
1 tablespoon tarragon mustard (at
    fine food shops)

1 tablespoon finely chopped
    parsley
1 tablespoon finely chopped
    chervil
Salt and pepper to taste
4 tablespoons heavy cream

Hard-cook the eggs for 8 minutes in simmering salted water. Remove the shells and cut the eggs into thick slices. Heat the butter in a frying pan, add the eggs, shrimp, mustard, parsley, and chervil. Season with pepper and salt. Stir in the cream, reheat, and serve on toast.

HIDE-AND-SEEK EGGS   SERVES 6

Butter, about 2 tablespoons
6 eggs
4 eggs, separated
1 teaspoon chopped parsley

1 teaspoon chopped chives
1 teaspoon capers, drained
3 anchovy fillets, drained of oil
    and crushed

Preheat oven to 300°.

Butter a good-sized casserole. Break 6 eggs into it, well spaced. Beat 4 egg yolks until creamy, the 4 whites until stiff. Fold together yolks and whites fast and lightly, adding the parsley and chives. Pour over the whole eggs. Set the casserole in a pan of hot water and bake until pale golden on top, about 20 minutes.

EGGS LUCCHESE

SERVES 2

1 onion, peeled and sliced
2 tablespoons butter
1 cup milk
4 hard-cooked eggs, shelled and halved
2 egg yolks

1 tablespoon chopped parsley
2 tablespoons grated Parmesan cheese
Pinch of cinnamon
Salt and pepper to taste
Juice of a half lemon

Cook the onion in the butter until golden, using a heavy saucepan. Add the milk and hard-cooked eggs, cook gently 3 to 4 minutes. Add the egg yolks, beaten until frothy with the chopped parsley, cheese, cinnamon, salt, and pepper. Stir over very low heat 6 to 8 minutes, then add the lemon juice. Serve at once.

Hot Climate, Cold Eggs

City winter forgotten as fast as pain. Trays of food on the terrace or a boat, by a pool, or for a picnic on a secret beach. An ice-cold eggy something to nibble between swims, rounds of sport, drinks, and naps. To eat lying down, sitting on a rock, or paddling at the water's edge looking for the perfect pink shell.

Three Ways to Present Cold Oeufs Mollets

These "in-between" eggs, like poached eggs in their tenderness, are first boiled 5½ minutes (jumbo size), cooled fast in cold water, chilled, then peeled. Then you might try:

OEUFS MOLLETS CARÊME

Put one egg in each puff-pastry tartlet shell (found at most good bakery shops) on top of a filling of cold salmon mixed with mayonnaise. Garnish with red caviar.

OEUFS MOLLETS NIÇOISE

Place one egg in each puff-pastry tartlet shell on top of a chopped mixture of cold cooked green beans, peeled and seeded tomatoes, and cold cooked potatoes, all seasoned and mixed with mayonnaise. Coat each egg with tomato sauce.

OEUFS MOLLETS WITH SEAFOOD

Place one egg in each puff-pastry tartlet shell on top of a layer of tiny shrimp (or chopped shrimp) mixed with mayonnaise or cream cheese. Garnish with a strip of smoked salmon.

Hard-Cooked Eggs, Two Ways

EGG SALAD WITH ASPARAGUS   SERVES 4

Mash the yolks of 6 hard-cooked eggs with 1 teaspoon Vinaigrette Sauce☆ and 1 tablespoon Mayonnaise.☆ Chop the whites, season with salt and pepper. Combine in a shallow serving dish. Garnish with asparagus tips and tomato and cucumber slices, all seasoned to taste.

POTTED EGGS AND SARDINES

For each serving sieve a hard-cooked egg and 4 boneless and skinless sardines into a bowl. Mix well with ½ tablespoon softened butter; moisten with a little cream. Season with pepper. Serve in a china ramekin with hot buttered toast.

SECTION II

CELEBRITY RECIPES

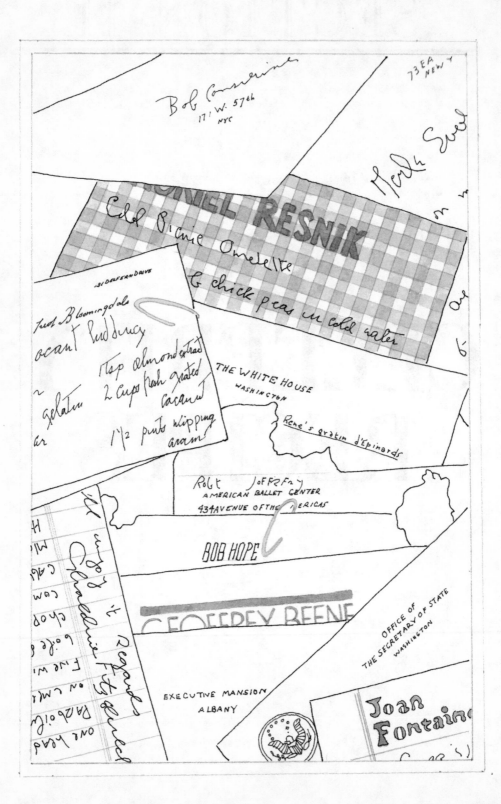

Most celebrities are tagged like luggage: movie star, politician, famous model, sports ace, Andy Warhol, rock-and-roller! They get stared at, pieces of their clothing are forcibly removed by their admirers, photographers pursue them right into their beds and bathrooms, their love affairs are chaperoned and exploited by a press agent. Somehow, some of them manage to cook a meal unmolested, so I am deeply grateful to them for handing me the results of their rare private enjoyment, as it were, on a platter.

Social celebrities are men and women who have created such an image for themselves that they are publicly recognized and adulated just for having done a good job on their own lives, for the clothes they wear, for their entertaining and first-nighting, for the time and efforts they give to public and cultural affairs, for being married to someone famous, for living some sort of charmed existence in which talent, beauty, cordiality, money, and gutsy know-how all combine. Some stars can also shine from special galaxies and be recognized mainly in the art world, in science, in fashion, among intellectuals, at dinner parties or locally as in New York, Cincinnati, or Los Angeles.

If most of my celebrity recipes are from East-Coasters, it is my fault: I live in New York. All across America and on the glamorous West Coast there are celebrated people with wonderful recipes that are not in this collection. I wrote to many and many letters were returned to me: so many people are on the move in this country. May these great cooks accept my apologies and give me a rain check for next time around.

All these recipes come from private homes and have been used countless times. Celebrity carries its own responsibilities, and good manners seem to be high on the list, for my requests were answered with admirable speed and graciousness. Jimmy Durante even added: "God bless you, my dear, for thinking of me!"

So, try these recipes and eat famously well!

Did one imagine that the Beautiful People lazed around in their Porthault sheets, waiting for a breakfast tray with one perfect rose? Not so . . . instant energy is a morning must . . . there may be a beauty appointment to keep, but there is often a lot more to handle in a day . . . a career . . . food to order . . . lunch and dinner parties to plan . . . children and school meetings . . . a flooded cellar in the country . . . a charity benefit . . . there's barely time to sit down for breakfast . . . thank God for whoever invented the blender . . . damn . . . there's the telephone again . . . put it on hold while I gulp this down, will you?

PART I

BREAKFAST/ BRUNCH

BORIS CHALIAPIN

EGGS WITH BLACK BREAD
SERVES 2

"This is a favorite with family and guests for brunch or breakfast on country weekends."

3 tablespoons butter
2 slices Westphalian pumper-
    nickel, cut into half-inch
    squares
4 eggs

1 tablespoon chopped scallions
1 teaspoon chopped fresh dill
Salt and pepper to taste
Chopped chives or parsley
    (optional)

Melt the butter in a skillet and sprinkle the diced pumpernickel into it in one layer. Cook over low heat for 1 minute. Break the eggs gently into the skillet. Sprinkle with the scallions, dill, salt, and pepper. Cook to desired doneness without turning the eggs. Garnish with chives or parsley and serve at once. For brunch, a glass of ice-cold beer goes particularly well with this.

FLEUR COWLES

BLINI WITH SMOKED SALMON
SERVES 4

"This recipe has been requested by dozens and dozens of American friends who come to my Sussex house at weekends. They have normally gone off without it in the confusion of departures, so I do know that there is a tiny group of anxious cooks waiting to get this one.

"The 'pancakes,' made from whole-wheat flour to give the unsweet taste of blini and large enough to be quite filling, are also used as the main course for Sunday luncheons. For the filling I use the less choice portions of smoked salmon."

PANCAKES

½ cake fresh yeast or 1 envelope
    dry yeast
Enough milk to make a good bat-
    ter (the consistency of cream)

2 eggs, beaten
¼ cup whole-wheat flour
Salt and pepper, a suspicion of
    each

½ pound smoked Nova Scotia
    salmon
3 tablespoons butter

2 onions, finely minced
1 cup white wine

FOR SERVING
Melted butter, about 1 stick

TO MAKE THE PANCAKE BATTER: Crumble the fresh yeast or sprinkle the dry yeast into 3 tablespoons of milk in a large bowl and let dissolve. Add the eggs, beat in the flour, then enough milk to give the batter the consistency of cream. Season with salt and pepper. Set aside in a warm spot, covered with a tea cloth, for 4 hours. When ready to use, stir well until satiny, then drop onto a lightly buttered hot griddle to form 4 large pancakes. Bake until done, turning once.

TO MAKE THE FILLING: While the blini batter is resting, make the filling. Cut the salmon into uneven chunks (they break up under heat). Melt the butter in a skillet and lightly fry the onions until they are golden. Add the wine, toss in the salmon, and let simmer on lowest heat for nearly an hour. Set aside and reheat while baking the pancakes. Two tablespoons of this hot mixture go onto each pancake. Roll each up and lay in a shallow baking dish, cover with aluminum foil and put into 300° oven for a few minutes until hot through. Pass melted butter with the blini.

ANDRÉ EMMERICH

MOCHA BRUNCH DRINK SERVES 1

"Here's an easy-to-prepare brunch drink that I've enjoyed for years. It's a perfect bachelor's breakfast, as it takes no great skill and very little time."

2 cups hot milk
1 tablespoon instant chocolate-
    drink powder
1 tablespoon freeze-dried coffee

powder
1 shot coffee liqueur (Kahlúa or
    Tia Maria)
1 egg, if you like

Fill a large mug (this makes a pint) halfway with hot milk and stir in the chocolate and coffee powders until they dissolve. Add a generous shot of coffee liqueur. Fill the mug with the remaining hot milk and stir gently. If very hungry, beat one egg and mix in after the mug is half filled, before adding the rest of the milk.

DAVID NIVEN

KEDGEREE

SERVES 4

½ cup rice, preferably the Patna
    variety
½ stick butter
Salt and pepper to taste
Good pinch of cayenne
½ pound cooked haddock or

salmon, skinned, boned, and
    flaked
2 hard-cooked eggs, whites and
    yolks chopped separately
1 tablespoon freshly chopped
    parsley and/or chives

Boil the rice, uncovered, in a lot of salted water for about 13 minutes from the time that the water containing it reboils. Drain it, rinsing under cold water, return it to the saucepan, and place in an oven set at "warm" to dry out for a few minutes. Melt the butter in another saucepan. When foaming, add the rice, salt, pepper, and cayenne. Add the cooked haddock and chopped egg whites, stir over heat, being careful not to crush the fish flakes. When heated through, pile in a pyramid on a hot serving dish. Sprinkle with the chopped egg yolks and parsley, and reheat in the oven for 15 minutes at 300°.

VIDAL SASSOON

YOGURT BREAKFAST

SERVES 1

"My best dish has to be a morning dish . . . this keeps me going all day."

1 carton (½ pint) plain yogurt
1 egg

2 tablespoons wheat germ
1 tablespoon honey

Empty the yogurt into a bowl. Add the raw egg, wheat germ, and honey. Mix well and serve—eat! It's delicious. Wash it down, if you must, with a glass of fresh carrot juice, which you have just made yourself.

ETHEL SCULL

SOUR-CREAM COFFEECAKE

SERVES 6 TO 8

1 stick butter
2 eggs, beaten
2 cups flour
1 teaspoon baking powder
1 teaspoon baking soda
¼ teaspoon salt

1 cup dairy sour cream
¼ teaspoon vanilla
½ cup sugar
½ cup chopped nuts
1 teaspoon cinnamon

Preheat oven to 350°.

Cream the butter, then add the eggs, blending well. Sift together the flour, baking powder, soda, and salt. Add the flour mixture to the creamed mixture alternately with sour cream and vanilla, beating until smooth. Mix in a separate bowl the sugar, nuts, and cinnamon. Put half the batter in a greased 9-inch tube pan. Sprinkle with half the nut and sugar mixture. Add the remaining batter, then top with the remaining nuts. Bake 45 minutes or until a tester inserted in the cake comes out clean.

NANCY KISSINGER

BASQUE OMELETTE

SERVES 6 TO 8

1 cup chopped green peppers
1 cup finely chopped onions
Olive oil as needed
1 clove garlic, minced, or ¼ teaspoon garlic powder
¼ teaspoon dried oregano
Salt and pepper to taste

4 tomatoes, peeled, seeded, and cut into thin strips
4 to 6 strips country ham, ¼ inch thick
8 to 10 eggs
2 tablespoons chopped fresh parsley

Cook the peppers and onions in 2 to 3 tablespoons of olive oil until tender but not browned. Add the garlic, oregano, salt, and pepper. Put the tomato strips on top. Cover and cook slowly for 5 minutes. Uncover, raise the heat and cook, shaking the pan, until the juices have evaporated. Set aside. Brown the ham strips lightly in a little oil in a separate pan. Set aside. When ready to make the omelette, reheat the vegetables and ham.

Beat the eggs with salt and pepper to taste until thoroughly mixed. Heat enough oil to cover the bottom of a large omelette pan, pour in the eggs, and stir rapidly until they have barely set into a creamy mass. Remove from the heat and spread over the omelette the vegetable mixture, blending it delicately into the eggs. Lay the ham over the top, sprinkle with parsley, and serve immediately.

JULE STYNE

POTATO KNISHES WITHOUT DOUGH

SERVES 8

6 medium-sized potatoes, peeled
Salt and freshly ground black
    pepper to taste
1 large onion, coarsely chopped

4 tablespoons chicken fat, or
    amount needed
2 eggs, beaten
3 egg yolks

Preheat oven to 350°.

Boil the potatoes, then mash them well. Blend in salt and pepper. Fry the onion in chicken fat until very crisp, add to the mashed potatoes. Blend in the 2 beaten eggs and stir well. Shape the mixture into 8 hamburger-sized cakes with a large spoon. Beat the 3 egg yolks until thick and brush each knish with yolk on both sides to form a crust. Place in a lightly greased baking pan. Bake until golden brown and crusty. Serve hot.

GLORIA VANDERBILT

BREAKFAST FOR TWO

6 eggs
½ stick butter
Freshly ground black pepper

Black or red caviar, about ½
    pound

ACCOMPANIMENTS
Pumpernickel
Champagne

The night before, remove the eggs from the refrigerator and leave in a bowl. They will be ready at room temperature by morning. Prepare a double boiler by putting a good-sized dollop of butter, about half a stick, in the top part. Add a few grinds of pepper but no salt. Place on the base of the double boiler, partly filled with warm (not hot) water, bring very slowly to a boil, stirring the butter occasionally until it is melted. Break the eggs into the melted butter. With a wooden fork, gently stir yolks and whites until lightly but smoothly blended, but not cooked at all. Remove the double boiler from the heat and allow the mixture to settle in. Eggs are most sensitive, and need time to adjust to new conditions.

Use your instinct to know when to replace the double boiler on the stove. Turn heat on the stove to very low. With a wooden spoon, stir the mixture, from time to time, so that it gradually begins to scramble. Now and then remove the double boiler from the stove to allow the eggs to take their own time. At no time should the mixture start sticking to the sides of the pan. The eggs are ready when they are loosely bound together in large curds. Remove from the heat immediately and divide onto two preheated plates. In the center of each serving put several large spoonfuls of large-grain caviar. Serve instantly with slices of dark pumpernickel and a split of ice-cold champagne.

GEORGE BRADSHAW AND RUTH NORMAN

CRAB MEAT IN A SKILLET

SERVES 4

2 tablespoons butter
Juice of a half lemon
1 pound cooked crab meat,
    picked over

Salt and pepper to taste
Jigger of cognac (optional)
Dash of paprika
4 slices hot toast, buttered

Heat the butter and lemon juice in a skillet; add the crab meat, salt, and pepper. Now shake the skillet constantly over medium heat so that the flavors mingle; don't stir, however. When the crab meat is hot, you can flame it with prewarmed cognac, if you like, shaking the pan during the flaming. Dust with paprika and serve on buttered toast.

TOM WOLFE

DRIED FRUITS OLYMPUS

"Since I almost never eat lunch or dinner at home, the only meal I have ever learned to fix is the main course for my breakfast, which is prepared as follows. All dried fruits must come from Fresno."

1 box of dried apricots from
    Fresno, California
1 bag of pitted prunes from

Fresno
1 box of golden seedless raisins
    from Fresno

Empty everything into a pot full of branch water and put it all on top of the stove and let it soak overnight. In the morning bring it to a boil, then let it simmer for 20 minutes, adding a few teaspoonfuls of lemon juice. Let it cool off, empty it all into a plastic container, and put it in the refrigerator.

The following morning (and each morning thereafter) spoon out 4 or 5 apricots, 3 or 4 prunes, and a bunch of raisins onto a cereal bowl full of:

1 part roasted wheat germ
1 part Familia or granola-type
    cereal

1 part raisin-bran flakes or plain
    all-bran cereal

Add milk.

Any time you are compelled to be at home for lunch or dinner, EAT THE SAME THING . . . If you are ever so unfortunate as to have to go on a camping trip, take some along and EAT THE SAME THING morning, noon, and night.

PART II

LUNCH

Aheavy lunch is a disaster unless one can go straight to bed or to a gym after it. Like breakfast, it should be energizing and also consist of food that looks attractive by daylight. The color of salads, green vegetables, golden-crusted casseroles, and the clear pink of a raspberry mousse are as important a choice as a pink silk shirt and pastel-tinted daytime make-up.

The colors of picnic food are even more affected by light and shade, sun and shadow. A picnic lunch never needs to be on grass. Take lunch to your office or your mate's and invite a friend or two; they'll love it. Stick lunch in your pocket and walk the hour and a pound or two away. Go to a museum and eat a delicious homemade snack in the garden or on the steps. Have an hour's rest, in bed with a tray, a book, a snooze, and start the afternoon refreshed.

Starters

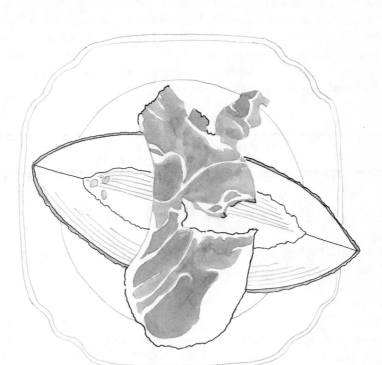

SYDNEY GRUSON

BRANDY-WINE SCALLOPS

SERVES 6

1½ pounds fresh small
    mushrooms
6 tablespoons melted butter
1 pound bay scallops, drained
½ cup flour
1 cup milk

Salt and pepper to taste
½ cup very dry white wine
1 tablespoon French brandy
2 tablespoons grated Parmesan
    cheese

In a large skillet cook the mushrooms in 4 tablespoons of the butter until their liquid has evaporated. Remove from skillet. Dredge the scallops in the flour. Add the rest of the butter to the skillet; sauté the scallops until opaque, shaking the skillet often (about 10 minutes). Add the cooked mushrooms to scallops. Gradually add the milk, stirring gently, simmer until the sauce thickens (5 to 10 minutes). Add salt and pepper. Gently stir in the wine, brandy, and cheese. Rewarm without boiling and serve hot.

TIPS   This dish may be cooked an hour or so before serving. The sauce should be about the consistency of heavy cream. If it seems too thick when ready for serving, add milk to bring to the correct consistency. This may be served as is, or in *vol-au-vent* shells.

DENISE HALE

CELERY ROOT REMOULADE   SERVES 4

2 medium-sized celery roots
    (celeriac)

2 tablespoons tarragon vinegar

DRESSING
1 cup Mayonnaise☆
2 tablespoons chopped parsley
2 tablespoons chopped scallions
2 tablespoons Dijon-style mustard

½ teaspoon dried tarragon,
    crumbled
½ teaspoon salt
Pinch of freshly ground pepper

Slice the celery root very thinly, soak overnight in water to cover, to which the tarragon vinegar has been added. Rinse thoroughly in cold water, drain. Cut the slices into very fine julienne strips. Mix the dressing ingredients and blend with the celery root. Serve at room temperature.

MAXIME DE LA FALAISE

PROVENÇAL SHRIMP AND RICE   SERVES 2

Marinate 6 large shrimp in 2 tablespoons olive oil, 1 teaspoon vinegar, pinches of salt and pepper, a crushed garlic clove, ½ teaspoon each McCormick's Italian and Lemon Pepper seasonings, for a few hours. Broil shrimp 4 to 5 minutes on each side, serve over rice.

Provençal Rice   boil ½ cup rice in plenty of salted water with 4 pieces of star anise. Drain when just tender, discard the anise. Season to taste.

CRÊPES ÉCOSSAISES

4 thin pancakes, made without
    salt or sugar

4 thin slices smoked salmon

MORNAY SAUCE
1⅓ cups Béchamel Sauce☆
1 egg yolk, beaten
Pinch of grated nutmeg
1 tablespoon grated Parmesan

cheese
1 tablespoon grated Gruyère
    cheese

Fill each crêpe with a slice of smoked salmon, covering the crêpe. Roll up
and place in a lightly buttered baking/serving dish. Make the Mornay
sauce: to the hot Béchamel sauce add the egg yolk, nutmeg, and cheeses,
mix well. Reheat without boiling and pour over the crêpes. Brown under
the grill and serve at once. Garnish with a few sprigs of parsley if desired.

SOLE CZARINA

4 fillets of sole
Fish stock to cover
1⅓ cups Béchamel sauce, unsalted

4 tablespoons caviar (fresh gray
    beluga if possible)

Gently poach the fillets in the stock (*not* white wine, which doesn't go well
with the caviar). Add as much caviar as you can afford to the Béchamel
sauce and spoon this over the fillets on a white serving dish. Top each fillet
with a generous spoonful of caviar.

DIONE LUCAS

PÂTÉ MAISON

2 pounds ground calf's or pork
    liver
1 pound bulk sausage meat or
    liverwurst
3 teaspoons salt
1 teaspoon pepper
⅛ teaspoon paprika

½ pound thinly sliced bacon
2 hard-cooked eggs, peeled and
    halved
6 chicken livers, trimmed
6 slices cooked ham or tongue
6 slices liverwurst, casing removed

Preheat oven to 350°.

Mix the first 5 ingredients together well with your hands or a large wooden spoon. Line an oblong 4-pound breadpan very carefully with very thin slices of bacon. Half fill the pan with part of the liver mixture; on top place the hard-cooked egg halves. Add a layer consisting of the chicken livers, slices of cooked ham or tongue, and slices of liverwurst. Cover this layer with the remaining liver mixture and press down well. Cover the top with doubled waxed paper and set into a deep baking pan half filled with water. Bake 1½ hours. When cooked (the juices will be clear when the pâté is pricked) remove the pan from the water bath and place a brick or other oblong weight on top of the waxed paper. Allow the pâté to get quite cool. Then place in the refrigerator until needed.

This will keep very well for a week or so, but do not turn it out of the breadpan until you want to eat it.

HENRY MCILHENNY

COLD TOMATO SOUFFLE SERVES 8 TO 10

2 pounds ripe tomatoes, skinned and seeds removed
2 cups thick Mayonnaise☆, home-made
½ cup finely minced onion (and/or celery)

Salt and pepper to taste
3 envelopes unflavored gelatin
½ cup tomato juice
1 cup heavy cream, whipped until stiff

GARNISH
¼ cup chopped parsley, or chopped aspic, or shredded

lettuce

Dice half of the tomatoes, set aside and keep cold. Put the remainder through a very fine sieve. Flavor the mayonnaise with the onion, salt, and pepper. Soak the gelatin in the tomato juice, then heat to dissolve. Add to the sieved tomato, then add to the mayonnaise base. Fold in the whipped cream. Tie an upstanding band of doubled waxed paper around a 1½-quart soufflé dish and fill with the mixture; set a glass in the center, rim uppermost. Put on ice until firm. When ready to serve, remove the glass and fill the center with the diced tomatoes, seasoned with salt and pepper. Sprinkle with the parsley, or garnish with chopped aspic or shredded lettuce.

ASHTON HAWKINS

SLICED BEEF AND MAYONNAISE

SERVES 6 TO 8

Ashton Hawkins, Secretary of The Metropolitan Museum of Art, gives, in A Culinary Collection from The Metropolitan Museum of Art, *this recipe:*

1 cup Mayonnaise☆
Dijon mustard to taste
Olive oil
Salt and pepper to taste
1 pound top round of beef sliced

paper-thin (by a kindly
butcher)
Chopped parsley
Lemon wedges

Combine the mayonnaise, mustard, olive oil (enough to thin the mayonnaise slightly), salt, and pepper; refrigerate. Arrange the slices of meat in one layer on plates. (It is best to do this just before serving, as the meat will dry out and turn brown if exposed to air for any length of time. If prepared in advance, wrap each plate tightly with plastic wrap and refrigerate.) Trickle onto each serving of meat several stripes of sauce, sprinkle with parsley, serve with a lemon wedge.

MITZI NEWHOUSE

MOLDED CHOPPED CHICKEN LIVERS

SERVES 6 TO 8

1 pound chicken livers
2 small onions, peeled and
    chopped
3 tablespoons chicken fat or but-
    ter, or more if needed

Salt, pepper, and paprika to taste
3 hard-cooked eggs
3 tablespoons ground almonds
3 tablespoons cognac

Wash and trim the livers and dry thoroughly. Fry the onions until golden brown in chicken fat or butter. Remove from the pan and sauté the livers for 10 minutes, adding more fat if needed. Chop together the livers, onions, salt, pepper, and paprika until the mixture is very fine. Add hard-cooked eggs and continue chopping until they, too, are very fine. Add the almonds and cognac. If needed, add more seasonings. Pack into greased mold and chill. Unmold and serve with thin-sliced pumpernickel or with sesame crackers.

MURIEL RESNIK

COLD PICNIC OMELETTE SERVES 3 TO 4

1 medium can chick-peas
2 tablespoons olive oil
1 onion, finely minced
½ teaspoon salt
1 teaspoon pepper

½ teaspoon ground sage
1 teaspoon ground thyme
6 eggs
2 tablespoons water
3 tablespoons butter

Rinse the chick-peas in cold water and dry well. Cook them in the olive oil with the onion, stirring over medium heat. When they begin to color, season with salt, plenty of pepper, sage, and thyme.

Preheat the broiler.

Beat the eggs with the water. Heat a large omelette pan, add the butter. Pour half the eggs into the pan and let set. Add the chick-pea mixture and spread evenly. Add the rest of the eggs. Put the pan under the preheated broiler until the surface is set. Remove to a platter and let cool. Chill, covered, in the refrigerator. This can be made a day ahead.

HAROLD ROSENBERG

BAKED SCHMALTZ HERRING AND SNORTS OF GIN

Figure one fat schmaltz herring for two. Look for it at your best local appetizing store. Douse each herring in flour and wrap in a single layer of brown wrapping torn from a clean grocery bag. Wrap this in several sheets of *The Forvitz* or any other Jewish newspaper, and drop onto white-hot coals in the kitchen stove, an empty-lot bonfire, or a barbecue hibachi. The package will flare up, but wait until the package becomes alarmingly charred and hard. Then remove and crack open. Inside the black shell is a fragrant, skinned, hot herring, ready to eat at once, accompanied by generous snorts of cold gin.

Soups

PAT BUCKLEY

MUSSEL SOUP

SERVES 8 TO 10

This soup may be made a day ahead. In that case don't add the cream; store the base in the refrigerator. At serving time, heat the soup base, then the cream, combine, and serve. This is good served before a hearty salad, accompanied by a good home-baked bread; cheese and fresh fruit for dessert.

9 dozen mussels
3½ sticks butter
2 bottles dry Chablis, or more if
    needed
Leaves only from 1 head celery,
    finely chopped

6 to 10 shallots, peeled and finely
    chopped
1 bunch parsley, finely chopped
6 tablespoons flour
1 to 2 cups heavy cream

Scrub the mussels thoroughly with a vegetable brush to remove sand and the mussels' beards. Rinse repeatedly, at least 4 or 5 times. In a large pot melt 1½ sticks of the butter; add the wine, chopped celery leaves, shallots, parsley, and the mussels. Cover, bring to a boil, turn the heat down, and simmer until all the mussel shells have opened, approximately 10 to 15 minutes; shake the pot from time to time. Remove the mussels (save the broth) and remove meat from the shells. Scoop out all the greenery (parsley, celery leaves, shallots) that has collected in shells, and reserve. Melt the remaining 2 sticks of butter in a large saucepan. When it is creamy and frothy, stir in the flour to make a *roux*. Over low heat add the mussel broth slowly, stirring constantly with a wooden spoon. If the consistency is too thick, add more wine. Add the mussels and the collected greenery from their shells, bring the soup to a boil for 30 seconds, and turn off heat. Add the cream, which has been heated (not boiled), using from 1 to 2 cups; stir and serve.

SISI CAHANE

SOLE AND CRAB MEAT SOUP   SERVES 6

¼ to ½ cup milk
1½ pounds fillets of sole
4 to 5 shallots
3 tablespoons butter
2 (7-ounce) cans minced clams,
    with their liquid

½ pound fresh crab meat, picked
    over
2 pints heavy cream
Bread crumbs, ½ to ⅔ cup
Salt and pepper to taste

Preheat oven to 300°.

Put a little milk in the bottom of a 9″ by 12″ casserole, just enough to cover the bottom. Line with the fillets. Cook the shallots in the melted butter in a skillet until wilted but not browned, and pour over the fish. Add the clams, crab meat, and cream. Season with salt and pepper and top with a thin layer of bread crumbs. Bake, covered, for 1½ hours, uncovering during the last 15 minutes. This is a chunky soup, really a fish stew.

Chicken Soups

BASIC CHICKEN BROTH MAKES ABOUT 2½ QUARTS

One 4-pound fowl, or 3 pounds   1 rib celery
    chicken necks, wings, and   1 sprig parsley
    backs and 2 gizzards   Salt and peppercorns
1 onion

Put the fowl or chicken parts into a deep pot with the onion, celery, parsley, salt to taste, a few peppercorns, and more water than is needed to cover the chicken. Bring to a boil. Skim off any scum, reduce heat, cover, and simmer for 2 hours. If you are using a whole fowl, remove it as soon as it is tender and cut the meat from the breasts, thighs, and drumsticks to reserve for salad or other dishes. Chicken parts can be cooked longer. Remove the bones from the broth and strain it through cheesecloth or a linen napkin. Let it cool until any fat that is left rises to the top. Skim this off. To serve, reheat the broth.

DOUBLE CHICKEN BROTH

To the finished Basic Chicken Broth (above) add another fowl and, if needed to cover it, a little water. Bring to a boil, reduce heat, cover, and simmer very gently 3 hours, or until the bird is tender. Remove the fowl, taste the broth for seasoning, and add salt if necessary. Strain through a linen napkin. Use the poached fowl for salad or any dish calling for cold cooked chicken.

VARIATION

Combine Basic Chicken Broth (above) with an equal amount of tomato juice. Add a slice of lemon and 1 small onion stuck with a clove. Simmer for 15 minutes, strain, serve hot.

BORIS CHALIAPIN

CHICKEN GIBLET SOUP WITH PICKLES *(RASSOLNIK)*

SERVES 8 TO 10

"This is a winter soup which utilized food from the storage room when fresh produce was gone. Nowadays, we save our unused, uncooked chicken parts in the freezer; of course no Russian household is without its large jar of pickles, 'from the barrel.'"

2 cups chicken giblets (liver, hearts, gizzards), chopped
1 dozen or so chicken parts (wings, necks, feet), broken or chopped into bite-sized pieces
2 quarts water
3 medium-sized sour dill pickles

(from the barrel), cut into large dice
2 cups pickle brine (get some when you buy the pickles)
4 tablespoons chopped fresh young dill; or 3 tablespoons dried dill weed
Freshly ground pepper

OPTIONAL GARNISHES:
Diced boiled potatoes (hot)
Sour cream

Wash the giblets under cold running water, trim off any fat. Cut off and discard the first joint of the feet. Place the giblets and chicken parts in a soup pot with the 2 quarts of water and simmer 30 minutes. Add the pickles, half the brine, and the dill; add pepper to taste. Add more of the remaining brine until the soup is satisfactorily piquant. Simmer another 30 minutes, or until the giblets are tender. If the soup seems too "crowded," add water and pickle brine. If potatoes and/or sour cream are used, add to individual servings.

HIRO

CREAM OF POTATO SOUP

SERVES 4 TO 6

"When it comes to eating, I go towards simple and healthy cooking. My favorite is, with no doubt, homemade soup, and here is one soup I usually cook in the wilderness of Canada:"

4 to 5 potatoes, thinly sliced or
    diced
1 medium onion (1 or 2 leeks
    would be better), cut up small

¾ to 1 cup celery, cut up small
3 tablespoons butter
1 cup milk
Salt and pepper to taste

Barely cover the potatoes, onion, and celery with cold water. Cook slowly, covered, until the potatoes are tender. Add the butter and milk. Heat to scalding, *but don't let it boil.* Season with salt and pepper. The potatoes can be mashed in the cooking liquid, if desired, before the butter and milk are added. This will make a thick soup.

CHARLES MASSON

CREAM OF PEAS LA GRENOUILLE

SERVES 8

3 quarts water
1 pound dried split peas, soaked
    overnight
1 pound fresh green peas, in their
    pods
½ pound potatoes, peeled
1 carrot, scraped
1 onion, peeled
6 leeks, trimmed, split, and
    washed

1 head lettuce, leaves separated,
    washed, and drained
1 bay leaf
Pinch of thyme
1 bunch (a handful) parsley
Salt to taste
Pinch of sugar
2 cups heavy cream
¼ pound sweet (unsalted) butter,
    cut up

In the 3 quarts water cook all the vegetables, together with the bay leaf and thyme (but not the parsley) until tender. Purée in a blender, first removing the bay leaf. Add water as needed to liquefy. Include the pea pods in the purée; they give a nice green color and flavor to the soup. Use a little of the purée to help liquefy the parsley in the blender. To extract the extra color from the parsley, add the liquefied parsley to the purée, strain again, and taste for seasoning. Add salt, sugar, cream, and butter. The soup should have the consistency of thick cream and be very green. (A drop or two of food coloring may be added if the color is not bright enough.) Reheat and serve with croutons.

MARION W. FLEXNER

ANDALUSIAN GAZPACHO
SERVES 6

1 clove garlic
1 teaspoon salt
1 cup soft bread crumbs
¼ cup wine vinegar
4 tomatoes, peeled (dip into boil-
    ing water, then cold water,
    and strip off skin)

2 medium cucumbers, pared,
    split, and seeds removed
    (reserve cores and peels)
2 medium green peppers
½ cup olive oil
4 cups very cold water
Salt to taste

Pound the garlic and salt well in a mortar; add the bread crumbs moistened with vinegar and work into a paste. Add two thirds of the tomatoes
and mash; add the cores of the cucumbers and two or three strips of the
peel. Purée in a blender. Place the purée in a bowl and mix with the rest
of the tomatoes, diced; the flesh of the cucumbers, diced; and the green
peppers, diced. Chill in the refrigerator. Before serving, stir in the olive oil
and water, add salt and extra vinegar if the taste is too bland. In Spain
gazpacho is often served in a tureen with croutons.

CLARE BOOTHE LUCE

CONSOMMÉ À LA DUCHESSE
SERVES 6

*"This is one of my favorite recipes," says Clare, "because while it comes off as a real
party entrée, it requires no cooking, and it only takes ten minutes to whomp it up."*

4-ounce package cream cheese
4 ounces mild processed cheese
    (Primula or a similar kind)
1 can consommé (the jellying
    kind)

1 teaspoon onion juice
1 clove garlic
1 teaspoon Worcestershire sauce
Salt and pepper to taste

Put two thirds of the consommé (reserve the rest) and all other ingredients
in a blender and process until very smooth. Pour into cups. Chill in the
refrigerator. When set, pour over a layer of the reserved consommé, which
should be at room temperature. Chill in the refrigerator until the glaze
has jelled.

JACQUELINE ONASSIS

NEW ENGLAND FISH CHOWDER
SERVES 6

A White House recipe from a former First Lady.

2 pounds haddock
2 cups water
2 ounces salt pork, diced
2 onions, sliced
4 large potatoes, peeled and diced
1 cup chopped celery

1 bay leaf, crumbled
1 teaspoon salt
Freshly ground black pepper
1 quart milk
2 tablespoons butter

Simmer the haddock in the water for 15 minutes. Drain, reserve the broth. Remove the bones from the fish. Fry the salt pork in a heavy pot until crisp; remove and set aside. Sauté the onions in the pork fat until golden brown. Add the fish, potatoes, celery, bay leaf, salt, and pepper. Pour in the fish broth and enough boiling water to make about 3 cups of liquid, simmer for 30 minutes. Add the milk and butter, simmer for 5 minutes. Check the seasoning. Serve the chowder sprinkled with the salt pork bits.

VIRGIL THOMSON

RAW SPINACH SOUP
SERVES 6

1 pound fresh young spinach, washed and thick stems discarded
2 scallions, cut up
2 cans beef consommé (the kind that jells)
Salt and pepper to taste

Pinch of freshly ground nutmeg
Dried dill weed, about 1 teaspoon
1 to 2 sprigs fresh tarragon, or ¼ teaspoon ground anise, or several sprigs of fresh chervil (hard to find unless you grow it)

Put the spinach leaves in a blender with the scallions, consommé, and seasonings. When thoroughly liquefied, put the soup in the refrigerator to cool and, with luck, jell a little (overnight is best). Before serving stir vigorously (very briefly) in the blender.

VARIATIONS: For thickening a little, add 2 tablespoons cracker meal when blending. For binding further, add either 1 tablespoon of good olive oil or 2 tablespoons of heavy cream (not both) during the blending.

Fish

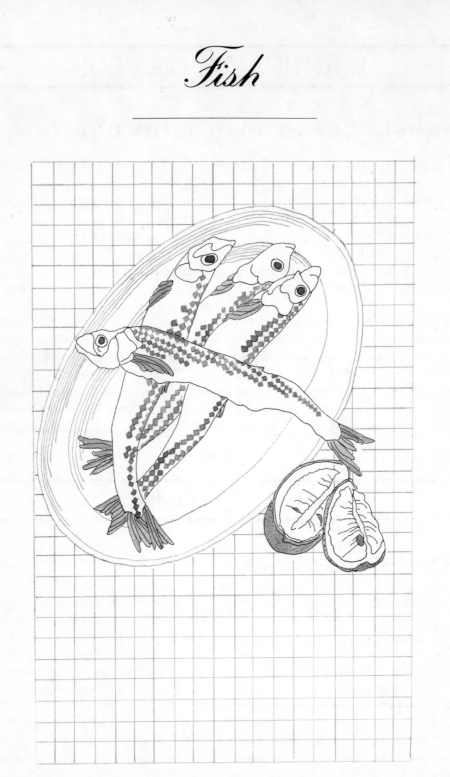

GEOFFREY BEENE

CRAB MEAT SOUFFLÉ

SERVES 4

½ cup chopped scallions
2 tablespoons butter
1 cup Béchamel Sauce☆
3 tablespoons chopped parsley

1 pound cooked crab meat,
    picked over
6 egg whites, beaten stiff

Preheat oven to 375°.
    Cook the scallions in the butter until soft but not browned, put into a large bowl. Add the white sauce and chopped parsley. Fold in the crab meat, then the egg whites. Bake in a greased 8-inch soufflé dish for 30 minutes. Serve at once with Hollandaise Sauce☆

JULIA CHILD

DARNES DE POISSON À LA CRÈME, KATHARINE
(Fish Steaks Simmered with Cream and Mushrooms)

SERVES 4

"This is an easy and perfectly delicious way to prepare firm-fleshed lean fish such as large cod, cusk, and particularly halibut. It's all done on top of the stove, so that you can cook and serve in the same utensil.
    "Ahead-of-time note: May be cooked in advance and reheated. If you do this, it is best to undercook fish slightly so it will not be overcooked when reheated."

⅔ cup finely minced onions
4 tablespoons butter
4 halibut steaks 1 inch thick (2
    pounds)
½ pound (2 cups) fresh mush-
    rooms, trimmed, washed, and
    quartered into ⅜-inch pieces

Salt and white pepper
½ cup dry white French vermouth
½ cup heavy cream
If needed: 1 tablespoon flour
    blended with 1 tablespoon
    soft butter
2 tablespoons minced parsley

Cook the onions slowly in the butter for 8 to 10 minutes, using a 9-inch sauté pan, a chicken fryer, or an electric skillet; cook until tender but not browned. Meanwhile, remove the skin from the fish steaks, but leave in the bones if you wish. When the onions are done, dry the fish and add to the pan, raising the heat slightly. Add the mushrooms. Shaking the pan frequently, sauté the fish lightly on one side for several minutes until it is barely golden, season with salt and pepper, turn, and sauté on the other side for 2 to 3 minutes. Season the fish again, then pour in the vermouth and let boil for 2 minutes to evaporate its alcohol. Pour in the cream and boil slowly, basting, for 3 to 4 minutes. Carefully turn the fish and cook another 3 to 4 minutes, basting several times. Cover, and simmer very slowly 8 to 10 minutes more (or 15 to 18 minutes in all). Remove to a side dish or hot platter and rapidly boil down the sauce to thicken it. (If the flavor is concentrated enough but the sauce remains thin, remove from heat, beat in flour/butter mixture, and bring to a boil.) Carefully correct the seasoning, stir in the parsley, pour the sauce and mushrooms over the fish, and serve.

CRAIG CLAIBORNE

CÔTELETTES DE SAUMON POJARSKI
(Salmon Cutlets with Brown-Butter Sauce)   SERVES 6

1¼ pounds skinless, boneless fillets of fresh salmon
1½ cups (approximately) fine fresh bread crumbs
1 cup heavy cream
Salt and freshly ground pepper to taste

¼ teaspoon nutmeg, or more or less to taste
Pinch of cayenne
4 tablespoons peanut, vegetable, or corn oil
8 tablespoons butter

Use the fine blade of a meat grinder and grind the salmon, putting it through once. (It could be chopped very fine, using a sharp knife on a flat surface.) It should not be processed in a blender. Put the salmon in a mixing bowl and add ½ cup of the bread crumbs and ⅓ cup of the heavy cream, stirring briskly with a wooden spoon. Add salt, pepper, and nutmeg. Add cayenne and continue beating rapidly with the spoon. Beat in the remaining ⅔ cup of heavy cream.

Lay out a length of waxed paper. Divide the mixture into 6 equal portions. Shape each portion first into an oval like a small football, then place each portion on the waxed paper and shape to look like a pork chop with bone. The "chop" should be about ¾ inch thick. Arrange them on a jelly-roll pan or cookie sheet and refrigerate until ready to cook. Then coat each on all sides with the remaining bread crumbs.

Using two skillets: Heat 2 tablespoons of oil and 2 tablespoons of butter in each skillet, and when hot add the salmon "chops." Cook on one side about 4 minutes, until golden brown, and turn. Cook 3 to 4 minutes longer, until golden brown on the second side. Transfer to a warm platter. Put the remaining 4 tablespoons of butter in one of the skillets and cook, shaking the skillet, until the butter starts to brown, no longer. Do not let the butter burn. Pour the hot butter over the salmon cutlets.

MARION JAVITS

MARION'S FISH DISH
SERVES 8

1 large onion
2 ripe tomatoes
½ pound mushrooms
3 pounds of fillets of any tasty
    fish, preferably bass
2 teaspoons chopped parsley
2 teaspoons chopped chives
Lemon juice

Salt and pepper to taste
White wine or light beer, as
    needed
1 stick butter, cut up
Arrowroot mixed with cold water,
    2 to 3 tablespoons of each
2 tablespoons grated cheese,
    Gruyère or Parmesan

Preheat oven to 375°.

Peel the onion and skin the tomatoes; slice thin. Place half of them in the bottom of a large shallow casserole; add the mushrooms. Arrange the fish over the vegetables. Sprinkle with the parsley and chives and lemon juice to taste; add salt and pepper. Lay the rest of vegetables over the fish and pour over white wine or beer to cover. Dot with butter bits. Cover and bake ½ hour. Drain off the liquid, thicken it with as much as you need of the arrowroot mixed with cold water. Pour the sauce back over the fish. Sprinkle grated cheese over the top and brown quickly under the broiler.

MARION W. FLEXNER

FRIED BASS FILLETS
SERVES 6

6 fillets of bass (or other fish)
Flour
2 eggs
1 tablespoon water

Salt and pepper to taste
2 cups cornflakes or Rice Krispies
½ cup lard

Roll each fillet in flour and then in the eggs, which have been well beaten with the water. Salt and pepper the fish and roll in the crushed cornflakes or Rice Krispies. (These make a nice change from bread crumbs or cracker crumbs.) Use a large iron skillet and put into it ½ cup lard, or enough to cover the bottom about ½ inch deep. Heat until it reaches 375° to 380°, or, if you don't own a kitchen thermometer, until the fat smokes and will fry a cube of bread in 40 seconds. Add the fish—do not crowd it in the pan. Lower the heat. Cook exactly 3 minutes by the clock, or until the underside becomes a lovely golden brown. Turn with a pancake turner and cook 2 to 3 minutes longer, or until the second side has browned. The time will depend on the thickness of the fillets. The outside should have a crunchy shell, but the inside should be tender and juicy. Pepper and salt again if necessary. Serve at once on a platter. Surround with lemon wedges and garnish with parsley. Serve with a Tartar Sauce☆ or with Aioli,☆ dear to the Frenchman's heart.

GEORGE BRADSHAW AND RUTH NORMAN

CLAM PIE   SERVES 8

THE FILLING

2 7-ounce cans minced clams

2 teaspoons grated shallots or
    onions

1 tablespoon finely chopped
    parsley

4 whole eggs plus 2 yolks

2 cups light cream

A pinch of nutmeg

Salt and pepper to taste

THE CRUST

Pastry for a one-crust pie,
    unbaked

Preheat oven to 375°.

Line a 9-inch pie plate with pastry. Drain the clams, reserve the liquid, and spread the clams, shallots, and parsley in the unbaked pastry shell. Beat the eggs and egg yolks thoroughly. Add the cream, reserved clam juice, nutmeg, salt, and pepper and stir. Pour into the shell. Bake until the custard has barely set and is golden, about 30 minutes. Let rest a few minutes; serve warm, not hot.

LOUISE NEVELSON

CRAB MEAT KIEV

SERVES 2 TO 4

6 tablespoons butter
1 pound cooked fresh crab meat,
    picked over
⅔ cup blanched and finely
    chopped almonds
Salt and pepper to taste

2 cloves garlic, passed through
    garlic press
8 rounds Russian black bread
4 tablespoons dairy sour cream
4 tablespoons chopped fresh dill

Melt 4 tablespoons of the butter in a skillet and lightly toss the crab meat over medium heat until delicately browned. In another skillet brown the almonds in the remaining butter. Set aside to cool. Gently toss the crab meat and almonds together, adding salt, pepper, and garlic to taste. Spoon onto rounds of fresh black Russian bread and top with sour cream and dill.

MISS MOLLY MALONEY

RED SNAPPER RING

SERVES 8 TO 10

1 3-pound red snapper
1 whole onion stuck with a clove
1 bay leaf
Few sprigs of parsley
1 rib celery
½ cup vinegar
1½ cups White Sauce☆

1 onion, grated
1 tablespoon finely chopped
    parsley
1 teaspoon lime juice
Salt to taste
4 eggs, separated
1 pint heavy cream, whipped

Preheat oven to 350°.

    Poach the snapper until tender in simmering salted water, seasoned with the onion, bay leaf, parsley, celery, and vinegar. Drain, remove the skin and bones, and grind the fish finely. To the white sauce add the grated onion, chopped parsley, lime juice, salt, and the egg yolks, well beaten. Add the fish, then fold in the egg whites, beaten until stiff. Fold in the whipped cream. Pour into a well-greased and floured large ring mold, place it in a pan of boiling water, which should come up ⅓ of the side of the pan before boiling. Cook in the oven until set, 30 to 40 minutes. Let rest 5 minutes, then unmold and fill the center with cooked lobster, shrimp and crab meat heated in Newburg sauce made by any good standard recipe.

FRANCESCO SCAVULLO

FILLETS OF HADDOCK FRANCESCO

SERVES 6

6 fillets of haddock
1 cup cider vinegar
6 tablespoons plain sesame oil
(not the roasted Oriental
type)
Salt and pepper to taste
½ teaspoon tamari sauce (obtainable in most Oriental food
stores)
3 yellow onions, peeled and
quartered
3 teaspoons herb-flavored or spicy
brown mustard
6 tablespoons Mayonnaise☆

Preheat broiler for 5 minutes.

Place fillets in one layer in a shallow fireproof dish. In a blender jar put all other ingredients and process until smooth. Pour this sauce over the fish. Broil for 10 to 15 minutes, or until fish flakes when tested; don't overcook.

Main Course
Poultry

BROOKE ASTOR

CHICKEN SUZANNE

SERVES 4

"Here is a recipe I have used for years. The whiskey gives it a very special flavor."

3 pounds small white onions
1 stick butter
1 broiler-fryer chicken (about 2½ pounds)
1 medium onion, stuck with a clove
1 carrot, cut up
1 rib celery, sliced
1 sprig dried thyme
1 small bay leaf
2 to 3 sprigs parsley
Salt and pepper to taste
1 cup heavy cream
1½ tablespoons whiskey

Peel the onions and put into the top of a double boiler with the stick of butter; cook over simmering water 1 hour, or until tender. Do not let the onions get brown. Poach the chicken for ½ hour, or until tender, in a covered pot containing water to cover that has first been boiled 10 minutes with the onion, carrot, celery, thyme, bay leaf, parsley, salt, and pepper. Take it out and skin it, cut into 4 to 6 pieces, arrange in a serving casserole, and keep warm. Add the cream to the onions slowly and heat thoroughly, add the whiskey, and pour the mixture over the chicken. Serve hot.

FROM GLEN BIRNBAUM, MORTIMER'S RESTAURANT

CHICKEN PAILLARDE WITH *ROSEMARY BUTTER*

SERVES 1

1 chicken breast, 4 to 5 ounces, skinned and boned
1 tablespoon melted butter
Salt and pepper to taste

Place the chicken breast, fillet side up, between two sheets of clear plastic. Beat the surface gently with a mallet until the meat is evenly spread and is about ⅛ inch thick. Brush with the butter and season. Cook quickly over a very hot charcoal grill (or at home in a very hot, well-oiled iron skillet). Garnish with grilled tomato halves and watercress. Serve with a slice or two of Rosemary Butter (below).

ROSEMARY BUTTER

SERVES 4

It is not practical to make this for just one serving, but it is practical and delicious to serve with any grilled meats.

2 sticks sweet butter
½ cup Dijon mustard
1 teaspoon dried rosemary,

coarsely chopped
1 teaspoon marjoram

Cream the butter and mustard together, add the herbs. Wrap in foil and form into a roll 1 inch in diameter; freeze. Cut into ¼-inch slices and serve, while still very chilled, with the chicken.

AMANDA BURDEN

BARBECUED SQUAB OR CHICKEN

SERVES 4

4 squabs or chickens, butterflied

MARINADE
1 cup olive oil
¼ cup imported soy sauce
½ cup sherry
1 teaspoon garlic salt
2 tablespoons mixed dried Prov-

ençal herbs (at fine food stores), or a combination of dried rosemary, thyme, sweet marjoram, and summer savory

Marinate the squabs or chickens, covered, in the well-mixed marinade in the refrigerator for at least 8 hours, turning them occasionally. Drain; keep the marinade for basting. Barbecue the squabs or chickens slowly over charcoal, basting often with the marinade and turning several times until done, 30 to 45 minutes. Serve with wild rice mixed with golden raisins and toasted almonds.

MRS. DWIGHT D. EISENHOWER

CHICKEN JEWEL RING

SERVES 8

CRANBERRY LAYER
1 envelope unflavored gelatin
1 cup cranberry-juice cocktail
1 can (1 pound) whole cranberry

sauce
2 tablespoons lemon juice

CHICKEN LAYER

1 envelope unflavored gelatin
¾ cup cold water
1 tablespoon imported soy sauce
1 cup Mayonnaise☆

1½ cups diced cooked chicken
½ cup diced celery
¼ cup coarsely chopped almonds,
    toasted

Prepare the cranberry layer: Sprinkle the gelatin on the cranberry-juice cocktail in a saucepan and let soften 5 to 10 minutes. Place over low heat, stirring constantly, until the gelatin is dissolved. Break up the whole cranberry sauce: stir into the gelatin mixture and lemon juice. Turn into a 6-cup ring mold; chill until almost firm.

    Prepare the chicken layer: Sprinkle the gelatin on the cold water in a saucepan and let soften 5 to 10 minutes. Place over low heat, stirring constantly until the gelatin is dissolved. Remove from heat; stir in the soy sauce. Cool completely. Gradually stir in the mayonnaise until blended. Mix in the remaining ingredients. Spoon on top of the almost firm cranberry layer. Chill until firm. Unmold on salad greens.

KITTY CARLISLE HART

ROAST CHICKEN

SERVES 4

"Herewith is my recipe for roast chicken, one of the rarest things to be found in all its crispy glory, outside one's own house."

3- to 3¼-pound chicken
2 sticks plus 2 tablespoons butter

Salt and pepper to taste
Poultry seasoning to taste

Preheat oven to 500°.
    Wash the chicken well inside and out; wipe dry and salt the inside well. Put into a roasting pan with the butter, salt, pepper, and poultry seasoning; put the pan over stove burner just until butter melts, then rub the butter and seasoning all over the chicken. Bake in the oven for about 10 minutes on its back; then reduce the heat to 400°, turn onto one side, roast 10 minutes, turn onto the other side, roast 10 minutes longer; then turn breast side up, lower heat to 300°, and roast for another 10 to 15 minutes, or until done. It will be done when its legs are loose. Then, at the last minute, pop it under the broiler till it's good and crispy—*et voilà!*

POULET À L'ESTRAGON
(Tarragon Chicken)   SERVES 6

A White House recipe:

3 whole skinned chicken breasts,
    each two halves left attached
    at the breastbone
1 onion, thinly sliced
1 carrot, thinly sliced
¼ teaspoon dried tarragon
½ cup white wine
4 cups water, or as needed

3 tablespoons butter
3 tablespoons flour
½ teaspoon salt
Pinch of pepper
2 tablespoons butter, cut into bits
1 egg yolk, lightly beaten
3 tablespoons heavy cream

Place the chicken breasts, onion, carrot, tarragon, and wine in a large saucepan. Add just enough water to cover, about 4 cups. Cover and bring to a boil over moderate heat. Lower the heat and simmer gently about 25 minutes, until fork-tender. Remove the chicken and keep warm. Cut apart into 6 servings. Strain the broth, then cook over high heat until it is reduced to 2 cups.

In a heavy saucepan melt the 3 tablespoons butter, stir in the flour, salt, and pepper. Gradually add the reduced chicken broth; cook, stirring, over moderate heat until thickened and smooth. Add the 2 tablespoons butter, simmer gently 5 minutes, stirring occasionally. Combine the egg yolk and cream. Stir into the hot sauce; don't cook further. Arrange the chicken breasts on a warm serving platter and pour the hot sauce over them.

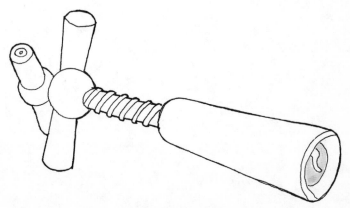

ELEVEN-MINUTE CHICKEN BREAST SAUTÉ

SERVES 4

½ cup olive oil or butter
2 whole chicken breasts (2 sides each), cut into 1-inch cubes
1 rib celery, cut into 1-inch pieces
½ sweet green pepper, cored, seeded, and cut into 1-inch squares
1 apple, peeled and cut into 1-inch pieces
4 large mushrooms, quartered
1 small onion, finely minced

½ cup chopped basil, or 1 tablespoon dried basil
1 teaspoon coarsely ground pepper
¼ cup Marsala wine (or sherry)
Juice of a half lemon
¼ teaspoon coarse (kosher) salt, or to taste
½ cup dairy sour cream, or more, to taste
¼ cup minced fresh dill

Heat the oil or butter in a skillet over medium-high heat, add the chicken, celery, green pepper, apple, mushrooms, onion, basil, and pepper; sauté, tossing often, for 11 minutes. Add the Marsala or sherry, lemon juice, and salt. Reheat briefly and serve immediately with the sour cream topped with fresh dill.

Main Course
Meat

CAROL BURNETT

CAROL BURNETT'S MEAT LOAF   SERVES 8

2 eggs
4 tablespoons milk
2 (8-ounce) cans tomato sauce
1 onion, chopped
1 green pepper, chopped
2 pounds ground round

Salt and pepper to taste
Onion salt or garlic salt (optional)
½ cup bread crumbs, or more if
    needed
Oil for the electric skillet

Beat the eggs with the milk in a big bowl. Add 1 can tomato sauce and beat. Add the onion, green pepper, and the meat and squish with hands (wash hands first). Add salt and pepper to taste, and onion or garlic salt, if you like. Add enough bread crumbs to hold it all together, pat into a greased loaf. Place the loaf in an electric skillet brushed with a little oil. Pour over it the second can of tomato sauce. Cover and cook about 1½ hours at a thermostat setting of 325°. (If you don't have an electric skillet, put the meat in a greased loaf pan, top with sauce, and bake in a 325° oven for 1½ to 2 hours.)

LEON LOBEL

OVERNIGHT STEAK   SERVES 4

"This marinade was created for all steak lovers, rich or poor, young and old—for steak on the barbecue, in the fireplace, or just in your broiler."

4½ pounds beefsteaks

MARINADE FOR STEAKS

4 tablespoons raw beef marrow
    (from the butcher)
½ stick butter
2 slices bacon, cooked crisp,
    drained and pulverized
1 large onion, minced very fine

3 cloves garlic, minced very fine
Pinch of thyme
¼ teaspoon salt
¼ teaspoon freshly ground
    pepper

The day before serving: In a medium-sized skillet melt the marrow, slowly mashing it as it melts. Add butter and blend well. Add the bacon, onion, garlic, and thyme, mix well, cover, and cook over very low heat 15 minutes. Add the salt and pepper, continue cooking, uncovered, 20 minutes longer, stirring often. Brush the steaks all over with the warm marinade (keep any extra), then refrigerate the meat until the next day.

Final preparations: Remove the meat from the refrigerator 2 hours before cooking. Reheat leftover marinade.

Preheat the broiler, or prepare a charcoal fire.

Broil the steak on one side the way you usually do, spread the marinade evenly over the uncooked side (turning the meat either before or after you do this, depending on whether the heat is above or below the meat), and finish broiling to the doneness you like.

LIZ SMITH

CHICKEN-FRIED STEAK WITH GRAVY
SERVES 6

3 pounds round steak, sliced thin
Pepper to taste
5 whole eggs
¼ cup cooking oil
⅓ cup all-purpose flour for
    dredging meat

2 to 3 tablespoons instant flour
    (for gravy)
Salt and pepper to taste
¼ cup water
¼ cup milk

Ask your butcher for *thinly cut* round steak for frying. (This is the most flavorful part of the steer, but most people never eat it except ground up, because it's tough.) Trim the meat slices and pepper them liberally on both sides. Then beat them with a wooden mallet, a hammer, or, as my pal Chuck Howard says, "Hit them with a Coke bottle like Mamma did." After pounding on both sides, cut each steak in small pieces, about 2 by 2 inches. Now beat up the eggs in a bowl and pour the all-purpose flour onto a flat plate. Put the oil in a skillet and get it very hot. Dip each piece of meat in egg, then coat it in flour and fry it quickly, turning it to brown on both sides. Sprinkle pieces with salt after putting them on paper towels; keep warm. Pour off any excess fat from the skillet and stir in the instant flour, lots of pepper and salt, and then the water and milk into the crunchy skillet leftovers. Stir, cooking over medium heat. Keep tasting it; the secret of good gravy is lots of pepper and salt.

ELI WALLACH

STEAK AND CORN ON THE COB

"My cooking is hearty, outdoors-type stuff," says actor Eli Wallach. "In the summer, I usually take over the main cooking chore over a charcoal grill: steaks, chops, chicken and occasionally fish. And corn on the cob, which I prepare as follows:

"Take an ear of corn, peel back the green husk and remove the silk; butter and salt the raw kernels; rewrap the corn in its husk, then wrap it in aluminum foil. Place directly on the grill; turn regularly . . . it makes for tender, steamed, and buttered corn.

"And this is the way I do the steak: I use sirloin steaks and insert several pieces of garlic in spaced cuts. Rub the meat with olive oil, then season with onion salt and mustard and marinate in red wine to cover for a few hours. Grill the first side 5 minutes, then turn, repeating turning every 5 minutes. The length of cooking depends on the steak's thickness— usually 40 minutes."

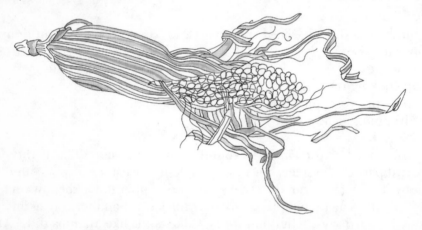

BETTY FORD

STUFFED PEPPERS

SERVES 6

A White House recipe:

1 pound ground beef
½ cup uncooked rice
1 (6-ounce) can tomato sauce
1 medium onion, diced

Salt and pepper to taste
¾ cup water
6 medium-sized green peppers

Preheat oven to 325°.

Mix the beef, rice, tomato sauce, onion, salt, pepper, and water. Remove the tops from the peppers and save them. Cut out all ribs and remove the seeds. Stuff the peppers, replace the tops, and place in a shallow baking dish. Bake for 2½ hours. Serve with tossed salad and French bread.

YOGI BERRA

SCALOPPINE DI VITELLO ALLA MARSALA (Veal Scallops with Marsala) SERVES 4

1 stick butter, or more if needed
½ pound fresh mushrooms, sliced
1 clove garlic, finely chopped
1 pound veal scallops, sliced

paper-thin
Flour for dusting veal
1 cup dry Marsala

In a heavy skillet or shallow fireproof casserole melt the butter over medium heat, add the mushrooms and garlic. Cook gently until the mushrooms are done. Remove the vegetables and place to one side. Take the veal scallops, roll them in flour, pat the flour in with the heel of your hand. Reheat the butter in the same skillet and brown the veal on both sides, adding a little more butter if it is needed. Add the mushrooms and Marsala, cover, and simmer gently 15 minutes. Serve with green noodles cooked *al dente,* tossed with hot butter.

ANGELO DONGHIA

VITELLO TONNATO
(Cold Veal with Tuna Sauce) SERVES 8 TO 10

3- to 4-pound boneless veal roast, tied tightly by your butcher into a small round, 2½ to 3

inches in diameter.
Salt and pepper
Garlic to taste, minced or pressed

TUNA SAUCE
1 egg
1 cup olive oil
Juice of a lemon

Salt and pepper
½ can (6½-ounce size) Italian tuna
Capers

Preheat oven to 375°.

Rub the veal with salt, pepper, and garlic, roast for approximately an hour or until done. Let cool, remove strings, and then slice. Cover and set aside.

To prepare the sauce: Place the egg in a blender. Blend for an instant at high speed. Pour in the olive oil very slowly in a steady stream. When thick, add the lemon juice, salt, pepper, and tuna. Blend at low speed until smooth. (If the sauce becomes thin or curdled, pour it into a container, then rinse and dry the blender container. Add another egg, blend for an instant, then pour in the sauce in a slow steady stream until the consistency of thin mayonnaise.) Check for taste and add seasonings if necessary. Pour the sauce over veal rounds on a serving platter and garnish with capers. May be made ahead and refrigerated, covered, for several hours.

BARBARA POSES KAFKA

VEAL AND HAM PÂTÉ

PASTRY

2 cups flour, sifted
1 stick butter at room temperature; or 6 tablespoons butter and 3 tablespoons lard; or 6 tablespoons butter and 2

tablespoons olive oil
1 teaspoon salt
2 egg yolks
¼ cup cold water

FOR THE PÂTÉ

1¾ pounds veal fillet, tenderloin, or leg
¼ cup cognac
2 pounds cold lean boiled ham
2 eggs, unbeaten
½ cup chopped mushrooms, both caps and stems
4 tablespoons lard

3 shallots, chopped
3 tablespoons chopped parsley
Salt, pepper, and allspice to taste
1 packet strudel dough or Greek filo pastry, at room temperature, for ornamenting crust
1 egg, beaten

OPTIONAL FOR COLD PÂTÉ

½ envelope (1½ teaspoons) unflavored gelatin

1 cup veal or beef stock
2 tablespoons dry sherry

THE PASTRY: Make it the day before you make the pâté. Put all the ingredients except the water in a large bowl, or make a well in the flour piled on the table, place in it all other ingredients except the water. Knead thoroughly, adding only as much water as necessary to make the dough hold together. Knead for several minutes; this should be a firm dough. Place it in the refrigerator overnight, or for several hours. When ready to make the pâté, remove the pastry from the refrigerator and allow to come to a temperature at which it can just be rolled without becoming soft.

THE PÂTÉ: Cut 1¼ pounds of the veal into strips the size of raw carrot strips. Marinate in the cognac. Cut up 1¼ pounds of the ham in similar fashion. Combine the remaining meat, finely diced, with the unbeaten eggs, mushrooms, lard, shallots, parsley, and seasonings. Process in a blender at high speed, or pass several times through a meat grinder fitted with its finest plate.

Grease a spring-mold loaf pan measuring 3½ by 12 inches and 3¼ inches deep. Line the pan with the rolled-out pastry. (If you do not want to unmold the pâté, use a regular loaf pan measuring about 5½ by 9¾ inches.) Fill the pastry-lined pan with alternate layers of the ground meat and the drained veal and ham strips (save the cognac), ending with a layer of ground meat. (If any filling is left over, it can be ground together and sautéed to make an excellent spread for canapés.) Pour the cognac in which the veal was marinated over the pâté.

Preheat the oven to 350°.

Cover the pâté, first with a thin layer of pastry and then, if you like, with pretty shapes cut from the strudel or filo pastry. Cut a hole through the crust to the meat, brush crust with beaten egg. Bake for 1 hour. Serve hot or cold.

FOR COLD PÂTÉ: Let it cool almost completely, then dissolve the gelatin in ¼ cup of the stock. Add the rest of the stock and bring slowly to a boil, stirring; cool and add the sherry. Pour into the opening in the top of the crust as much of the liquid as you can without soaking the crust and place the pâté in the refrigerator for at least 5 hours. Any remaining aspic can be chilled, chopped, and served as a garnish around the pâté, when released from the pan.

Vegetable Accompaniments

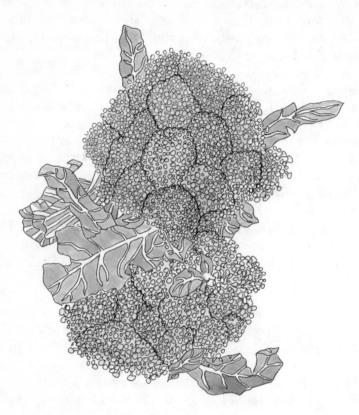

JAMES MERRILL

TSATZIKÍ (Greek Yogurt with Cucumber)

1 quart dairy yogurt
1 cucumber, peeled
Salt

2 cloves garlic, peeled and very
  finely minced or passed
  through a garlic press

Drain the yogurt for 6 hours in a sieve lined with paper toweling; discard the liquid that drains off. Grate the cucumber, then salt it, let it stand ½ hour, then squeeze it in a twisted towel to rid it of surplus moisture. Add the cucumber and garlic to the yogurt. Refrigerate 1 hour, then serve with a good "peasant" bread or hot toast.

BELLA ABZUG

EGGPLANT AND GREEN BEAN CASSEROLE

SERVES 6

1 cup olive oil, or as needed
1 large eggplant (1½ pounds),
    peeled and sliced
1 9-ounce package frozen Italian
    green beans, thawed
Salt and pepper to taste

Oregano to taste
1½ cups freshly grated Parmesan
    cheese
1 (17-ounce) can peeled Italian
    tomatoes

Preheat oven to 375°.

Pour the olive oil to the depth of about ⅛ inch in a large heavy skillet. Fry the eggplant slices quickly until lightly browned on both sides, cooking in two or more batches and adding oil as you need it. Layer the browned slices with the green beans in a 2-quart baking dish, sprinkling each layer with salt, pepper, and oregano and the grated Parmesan cheese. Pour the tomatoes over all and bake for 45 minutes, or until all is tender.

AMANDA BURDEN

GRATED ZUCCHINI

SERVES 4

"The easiest and most delightful vegetable dish I know."

6 zucchini
Salt and freshly ground black

pepper
½ stick butter

Grate the zucchini on the medium side of a grater. Sprinkle fairly generously with salt, let stand in a colander for 15 minutes. Dry well on paper towels. Melt the butter, and when hot add the zucchini, stir-fry for *barely one minute.* Serve immediately, lavishly sprinkled with freshly ground black pepper and additional salt if needed.

BILL BLASS

HOMINY AND CHEESE SOUFFLÉ

SERVES 4 TO 6

"This is great instead of rice or potatoes. Sensational with roast beef as well as roast chicken. It's the texture as well as taste that makes it good."

1 cup water
1 cup milk
1 teaspoon salt
½ cup hominy grits (regular, not
    instant)
3 egg yolks
6 tablespoons grated Parmesan

cheese
½ teaspoon salt
¼ teaspoon pepper
1 tablespoon snipped chives
3 tablespoons butter, melted
4 egg whites

Combine the water and milk in the upper part of a double boiler, bring to a boil over direct heat. Add the salt and grits, stirring constantly, over low heat. Place over hot water in the boiler base and cook 45 minutes, stirring occasionally. Remove from the heat and set aside to cool for 15 minutes.

Preheat oven to 325°.

Meanwhile, beat the egg yolks in a bowl until light in color. Add the cooked grits, beating steadily until smooth. Add the cheese, salt, pepper, chives, and butter, mix well. Beat the egg whites until stiff but not dry. Fold them into the soufflé mixture carefully. Pour into a buttered 1½-quart soufflé dish. Bake 40 minutes. Serve at once.

EVANGELINE BRUCE

SPINACH SOUFFLÉ SURPRISE

SERVES 4

4 eggs for poaching
1 teaspoon vinegar
½ cup milk
1 onion, finely minced
1 pound fresh spinach, leaves
    only
3 tablespoons butter

3 tablespoons flour
Salt and pepper to taste
Pinch of nutmeg
4 eggs, separated, for the soufflé
2 additional egg whites
3 tablespoons grated Parmesan
    cheese

Poach 4 eggs in water and vinegar, removing them while they are still very soft. Drain and refrigerate.

Preheat oven to 375°.

Place in a blender the milk, onion, and spinach, process until smooth. In a saucepan melt the butter, add the flour, and stir over medium heat until thickened. To this *roux* add 1½ cups of the spinach mixture. Add salt, pepper, and nutmeg, continue to cook, stirring. When the mixture has become quite thick, remove from the stove and beat in gradually the 4 egg yolks, which have been beaten together. Allow to cool. Beat the 6 egg whites until stiff. Then quickly stir one fourth of them into the soufflé base. Fold in the remaining whites carefully, keeping as much air as possible in the mixture. Place one fourth of mixture in an unbuttered 8-inch soufflé dish. Arrange the cold soft-poached eggs on this layer and cover with the remaining soufflé mixture. Sprinkle with the cheese and bake 25 minutes or until done. Serve hot.

SHIRLEY HUNTINGTON

GREEN CHILI AND CHEESE FLAN

SERVES 6

"This dish may be served as a luncheon entrée or as an accompaniment to a roast of beef or steak in place of a vegetable or starch. It may also be served hot or cold as a buffet dish. You can vary the amount of chilies according to taste."

7-ounce can whole green chili
    peppers (mild)
2 cups tomatoes, fresh or canned,
    coarsely chopped
⅔ cup finely chopped onions
    (preferably red)
1½ cups grated sharp Cheddar
    cheese
Pinch of dried basil
Pinch of dried thyme
8 eggs, beaten until fluffy with ¼
    teaspoon salt
6 ounces Monterey Jack cheese,
    thinly sliced

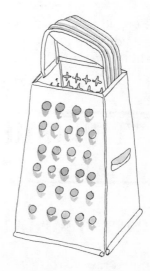

Preheat oven to 375°.

Butter the bottom of a 12-inch-square or 12-inch-long oval baking dish about 2 inches deep. With a sharp knife, slit the chilies lengthwise and spread them flat, discarding seeds and stems. Cut each pepper into four strips lengthwise. Place the strips in the baking dish in a solid layer, side by side. Add, in successive layers, the tomatoes, onions, and Cheddar cheese. Sprinkle on top the basil and thyme. Pour the eggs over the layers in the baking dish. Bake 15 to 20 minutes, until the top is somewhat firm. Now take the Monterey Jack slices. (The ones bought ready-sliced in the market will do nicely, but if you slice your own make the slices not thicker than ⅛ inch.) Remove the dish from the oven and carefully lay the cheese slices on top, slightly overlapping them to form a complete crust. Bake 40 to 45 minutes longer at the same temperature (total baking time, about 1 hour). To serve, cut into squares or rectangles and lift portions with a spatula or pie server.

JOAN FONTAINE

CURRIED TOMATOES
SERVES 2 TO 4

1 tablespoon olive oil
1 teaspoon curry powder, or to taste
1 medium onion, sliced
4 tomatoes, peeled, quartered,

and seeded
Dash of hot pepper sauce
Dash of Worcestershire sauce
Salt and pepper to taste
Chopped parsley

Heat the oil, add the curry powder and onions. Cook over medium heat until the onions are just *al dente*. Add the tomatoes and heat—*don't* cook them. Add the seasonings and serve, sprinkled with parsley.

"THE CHILDREN'S HOUR," VOGUE 1932

CARROT TIMBALES
SERVES 6

2 cups grated raw carrots
½ cup bread crumbs
2 eggs, beaten

1 teaspoon salt
2 tablespoons melted butter
½ cup milk

Preheat oven to 300°.

Mix all ingredients together. Fill 12 greased small timbale molds with the mixture, set in a pan of hot water, and bake until firm, about 20 minutes.

FELICIA AND MICK JONES

SAUTÉED MUSHROOMS AND SNOW PEAS

SERVES 4

½ pound snow peas (trimmed at each end but left whole)
½ pound medium-sized white mushrooms (wiped clean, not washed)
1 tablespoon sesame oil
1 tablespoon soy sauce
Juice of a half lemon

Wash the snow peas and shake out any excess moisture. Put the mushrooms, snow peas, and sesame oil in an iron skillet on low heat. Stir continuously for about 7 minutes, then sprinkle with the soy sauce while still on the heat. Shake the pan around for a few seconds, remove from the heat, and squeeze lemon juice over the top. Serve immediately. This is great with brown rice.

CHARLES MASSON

FONDS D'ARTICHAUTS PAULINE
(Artichoke Hearts Pauline)

SERVES 1

This recipe is named for Pauline Trigère, who asked the late Charles Masson to reinvent the dish that she had eaten during a visit to France.

For each serving, prepare 2 artichoke bottoms. Either poach them, then remove the leaves and the choke, or trim off the leaves, remove the chokes, and then poach the bottoms in a *blanc* for vegetables (boiling water with some flour and lemon juice added to preserve color). The easier method is the first. Then warm up both artichoke bottoms, finely dice *one* of them, and fill the other with the artichoke dice. Cover with the mustardy vinaigrette (below), with chopped parsley or tarragon added, and serve warm. For each serving blend the following ingredients:

½ teaspoon Dijon-type mustard
¼ teaspoon salt
¼ teaspoon pepper
1½ teaspoons vinegar

2 tablespoons salad oil
1½ teaspoons chopped fresh parsley or tarragon

JACQUELINE ONASSIS

WHITE HOUSE CHEF RENE VERDON'S GRATINEED SPINACH SERVES 6

This White House recipe was adapted by Anne Lincoln.

2 pounds fresh spinach
½ pound fresh mushrooms
3 tablespoons butter
1 cup Béchamel Sauce☆
Salt and pepper to taste
Freshly grated nutmeg

2 tablespoons grated Gruyère
    cheese
2 tablespoons grated American
    cheese
Buttered bread crumbs

Preheat oven to 375°.

Wash the spinach repeatedly, using tepid water for the final rinse. Blanch in a large pot of boiling water; cool quickly under cold water; drain, and dry in a towel. Set aside in a cool place. Peel the mushrooms and mince them. Cook them in the butter 4 to 5 minutes over a gentle flame; do not brown. Drain the butter and mix the mushrooms with the Béchamel sauce. Season with salt, pepper, and nutmeg. Arrange a layer of spinach in a buttered baking dish, cover with one third of the mushroom mixture, and repeat until the dish is full. Sprinkle over the Gruyère and American cheeses. Top with a thin layer of buttered bread crumbs, set the dish in a pan of hot water. Bake about 35 minutes, until the top is brown and bubbly.

CHESSY PATCÉVITCH

CUCUMBER MOUSSE

SERVES 4 TO 6

2 whole cucumbers, peeled
1 envelope unflavored gelatin
¼ cup cold water
¼ cup boiling water
½ cup Mayonnaise☆
1 teaspoon Worcestershire sauce
Juice of 1 lemon
Salt and pepper to taste
½ cup heavy cream
Slices of cucumber and sprigs of
    parsley as garnish

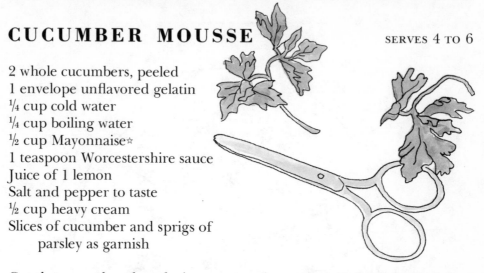

Cut the cucumbers lengthwise, remove the seeds, and shred the flesh into a mixing bowl. Soften the gelatin in the cold water, then dissolve by adding the boiling water. Set aside to cool. Combine the mayonnaise, Worcestershire sauce, lemon juice, and the cooled gelatin. Add salt and pepper. Whip the cream to soft peaks and fold into the mixture. Fold into the cucumber and place the mixing bowl in the refrigerator until the mousse just begins to set. Spoon it into a chilled 1-quart mold and chill for at least 2 hours, or until firm. To serve, unmold and decorate with cucumber and parsley.

Desserts

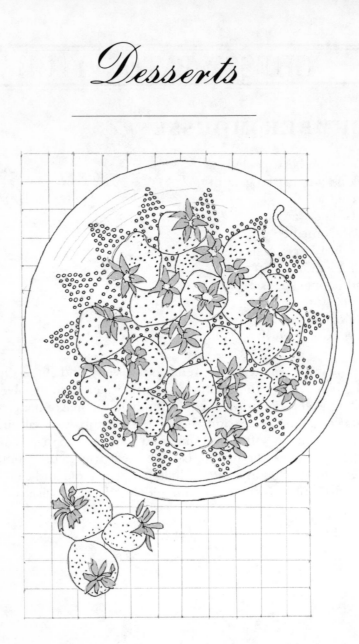

GORDON TEVIS, 1948

BLUEBERRY ICE-CREAM PIE
SERVES 8

A baked and cooled 10-inch
   piecrust
1 pint rich vanilla ice cream
2 cups rinsed and well-drained

blueberries (or other berries
   in season)
3 egg whites
3 tablespoons sugar

Have oven preheated to 450° during dinner.

Ten minutes before time to serve dessert, spread in the crust a layer of rich vanilla ice cream, then a layer of blueberries; set in the freezer. Beat the egg whites, gradually adding the sugar as they thicken, until you have a stiff meringue. Pile quickly over the berries, making sure the meringue touches crust all around. Place the pie plate on a board and put into a very hot oven just until the meringue browns; this should not take more than 3 minutes. Serve instantly.

ROBERT L. GREEN

COFFEE GRANITA SUNDAE
(Coffee Sundae Italian Style)

SERVES 6

⅔ cup sugar
⅔ cup water
4 rounded tablespoons instant

coffee powder
2 cups chopped ice and water,
   mostly ice

SAUCE
⅔ cup chocolate syrup
⅔ cup heavy cream, whipped

½ cup chopped nuts

ACCOMPANIMENT
Crisp sugar cookies

Combine the sugar and ⅔ cup water in a heavy 1-quart saucepan; bring to a boil over medium heat, stirring constantly. Stir in the instant coffee; add the ice and water; stir until the ice is melted. Pour into a metal ice-cube tray and place in the freezer. Freeze until almost solid, about 45 minutes.

Break up the mixture; place in a large electric-mixer bowl. Beat at low speed until the consistency of applesauce. Return to the tray and freeze 1 hour. Again break up the *granita* and beat again. Return to the tray and freeze until firm, about 1 hour. Scoop the *granita* into 6 sherbet glasses. Pour the chocolate syrup over, top with whipped cream, and sprinkle with nuts. Serve with crisp sugar cookies.

MARION W. FLEXNER, 1946

TRANSPARENT PIE

SERVES 6 TO 8

A 9-inch piecrust, lightly baked,
    or 6 small piecrusts (tartlets),
    lightly baked
8-ounce jar of tart fruit jelly or

preserves
2 sticks sweet butter, softened
1 cup sugar, sifted
3 eggs, beaten

Preheat oven to 400°.

Into the baked piecrust or tartlet shells, spread the jelly or the preserves evenly. (Raspberry or currant jelly is preferable, but plum, grape, blackberry, or any good jelly will do; some Damson plum preserves are also acceptable.) Cream the softened butter with the sugar. Add the eggs and continue to beat the mixture until it is light and spongy. (This filling, which in old English cookery books is called a "chess," is probably the ancestor of our Southern "chess pies," the word *chess* being an Old World term for "cheese.") At any rate, the filling is poured over the jelly and spread evenly. Put the pie or small pies into the preheated oven and let remain 20 to 25 minutes, until the filling sets; test by slightly shaking the pan. When the center of the filling is firm (be careful not to overcook), remove and cool on a rack. Serve warm or cold but not hot.

SHEILA HIBBEN, 1948

MADEIRA JELLY

SERVES 6

2¼ cups water
Rind of a half lemon
3 cloves
Rind of a half tangerine
Small cinnamon stick
½ cup sugar, or more if needed

1 envelope unflavored gelatin
    soaked 5 minutes in 1 table-
    spoon water and juice of 1
    lemon
1 cup sweet Madeira
Heavy cream

Put the cold water in a saucepan with the lemon rind, cloves, tangerine rind, cinnamon, and sugar. Let simmer over low heat 8 minutes. Pour the hot mixture over the soaked gelatin and stir until entirely dissolved. Add the Madeira and let stand until cool; taste and add more sugar if necessary.

Strain into a screw-top jar and cover tightly; let stand in the refrigerator overnight. Turn into a well-chilled glass bowl and serve with a jug of rich cream. The jelly should not be stiff enough to mold.

BOB HOPE

BOB HOPE'S FAVORITE LEMON PIE

SERVES 6

A 9-inch baked pie shell
3 tablespoons cornstarch
1 cup plus 2 tablespoons sugar
Pinch of salt
1 cup boiling water

3 egg yolks
2 tablespoons butter
Grated rind of 1 lemon
¼ cup lemon juice

MERINGUE
3 egg whites
2½ tablespoons sugar

Preheat oven to 325°.

Prepare the pie shell. Combine the cornstarch, sugar, and salt in a saucepan. Add the boiling water slowly, stirring constantly, and cook over medium heat until thick and smooth. Beat the egg yolks lightly and add, stirring rapidly, to the hot mixture. Add the butter, lemon rind, and juice, cook 2 or 3 minutes, stirring. Pour into the pie shell and let cool to luke-warm. Prepare the meringue: Beat the 3 egg whites, gradually adding sugar as the whites stiffen. Heap the meringue over the filling and bake 15 minutes or until the meringue is light brown. Cool on a rack.

JOEY ADAMS

EASY BLENDER ICE CREAM—A DIET DESSERT

SERVES 3 TO 4

"Being a sweets buff and a dessert lover, I either go on a diet or let out my cinch; I decided to find some great recipes where I can have my cake and eat it and stay as sweet as I am—after all, if I don't watch my figure, the girls won't. Here is a great diet recipe."

⅓ cup dried skim milk
⅓ cup water
2 individual serving packets non-
    caloric sweetener
½ teaspoon vanilla

½ cup unsweetened pineapple
juice (frozen), or ½ cup fro-
zen or canned dietetic
peaches

Process all the ingredients in a blender to ice-cream consistency. Pour into an ice-cube tray and freeze.

CHARLES MASSON

TARTE AUX POMMES LA GRENOUILLE
(Apple Tart La Grenouille) SERVES 6 TO 8

THE PASTRY
4 cups pastry flour (flour with low
    gluten content)
2 sticks sweet butter
1 teaspoon sugar

Pinch of salt
1 cup lukewarm milk
1 egg

THE FILLING
Sugar for sprinkling crust
4 to 6 greening or similar tart
    apples

Juice of a half lemon
Extrafine sugar
Apple jelly, about ½ cup

TO MAKE THE CRUST: Work up the flour and butter by breaking the butter into the flour with your finger until the lumps are very fine. Dissolve the sugar and salt in the milk. Beat in the egg and add to the mixture of flour and butter. Mix well together. Wrap and place in the refrigerator until needed.

TO MAKE THE TART: *Preheat oven to 375°.*
Roll out the dough and line a 9-inch pie plate or tart pan, trim the edges. Sprinkle the bottom with a little sugar. Peel and slice very thin enough apples to fill the shell, generously squirting them with fresh lemon juice as they are sliced. Lay the slices in overlapping fashion in the shell, forming circles. Sprinkle with sugar. Bake until done—the apples should be tender. Brush with apple jelly, which has been melted with 2 to 3 tablespoons water, for extra gloss. That's all.

HAPPY ROCKEFELLER

NEW YORK STATE FLAT APPLE PIE
SERVES ABOUT 12

CRUST

½ cup butter
½ cup margarine

2 cups flour
3 to 4 tablespoons ice water

FILLING

11 to 12 New York State apples,
    medium size
1 cup sugar
1 tablespoon cinnamon

Juice of a half lemon
½ cup New York State maple
    syrup

ACCOMPANIMENT

New York State sharp cheese,
    sliced

TO MAKE THE CRUST: Cut the butter and margarine into the flour with two knives or a pastry blender until like cornmeal. Add the ice water gradually, using just enough to hold the dough together. Roll out on a board or marble slab (lightly floured) until 1 inch thick and place in the refrigerator for 20 minutes. Remove and roll again, this time to ⅛-inch thickness. Line a 10- by 15-inch jelly-roll pan with prepared pastry.

Preheat oven to 450°.

Peel, core, and cut each apple into 6 sections. Arrange in one layer on the crust. Mix the sugar and cinnamon and sprinkle over the apples, then sprinkle with lemon juice. Bake at 450° for 20 minutes, then reduce heat to 350° and bake for 30 minutes more. Remove from the oven, sprinkle with the maple syrup, and serve while warm.

PEGGY D'UZÈS

SOUFFLÉ DE PAMPLEMOUSSE
(Grapefruit Soufflé)
SERVES 6

3 large grapefruit
1 ounce cornstarch
2 tablespoons milk

7 ounces sugar
3 eggs, separated
3 additional egg whites

Preheat oven to 400°.

Cut the grapefruit in half and scoop out the pulp without damaging the skin; set aside the grapefruit shells. Press all the juice out of the pulp and strain it. Pour the cornstarch into the milk a little at a time and mix well until smooth. Add the grapefruit juice and the sugar and mix. Cook until thickened over low heat; remove from heat. Beat the egg yolks and mix into the soufflé base. Beat the 6 egg whites until stiff and fold in gently. Fill the grapefruit shells with the soufflé mixture and set them on baking sheet. Bake about 15 minutes or until delicately firm and lightly browned. Serve hot.

F. LEE BAILEY

"I MAKE IT EVERY WEEKEND" CAKE

SERVES 6 TO 10

2 sticks butter
2 cups sugar
2 cups thick applesauce
3 cups flour
1 teaspoon cinnamon

1 teaspoon nutmeg
1¾ teaspoons baking soda
1 cup chopped pecans
1 cup raisins
1 teaspoon vanilla

Preheat oven to 325°.

Cream the butter and sugar. Fold in the applesauce. Sift the flour, cinnamon, nutmeg, and soda together. Remove ¼ cup of this mixture and toss with pecans and raisins. Fold the flour mixture into the sugar-butter-applesauce mixture. Add the vanilla. Fold in the floured pecans and raisins. Pour into a greased and floured 9-inch tube pan. Bake 1½ hours. Allow to cool in the pan before turning out. Spread on the following frosting:

FROSTING

2 cups light brown sugar, packed
6 tablespoons heavy cream
4 tablespoons butter

1 teaspoon vanilla
1 cup confectioner's sugar

Put the brown sugar, cream, and butter in saucepan, heat slowly, stirring until the mixture reaches a rolling boil. Remove from heat, stir in the vanilla and confectioner's sugar. Beat until thick and spread on cake.

PART III

DINNER

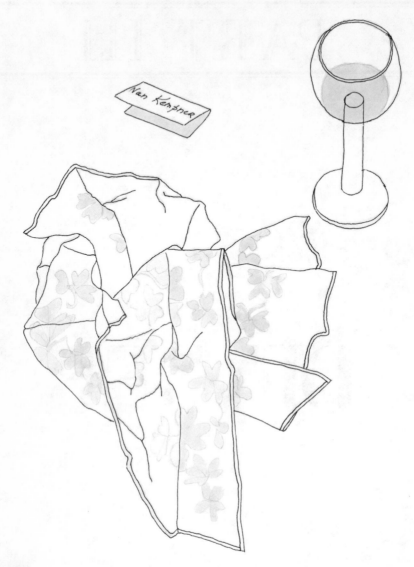

Most guests take a lot of trouble with their appearance; the women are wearing their latest evening creations and have coaxed their faces into glowing freshness or sultry glamour. A hostess should take as much trouble with the dinner and the table setting. Make diners enjoy the season and its fruits; a new dish (tested quietly at home beforehand to be on the safe side), a lovely wine, a truly irresistible dessert.

Drinks before dinner should not last too long, nor should punctuality be overstressed. It is good to remember that there will always be someone invited who can only take Sanka after dinner, or who longs for a refreshing non-alcohol drink such as real barley water, lemonade in summer, tea made with freshly diced ginger and hot water in the fall.

Starters

HELEN GURLEY BROWN

STUFFED GRAPE LEAVES

SERVES 8

"This is from The Single Girl's Cookbook. *Not sure this is sexy but it's good!"*

1 jar (1 pound) grape leaves in
    brine
2 pounds uncooked lamb, ground
½ cup uncooked rice
⅛ teaspoon pepper
2½ teaspoons dried thyme

1 teaspoon dried oregano
1 teaspoon dried marjoram
1 small onion, minced
3 medium-sized onions, sliced
2 tablespoons butter
3½ cups chicken broth

Rinse the grape leaves and drain. Mix the meat, rice, seasonings, and minced onion in a bowl. Cook the sliced onions in the butter in a large heavy pan without browning, then add half the chicken broth; heat. Place 1 tablespoon of the meat-rice mixture on each grape leaf, fold the sides in, and roll into a small package (it will stay put). Place all the packages, seams down, in the heated broth, then add the rest of the broth and cover. Simmer over low heat for 45 minutes, or until the rice in the stuffing is done; bite a sample to see. Place on a serving dish, cool, cover, and refrigerate. Serve cold. You can freeze any leftovers, but if you serve these at a party, you probably won't have that problem.

FROM "FOR THE HOSTESS," FEBRUARY 1929

CHILLED CASABA TROPICAL

The casaba melons used for this dish must be very cold. Just before serving, each portion is sprinkled with lime juice and paprika, together with a few drops of orgeat syrup [available at delicacy shops]. To add to the unusual flavor, mint leaves may be crushed fine and marinated in the lime and orgeat. The mint is removed just before serving.

THE BORIS CHALIAPINS

SALTED FRESH SALMON   SERVES 8 TO 10

This planked salmon, easily prepared, is a delicious alternative to smoked salmon.

1½ pounds fresh salmon, prefera-   piece
    bly from tail end, in one   Kosher salt

Split the salmon lengthwise and remove all bones. Place it, skin side down, on a board. Sprinkle well with kosher salt and cover with another board. Weight it down with a heavy object (a rock or canned goods) and place in the refrigerator overnight. (Place the boards inside a large pan to avoid drips in the refrigerator.) To serve, cut the fish in thin slices, on the slant, down to the skin. Delicious on firm white buttered bread, accompanied by ice-cold vodka.

BOB CONSIDINE

EGGS CONSIDINE

SERVES 1

"New York's incomparable '21' has a dish on its supper menu with the mind-bog-gling name of 'Eggs Considine.' I cannot claim authorship. The original alchemist was the restaurant's great captain, Vincent, long since retired to his native Italy. The way I got into the act was to provide an enthusiastic appetite for them. Here's the recipe for one serving:"

Steal 2 eggs
Break into small pieces 3 rashers
    of lean cooked bacon, prefer-
    ably Irish (no fat, please)
1 tablespoon chives (never onion)
2 tablespoons roughly grated

imported Parmesan cheese
2 stewed tomatoes (can be
    canned)
1 teaspoon sea salt
1 teaspoon freshly ground pepper
4 drops Worcestershire sauce

Mix this precious mess in a slow-heating, buttered frying pan and stir ten-derly with a fork until semi-firm. Eat the whole thing; don't let leftovers simmer or grow cold. Goes nicely with what we used to call "shoestring potatoes" and with a bottle of Dom Perignon.

SHEILA HIBBEN, 1950

SWISS CHEESE CHARLOTTE

SERVES 4 TO 6

3 medium-thick slices French
    bread
White wine to cover bread
4 eggs, slightly beaten

1½ cups light cream, scalded
2 cups grated Swiss cheese, pref-
    erably imported
¼ teaspoon salt

Preheat oven to 350°.
    Soak the bread in enough dry wine to saturate it. Mix the eggs and cream, then strain onto the grated cheese, add salt, and mix. Line a but-tered shallow baking dish with the bread slices; pour on the cheese mix-ture, set in a pan of hot water, and bake for about 20 minutes, or until the custard is set. Serve in the baking dish.

JOHN RICHARDSON

SEVICHE OF BAY SCALLOPS

SERVES 4

1 pound fresh bay scallops,
    drained
½ teaspoon red pepper flakes

½ teaspoon salt
Juice of about 6 limes, or enough
    to cover the scallops

Put the scallops into a bowl, sprinkle them with the red pepper flakes and
the salt, then add enough lime juice to cover them completely. Mix, cover,
and refrigerate for 2 hours. Drain and serve as a first course.

"THE BEST FOOD OF AUSTRIA," 1960

Three Hors d'Oeuvre from the Goldener Hirsch

POACHED EGGS WITH SAUCE VERTE

SERVES 6

6 eggs
1 tablespoon good vinegar

SAUCE VERTE (GREEN MAYONNAISE)
Handful of watercress
Handful of spinach leaves, with-
    out coarse stems
6 sprigs parsley

½ teaspoon dried tarragon
½ teaspoon chopped chervil
1 cup Mayonnaise*

GARNISH AND ASPIC
Small jar pickled mushrooms
½ package (1½ teaspoons) unfla-

    vored gelatin
1 cup chicken consommé

Poach the eggs in simmering salted water to which has been added the
vinegar. When the whites are quite firm, remove the eggs from the water
with a slotted spoon and place them to drain and cool on a folded napkin.

Immerse the watercress, spinach, parsley, tarragon, and chervil in a little boiling water for a few minutes to bring out the bright green color. Drain well, pressing out the water from the spinach. Place the greens and the mayonnaise in a blender and process at high speed for a few seconds, just long enough to pulverize the greens.

Trim the eggs neatly and coat them well with the *sauce verte*. Garnish each egg with a whole or sliced pickled mushroom.

TO MAKE THE ASPIC: Soak the gelatin in the chicken consommé, then heat until melted. Cool the aspic and use some of it to coat the eggs; pour the rest ½ inch deep into a flat dish. Chill the eggs and the aspic. When the rest of the aspic has set, cut it up and place around the eggs, which have been arranged on a serving dish.

SALMON CORNUCOPIAS   SERVES 6

½ cup heavy cream
½ cup fresh horseradish, grated,
   or prepared horseradish,
   drained well
Salt (if needed) and pepper for

the horseradish
6 slices smoked salmon
1 lemon
2 teaspoons chopped parsley

Whip the cream and mix with the fresh horseradish. Season with salt and pepper. (If prepared horseradish is used, salt only after tasting.) Place 2 heaping tablespoons of this mixture on one end of each salmon slice and roll the slice into a cornucopia shape. (If the slices are very wide, fold them in half on their width before filling.) Slice the lemon into 6 thin rounds and place a salmon cornucopia on each slice. Sprinkle a little chopped parsley on the open end of each cornucopia and chill well.

CHICKEN IN ORANGE SHELLS   SERVES 6

2 cups cooked chicken, finely
   diced
¾ cup Mayonnaise☆
Juice and grated rind of one

orange
Salt and pepper to taste
3 whole oranges
Parsley sprigs

Combine the chicken, mayonnaise, orange juice, rind, salt, and pepper. Cut the oranges in even halves, removing a thin slice from each bottom so that the shells will sit properly. Remove the pulp, leaving the inside of each shell clean and white. Fill with the chicken mixture and decorate with sections of the removed orange flesh and a little sprig of parsley. Chill before serving.

FROM "FOR THE HOSTESS," 1929

BLUE CHEESE CHARLOTTES
SERVES 12

½ small package cream cheese
1 tablespoon crumbled Roquefort
    cheese (or blue cheese may be
    used)
Enough light cream to soften
    cheeses

1 envelope unflavored gelatin
1 cup heavy cream
Salt and paprika to taste
12 small pastry cases, baked and
    cooled
1 cup grated Parmesan cheese

Mash the cream cheese smoothly with the Roquefort (or blue) cheese and enough light cream to make the mixture soft. Soak the gelatin in a little of the heavy cream, heat until dissolved, then cool. Add to the Roquefort mixture; add the remaining heavy cream, salt, and paprika. Fill the pastry cases and sprinkle the grated Parmesan over the charlottes. Chill before serving.

JERRY ZIPKIN

FLAGEOLETS AND CAVIAR
SERVES 4

"Here is my Ying and Yang recipe . . ."

2 cups dried flageolets
1 tablespoon butter
1 pound (actually 14 ounces) Ira-
    nian caviar

2 cups liquid from cooking
    flageolets
3 teaspoons sweet butter

Soak the flageolets overnight in cold water, reserve the soaking liquid. Rinse them in a colander with cold water. Combine them with 1 cup of the reserved water and the 1 tablespoon of butter in a heavy skillet. With a lid on simmer over low heat for about 1 hour, adding more flageolet liquid when needed. When cooked, drain the flageolets and cool until lukewarm. Toss gently with caviar and the 3 teaspoons of sweet butter. Serve immediately.

CLAUS VON BÜLOW

RISSOLES OF FOIE GRAS
(Goose Liver in Pastry)   SERVES 8

"This is, I believe, original. At any rate, I will add only one point to the list of instructions: As it is very rich, reserve rooms for a cure at Montecatini if you take seconds."

1 whole egg
1 small whole truffle
8-ounce block of canned *foie gras*

14 ounces strudel dough or Greek
    filo pastry
Oil for deep frying

S A U C E

½ cup heavy cream
3 egg yolks
Salt and pepper to taste

1 tablespoon minced truffles
    (peelings can be used)

Break the egg into a bowl and beat it. Cut 8 thin slices from the truffle and mince the rest. Slice the *foie gras* into 8 pieces. Flatten the strudel or filo dough into a large rectangle, 3 millimeters (about ⅛ inch) thick, and cut it into 16 pieces, each 1 inch or so wider and longer than a slice of *foie gras*. Place a slice of *foie gras* on each of 8 of the pastry sections; paint the 8 remaining pastry pieces with the beaten egg. Place a slice of truffle on each piece of *foie gras* and cover with one of the remaining pastry pieces, the egg-coated side down; pinch to seal the edges firmly. Gently heat the oil to 375°. When hot, lower the *rissoles* into fat a few at a time and deep-fry over high heat for 5 minutes, or until golden; keep hot until served.

    FOR THE SAUCE: Beat the cream and egg yolks together, cook gently in a double boiler over simmering water, stirring until thick. Season with salt and pepper and add the minced truffles. Serve in a sauceboat with the *rissoles*.

JELLIED WHITEFISH OR SALMON

SERVES 6 TO 8

THE STOCK

Head and bones of 2 to 3 pounds
(weight after filleting) salmon
or whitefish, whichever you
are using
2 small onions
1 carrot
½ parsnip

2 ribs celery
2 slivers fresh ginger
2 allspice berries
8 peppercorns
2 slices lemon with rind
2 cups chicken broth
3 cups water

THE FISH

2 to 3 pounds salmon or whitefish
fillets
Salt to taste

White pepper to taste
Juice of 1 lemon
2 envelopes unflavored gelatin

TO MAKE FISH STOCK: Wash the fish head and bones and put into a soup pot. Add all other stock ingredients, cover the pot, and cook over moderate heat until the vegetables are soft, no more than one half to three quarters of an hour. Strain the broth, reserving the carrot and the parsnip.

Wash and dry the fish with paper towels. Take out any remaining bones and sprinkle the fish lightly with salt, white pepper, and lemon juice. Place in a fish kettle or large pan, pour over it the fish stock, bring to a boil, lower heat, and poach the fish just until it flakes. Rinse an oblong baking dish, slice the carrot and parsnip saved from the fish stock, and make a design in the dish with the vegetables. Remove the fish from the broth and cut out any brown spots from the fish because they are fat and likely to smell strong. Arrange the fish over the vegetable design.

Soak the gelatin in 4 tablespoons of the fish stock, then add 4 cups of the stock, put back on the stove, and simmer about 15 to 20 minutes. Strain through a very fine strainer, then spoon over the fish. Cool, then place overnight in the refrigerator. When needed, loosen the sides of the jelly with a spatula, put salad greens on a nice platter and turn fish out onto the platter—the bottom will now be on the top. Serve with Horseradish Sauce.✧

Soups

KATHARINE CORNELL

JELLIED CREAM CONSOMMÉ
SERVES 6

2 cans condensed beef consommé
    (the kind that jells)
1 cup dairy sour cream
3 tablespoons minced chives

1 hard-cooked egg yolk, riced
2 tablespoons finely minced
    parsley

Combine the consommé, sour cream, and chives, beat with a rotary beater until well blended. Refrigerate in individual covered soup cups for 24 hours. Just before serving, garnish each cup with the riced egg yolk and parsley.

AMANDA BURDEN

CHILLED AVOCADO SOUP
SERVES 8

2 ripe avocados
2 cans regular-strength chicken
  broth (14-ounce size), or
  more if needed
1 pint dairy sour cream, or
  drained yogurt, or cottage
  cheese puréed in a food
  processor
2 tablespoons lemon juice
1 medium yellow onion, chopped
Salt and pepper to taste

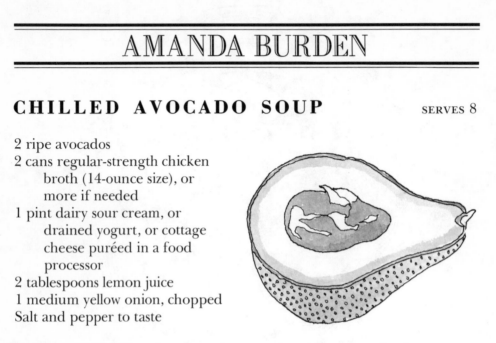

Purée everything but the salt and pepper in a blender or food processor. If too thick for your taste, add more chicken broth. Season to taste with salt and pepper and chill. Serve very cold.

GENEVIEVE DI SAN FAUSTINO

CUCUMBER AND CARROT SOUP
SERVES 8

2 cucumbers, peeled and coarsely
  chopped
6 carrots, coarsely chopped
1 large white onion, peeled and
  coarsely chopped
1 quart chicken broth
1 tablespoon chopped fresh dill
1 tablespoon chopped fresh
  parsley
Salt and pepper to taste
1 cup heavy cream

Simmer the vegetables for 1 hour in the chicken broth with the dill, parsley, salt, and pepper. Pass the cooked mixture through a sieve, or process at medium speed in a blender. To serve, add the cream and heat gently without letting the soup boil.

ELEANOR LAMBERT

PERNOD SOUP
SERVES 10

"This is my version of Billi-Bi, using clam juice and broth instead of mussels. I usually make it for buffet parties, passing around cups to get people moving into the dining room."

2 cups clam juice (to be found at good fish markets)
2 cups bottled clam broth (at supermarkets and fish markets)

1 rib celery, cut up
Celery salt and garlic to taste
Sea salt and white pepper to taste
3 cups heavy cream
½ cup Pernod

In a blender process until smooth part of the clam juice or clam broth with the celery, celery salt, garlic, sea salt, and pepper. In a saucepan stir the purée, the remaining clam juice or broth, the cream, and Pernod together while heating slowly. Serve hot.

MISS MOLLY MALONEY, 1963

CLARET CONSOMMÉ
SERVES 6

1½ cups claret wine
1 small cinnamon stick
1 tablespoon sugar

1 quart chicken or beef consommé
1 lemon, thinly sliced

Heat the claret with the cinnamon stick and sugar, simmer 10 minutes. Remove the cinnamon stick. Add the consommé, heat. Garnish each serving with a thin slice of lemon.

MRS. CHARLES SEYBURN WILLIAMS

CONSOMMÉ WITH OKRA NEW ORLEANS

SERVES 6 TO 8

3 cans consommé, either beef or
    chicken
3 cans water

6 okra pods, cut into ½-inch
    pieces
2 to 3 tablespoons sherry

Empty the consommé into a saucepan and set aside. Simmer the okra in
the water in another saucepan until done but not overcooked, about ½
hour. Combine with the consommé, bring to a boil, add the sherry, and
serve. Sometimes the sherry is passed for the guests to help themselves.

MAURICE MOORE-BETTY

CONSOMMÉ, OEUFS POCHÉS
(Chilled Consommé with Poached Eggs)

SERVES 8

CONSOMMÉ
2 quarts strong chicken stock
4 to 6 fresh ripe tomatoes,
    coarsely chopped
2 green tomatoes
1 medium onion, coarsely
    chopped with its skin on

2 ribs celery, coarsely chopped
2 carrots, coarsely chopped
1 bay leaf
10 peppercorns
Small bunch of parsley stalks
1 cup dry white wine

GARNISH
8 eggs
Chopped parsley

Simmer together in a covered pot all the consommé ingredients except the
wine, taking care not to allow the soup to boil. Slow, gentle cooking does
it. Turn the heat off after an hour and allow the pot to cool, uncovered.
Strain through a fine wire strainer. Strain a second time through four
thicknesses of cheesecloth soaked in cold water and wrung out. By now the
consommé should be reasonably clear. Refrigerate.

TO MAKE THE GARNISH: Poach the eggs in barely simmering water, a few at a time, for 4 minutes each. Lift them out and put them in a bowl of ice water, where they will sit without coming to any harm till you are ready to dine.

TO SERVE: Mix the wine with the consommé. Put a drained poached egg in the bottom of a chilled soup plate and fill it three quarters with chilled consommé, which should be of the consistency of rather liquid jelly. Sprinkle finely chopped parsley over the egg.

GEOFFREY BEENE

CREOLE GUMBO SERVES 10 TO 12

This is traditionally served as a soup with the consistency of a chowder. "I prefer it much thicker and as a main course with a crisp green salad and garlic bread," says Geoffrey.

8 thick slices bacon, cut up
6 tablespoons flour
2 cups sliced celery
2 medium green peppers, coarsely chopped
2 onions, peeled, chopped
4 cloves garlic, minced
2 medium cans tomato wedges
1 can beef consommé
1 consommé can water
6 hard-shell crabs, cleaned, boiled, and halved
Salt and pepper to taste
2 cups okra, halved lengthwise
2 pounds shelled raw shrimp
1 pound backfin crab meat
2 dozen shucked oysters, with their liquor
Gumbo filé powder, dried and pounded sassafras leaves, or a blend of thyme and sassafras (at fine food shops)

In a large cast-iron Dutch oven, cook the bacon until all the fat has been rendered. Remove bacon and set aside. Lower the heat and add the flour, slowly stirring it into the bacon fat with a wooden spoon and cooking until it is dark, dark brown, taking great care not to burn the *roux*. This takes about 45 minutes. Add the celery, peppers, onions, and garlic, cook until the garlic is brown. Add the tomatoes and their juice, the consommé, and one consommé can of water. Add the cooked bacon. Add the crabs, taking care not to discard their orange-colored fat. Add salt and pepper, and simmer the gumbo for 1 hour. Add the okra and cook for an additional half hour. Add the shrimp, crab meat, and oysters with their liquor, simmer for another 30 minutes. When ready to serve, remove the pot from the heat and add gumbo filé to taste, about 1 teaspoon per quart of gumbo. (Never let gumbo boil after filé has been added, or its texture will be spoiled.) Serve the gumbo hot, over boiled white rice in soup plates.

Fish

MAXIME DE LA FALAISE

COLD SALMON WITH DILL MAYONNAISE

SERVES 8 TO 10

A whole medium-sized salmon, 5 to 6 pounds

1 large bunch fresh dill
3 lemons, sliced

BROTH (SEE RECIPE INSTRUCTIONS)

1 part orange juice
1 part grapefruit juice
1 part tarragon vinegar
1 teaspoon crushed red pepper
2 tablespoons salt
6 carrots, coarsely chopped

2 onions, each stuck with 1 clove and halved
2 bay leaves, crushed
2 oranges, sliced
2 lemons, sliced

Watercress sprigs   quartered
3 ripe tomatoes, peeled and

Place the salmon in a fish poacher and pour cold water over until fish is barely covered. Remove fish and measure the amount of liquid used. Throw away water. On the poacher rack lay one third of the fresh dill. Place the fish on top and fill the cavity with sliced lemons and another third of the dill. Place the remaining branches of dill on top of fish.

Having measured the amount of liquid you need to cover the fish, divide this quantity into three parts. Mix one part orange juice, one part grapefruit juice, and one part tarragon vinegar, pour into the fish poacher, and lower the rack with the fish into it. Season with crushed red pepper and salt. Now add the carrots, onion halves, bay leaves, orange and lemon slices. Cover, bring to a boil, lower the heat, and simmer very gently 18 to 20 minutes. Turn off the heat and let the fish rest, covered, for 30 minutes. Remove the lid of the poacher when you can put your hand into the broth without scalding it. Set the pan in the sink. Pull up the rack and set it across the fish poacher to drain. When fully drained, remove any clinging seasonings and reverse the fish onto a long serving platter. Cool, then refrigerate if the fish is not to be served within 2 hours.

Remove the skin from the fish just before serving time. To remove it, use your fingers to avoid marring the smooth surface just beneath; it will lift off easily. When possible, save the skin and the dill adhering to it. Replace them on leftover fish before returning to refrigerator. Garnish with watercress and tomatoes and serve with Dill Mayonnaise:

DILL MAYONNAISE

4 egg yolks $\frac{1}{4}$ cup cider vinegar
1 teaspoon salt (more if desired)   1 cup salad oil
$\frac{1}{8}$ to $\frac{1}{4}$ teaspoon cayenne, to taste $\frac{1}{4}$ cup finely chopped fresh dill
1 teaspoon dry mustard (more if $\frac{1}{4}$ cup light cream
   desired)

Lightly beat the egg yolks in a small bowl. Mix in the salt, cayenne, mustard, and vinegar. Slowly pour in the oil, beating, until the mayonnaise is firm. Stir in the dill and cream; chill.

ELIZABETH DE CUEVAS

BAKED STRIPED BASS

SERVES 10

1 whole striped bass (about 6
    pounds including head),
    cleaned
Juice and rind of 2 limes or 2
    lemons
Salt and pepper to taste
2 onions, peeled and sliced

½ cup minced parsley
⅓ cup olive oil
5 thin slices of fresh ginger root,
    peeled and slivered
½ cup dry sherry
2 whole limes or lemons, sliced

Preheat oven to 400°.
    Wash the bass and lay it on aluminum foil in a large baking pan. Pour over it the lime or lemon juice and season with salt and pepper. In a skillet, cook the onions and parsley gently in the olive oil for a few minutes only—the onions should not wilt. Place half of the slivers of ginger inside the fish and sprinkle the rest on top. Pour the onion and parsley mixture over the fish; pour sherry over all. Spread the sliced limes or lemons evenly on top of the fish. Bake 10 minutes per inch of thickness of the fish, measured at its thickest point; be careful not to overcook.

OSCAR DE LA RENTA

DOMINICAN CRAB MEAT PIE

SERVES 6

PIE OR TART SHELL
6 tablespoons chilled butter, cut
    into ¼-inch pieces
2 tablespoons chilled vegetable
    shortening

1½ cups all-purpose flour
¼ teaspoon salt
4 to 6 tablespoons ice water

CRAB MEAT FILLING
3 tablespoons butter
1 tablespoon very finely chopped
    onion
3 tablespoons flour
¼ teaspoon salt
1 teaspoon curry powder

1 cup coconut milk (*see Note below*)
1 cup cooked crab meat, picked
    over
½ cup grated fresh coconut for
    garnish

MAKE THE PIE SHELL   In a previously chilled mixing bowl combine the butter, shortening, flour, and salt. Use your fingertips very fast to combine the flour and fat until they blend and look like flakes. Put in 4 tablespoons of the ice water all at once and gather the dough into a ball; add as much as you need of the remaining 2 tablespoons of water if the dough seems too crumbly. Form into a ball and dust with a little flour. Wrap in waxed paper and refrigerate for 3 hours. When ready, place the pastry on a floured board and roll out, dusting with a little flour from time to time, until about ⅛ inch thick.

For a tart shell, butter the sides and bottom of a 9-inch loose-bottomed tart pan and lift the pastry into it. Gently press against the bottom and sides of pan, fitting it into the flutings of the pan sides. Trim off excess pastry at the edge.

For a pie shell, fit the pastry into a 9-inch pie dish. Cut off the pastry ½ inch beyond the rim of the pan, fold under the excess, and flute the edges with fingers and thumb.

BAKING   *Preheat oven to 400°.* To keep the bottom of the pastry from puffing up, spread a sheet of buttered aluminum foil, buttered side down, across the bottom and slightly up the sides; press gently. Weight with a cupful of rice, beans, or pebbles. Bake on the middle shelf of the oven 10 minutes, then remove the foil and leave until the edges start to brown, 3 or 4 minutes more for a partly baked shell; remove from the oven and allow to cool. The tart or pie shell is now ready for filling and completion of baking.

TO COMPLETE THE PIE   *Preheat oven to 400°.* Put the butter in the top of a double boiler and add the onion, cook for about 4 minutes over boiling water. Stir in the flour, salt, and curry powder. Add the coconut milk slowly, bring almost to the boiling point, always stirring. Add the crab meat. Remove from the heat and pour the mixture into the partly baked shell. Sprinkle with the coconut and bake 15 minutes.

NOTE   To make coconut milk, take the meat of a whole coconut, grated, mix with 1 cup milk or with ½ cup milk and ½ cup heavy cream. Press the mixture several times through a cloth or very fine sieve, setting aside the strained liquid each time, until the coconut is dry. Discard it. The liquid is the coconut milk.

ROBERT DENNING

BAY SCALLOPS IN CREAM   SERVES 8 TO 10

"If you don't like scallops, you can make this same thing with chicken breasts. Cook them for 45 minutes, starting the oven at 500° and reducing after 15 minutes to 400°."

2 pounds bay scallops

2 tablespoons flour mixed with 1 teaspoon salt

3 to 4 red Italian onions or 12 scallions (including green tops), chopped

1 quart heavy cream

1 teaspoon fennel seeds

⅓ cup Pernod

2 teaspoons coarsely ground black pepper

6 tablespoons butter in small pieces

1½ cups grated Parmesan cheese

Preheat oven to 425°.

Dust the scallops in the salted flour. In an ovenproof casserole make a bed of the onions or scallions. Add the scallops. Flood in the heavy cream, then add the fennel seeds, Pernod, and pepper. Dot with the butter, cover with a heavy coat of Parmesan cheese, bake 5 minutes or until golden-brown and bubbly.

PRINCESS GRACE OF MONACO

BARQUETTES DE HOMARD FROID MATIGNON
(Salad of Zucchini Stuffed with Lobster)

SERVES 6

3 large zucchini (about 6 inches), peeled

White wine to cover zucchini

1 tablespoon salad oil

Salt and pepper to taste

1 onion, minced

½ teaspoon dried thyme

1 bay leaf

1 tablespoon chopped parsley

1 tomato, peeled, seeded, and chopped

Juice of a half lemon

Meat of a 2-pound boiled lobster,

diced

3 artichoke hearts, cooked and diced

3 medium-sized mushrooms, sliced

5 to 6 tablespoons Mayonnaise,☆ colored pink with tomato ketchup

3 tablespoons mayonnaise colored green with a purée of parsley and cooked spinach

3 tablespoons plain mayonnaise

GARNISH

18 medallions of lobster (slices of cooked lobster tails)

2 cups shredded lettuce

3 eggs, hard-cooked, peeled, and

quartered

3 tomatoes, peeled, quartered, and seeded

Cut the zucchini in half lengthwise, hollow the centers by removing the seeds with the tip of a spoon. Poach the zucchini barquettes until just tender in a wide pan with white wine barely to cover, oil, salt, pepper, onion, thyme, bay leaf, parsley, tomato, and lemon juice. Drain and chill the barquettes. To serve, fill the zucchini with the diced lobster, artichoke hearts, and mushrooms, all moistened with the ketchup-tinted mayonnaise. Place 3 medallions of lobster meat atop each barquette. Mask 2 barquettes with green mayonnaise, 2 with mayonnaise tinted with tomato ketchup, and 2 with plain mayonnaise. Serve them on a bed of shredded lettuce, garnished with the hard-cooked eggs and the tomatoes.

THEODORE ROUSSEAU

LANGOSTA CON POLLO CATALANA
(Lobster and Chicken Catalana) SERVES 10 TO 12

"A local Catalonian recipe which is unusual and awfully good—if you are feeling strong. This should be served with rice and accompanied by a strong red wine, preferably Spanish—something like a Priorato from Tarragona. The combination should arouse all your wildest and most primitive instincts."

2 onions
2 to 3 tablespoons olive oil
2 ripe tomatoes
4 cloves garlic, peeled
2 tablespoons chopped parsley
Beef bouillon, as needed
6 quarters of chicken, fried

3 to 4 fresh lobsters
A little butter and flour
⅓ cup ground almonds
1 square (1 ounce) unsweetened
   chocolate, grated
3 to 4 tablespoons cognac

Slice the onions, sauté them in the olive oil in a heavy saucepan until quite brown; add a little water and keep them on the stove until they are well cooked. Purée and strain the tomatoes and add, together with the garlic, well ground in a mortar with the chopped parsley. Cook over a low fire for a half hour, adding enough bouillon from time to time to keep the sauce ingredients from sticking. Process in a blender to make a smooth sauce. Pour the sauce into a casserole containing the fried chicken.
   Preheat oven to 450°.
   Split open the lobsters and remove stomachs; rub them with a little butter and flour, put for a few moments into the oven until they are pink. Add them to the sauce and the chicken in the casserole, together with the ground almonds and chocolate. Warm the cognac in a ladle or small sauce-

pan, flame it, and add it to the casserole. Allow to cook over very slow stove-top heat fire 1 hour, stirring from time to time to prevent sticking. A little more bouillon can be added if needed.

FELICIA AND MICK JONES

A VERY EASY FISH DISH
SERVES 4

1 whole sea bass or bluefish, 4 to 5 pounds
1 cup chopped celery, white part only
1 cup chopped parsley
1 onion, sliced
8 medium-sized clams
8 large shrimp, peeled
1 cup natural yogurt
1 tablespoon grated fresh ginger
1 teaspoon Dijon mustard
Salt and pepper to taste
1 dessertspoonful sesame oil

Preheat oven to 400°.

Line a flat baking dish with heavy duty aluminum foil, leaving at least 8 inches on the sides for folding over the fish. Place the fish on the lightly oiled foil and stuff with the celery and parsley, garnishing it with the sliced onion, clams, and shrimp. Mix together the yogurt, ginger, mustard, salt, pepper, and sesame oil, spoon over the fish, clams, and shrimp. Fold the foil over the fish and roll up the ends until the foil fits the shape of the fish. Bake in the oven for 20 to 30 minutes.

MAXIME DE LA FALAISE

SCALLOPS FOR LESTER PERSKY SERVES 4

1 large shallot, peeled and minced
1½ sticks butter
1 pound bay scallops, drained
1 teaspoon crumbled dried tarragon
½ cup chopped chives
½ cup dry white wine
2 tablespoons cornstarch mixed smoothly with an additional ½ cup dry white wine
Salt and pepper to taste
3 tablespoons brandy

In a good-sized skillet cook the shallot in a half stick of the butter until golden. Add the scallops, tarragon, and ¼ cup of the chives, lower the heat, and cook until the scallops have rendered most of their liquid and are half cooked. Pour off the liquid into a small saucepan and add ½ cup wine to it. Set the scallops aside in their skillet. Reduce the liquid in the saucepan by half over sharp heat; as it reduces, add the remaining stick of butter, cut into small pieces. Stir in the mixed cornstarch and wine, cook gently until the consistency of light cream. Return the sauce to the scallops; season with salt and pepper. Reheat gently. Flame the brandy in a ladle or small pan, add to the scallops, and continue to cook gently, stirring once or twice, until they are just done (firm and opaque). Garnish with the remaining ¼ cup chives.

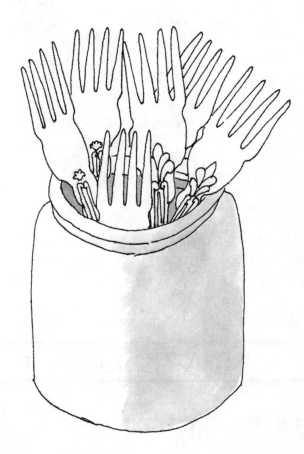

Poultry and Game

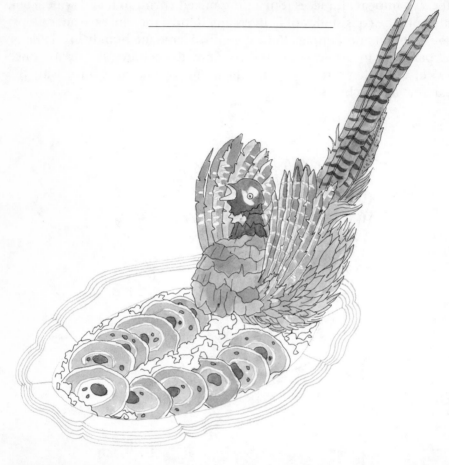

BING CROSBY

COMPOTE OF GAME BIRDS

"First capture yourself a Nimrod!

"You need pheasant, duck, and quail in stew proportions, with ham and sweetbreads if you like.

"Start by boiling the bones with celery, carrots, onions, etc. Strain and add the meat. Cook slowly in Madeira sauce. Add the sweetbreads the last 15 minutes.

"The sauce is part espagnole, *part tomato sauce, and part Madeira wine. Fear not the alcohol, which boils out, leaving only flavor.*

"It takes two days to make espagnole, *so get it in a can at a gourmet store.*

"Serve it with half wild rice and half brown rice, or all wild if you prefer, but brown rice adds body."

Here is my version, with measurements, of Bing Crosby's Compote of Game Birds (preceding recipe). It serves ten to twelve.

5 pounds chicken or game-bird
    bones
3 quarts cold water
5 to 6 ribs of celery
2 to 3 carrots, sliced
1 onion, stuck with 1 clove
Salt to taste
Small bunch of parsley

1 pheasant, plucked and cleaned
1 wild duck, plucked and cleaned
1 quail, plucked and cleaned
2 cups coarsely diced boiled ham
2 sweetbreads, presoaked in acid-
    ulated water, all membranes
    removed

MADEIRA SAUCE

¾ cup frozen or homemade
    brown sauce or *espagnole*
    sauce (obtainable frozen at
    fine food stores: Saucier
    brand)
1 teaspoon *glace de viande* (meat
    glaze, (obtainable frozen at

fine food stores: Saucier
    brand)
1 tablespoon tomato paste
½ cup Madeira wine
Salt and pepper to taste
1 to 3 tablespoons sweet
    (unsalted) butter

Boil the bones in the 3 quarts water with the vegetables, salt, and parsley; lower the heat and simmer for about 2½ hours; during cooking the quantity of stock should reduce to about 6 cups. Strain it into a stewpan. Add the pheasant and duck, bring to a boil, and simmer for about 1½ hours or until birds are tender.

Meanwhile make the Madeira sauce by boiling up all sauce ingredients except the butter. Reduce the heat, then swirl 1 tablespoon butter around in it. Add it to the stewpan. Add the quail, ham, and sweetbreads, bring to a boil, then simmer for 15 to 20 minutes, first removing the duck and pheasant if already tender. Remove all meats, carve, and arrange on a warm serving platter. Keep warm. Strain the sauce and reduce until rather thick, swirling in an extra 1 to 2 tablespoons sweet butter to finish the sauce. Pour it over the game birds and serve.

PASTEL DE CHOCLO
(Corn Pie with Chicken and Beef)   SERVES 4

"I really think this is delicious. I hope you will try it and think of Josh and me."

1 cup raisins
1 pound ground chuck beef
2 teaspoons cumin
Salt and freshly ground black
     pepper to taste
¼ teaspoon paprika
3 to 4 medium onions, chopped
1 cup pitted small black olives
⅛ teaspoon dried chili peppers,

ground or crushed
3-pound chicken, quartered
4 tablespoons butter
½ cup dry white wine, or more if
     needed
1 cup chicken stock, or amount
     needed
1 package frozen whole-kernel
     corn, thawed

Preheat oven to 350°.

Soak the raisins in water to cover 10 minutes; drain. Lightly brown the beef in a skillet, stirring. Add the cumin, salt, pepper, paprika, onions, olives, chili peppers, and drained raisins. Remove from heat and reserve. Brown the chicken quarters lightly in the butter. Put the beef mixture in a casserole, place the chicken pieces on top, add the wine and stock to cover, and top with corn. Bake, covered, until the chicken is done, about 30 minutes. Serve hot.

From "Danish Recipes," 1948

GAASESTEG
(Roast Goose)   SERVES 6 TO 8

A 10- to 12-pound young goose
Goose giblets, neck, and wing tips
1 carrot
1 large onion
3 cups water

Salt and pepper to taste
6 to 8 apples, sliced
20 prunes, pitted
1 teaspoon sugar
3 tablespoons ice water

Clean the goose. Cut up the giblets, neck, and wing tips, put them into a pot with the carrot and onion, and simmer with salt and pepper in 3 cups water; cover the pot and cook about an hour. Use this broth for basting and making gravy.

Preheat oven to 350°.

Rub the goose liberally with salt and pepper, inside and outside. Stuff it with the mixed apples and prunes, which have been mixed with the sugar. Truss the goose and roast in the oven for about 2½ hours. Baste frequently, using the giblet broth. When done, baste with the ice water to make the skin brittle, put the goose on a warm platter, turn off the oven, and return the goose to it, with the door slightly open.

To make the gravy, pour off most of the fat from the drippings in the roasting pan. Add the remaining broth from giblets to the pan and heat, stirring up and dissolving the brown bits. Season to taste and reduce, if necessary, to a proper consistency. If you like, you can thicken the gravy lightly with a little cornstarch mixed smoothly with a little water.

From "The Game Course at Dinner," 1930s

BREASTS OF PARTRIDGE SAUTÉ SERVES 4

4 partridge breasts (or squab)	¼ teaspoon salt
Legs and livers of the partridges	⅛ teaspoon cayenne
Salt and pepper to taste	5 slices of French bread
½ cup broth (see directions below)	⅓ cup cooked chopped mush-
½ cup sherry	rooms or truffles, or a mix-
1½ sticks butter, or amount	ture (optional)
needed	

Partridge prepared in this fashion is a delicious product of New England colonial cookery. The breasts are cut from 4 partridges, divided in half, and laid aside. The legs and livers of the birds are simmered in salted water until quite tender, then the meat is removed from the bones and, with the livers, is rubbed through a very coarse sieve. This pulp is put into a saucepan with ½ cup of the broth in which it was boiled, the sherry, 2 tablespoons of the butter, ¼ teaspoon salt, and a bit of cayenne. This is allowed to become very hot and is kept so while the breasts are sautéed (after being seasoned with salt and pepper) in about 4 tablespoons of the remaining butter until tender and light brown.

The slices of bread, which have been fried in the remaining butter, are then arranged in a circle upon a platter and the breasts are placed on these. The sauce made from the legs and livers is served upon a round of fried bread placed in the center. The chopped mushrooms, truffles, or a combination of both may be added to the sauce before it is served.

SALLY GANZ

BROILED SQUABS ON TOAST   SERVES 6

6 small squabs
6 squab livers
Salt and pepper to taste
¼ teaspoon powdered ginger
1¼ sticks sweet (unsalted) butter
2 tablespoons imported soy sauce

1 small clove garlic, finely minced
1 tablespoon cognac
6 slices French bread, diagonally
    cut about ½ inch thick
Chopped parsley for garnishing

Have the squabs split, reserving the livers. Rub the squabs with salt, pepper, and powdered ginger. Melt 1 stick of the butter in a small saucepan; add the soy sauce and garlic. Coat the flesh side of the squabs thickly with this mixture and refrigerate at least 4 hours, more if possible. Preheat the broiler for about 15 minutes, then reduce heat to low, place the birds on a rack in a roasting pan, and place as far as possible from the heat. Broil for 20 minutes, basting as often as possible with pan juices; turn and continue to broil and baste. The squabs should be cooked to a rich gold color. Length of cooking depends on their size—about 45 to 50 minutes is generally right.

While the squabs are cooking, sauté their livers lightly in 2 tablespoons butter in a small skillet. The livers should be firm outside and pale pink inside. Season well with salt and pepper. Warm the cognac, pour over the livers, and flame, shaking the pan. Mash the livers to a paste and keep warm.

Melt the remaining ½ cup butter in a skillet large enough to hold the 6 slices of French bread. Fry bread on both sides to a pale toast color. Spread with liver paste. Place the squabs on top, pouring over them any juices remaining in the roasting pan. Sprinkle with chopped parsley.

ROAST QUAIL, HENRIETTE

SERVES 6

This method of preparing quail was devised by a Boston Cordon Bleu, Miss Henriette Sowle, whose inventiveness and incomparable menus were justly well known.

6 quail
6 quail livers (or 3 chicken livers), trimmed
12 chicken livers, trimmed and chopped fine
¾ cup salt pork, chopped fine
⅓ cup minced parsley
Few drops onion juice

Salt to taste
⅛ teaspoon cayenne
1 tablespoon fine bread crumbs
1 egg, beaten
8 tablespoons melted butter for basting and sauce
Juice of 1 lemon

The quail are singed and prepared as for roasting. Their livers (or 3 chicken livers as a substitute) are chopped fine and mixed with the 12 chopped chicken livers and the salt pork. The parsley, onion juice, salt, cayenne, bread crumbs, and egg are added to bind it together. The quail are then stuffed with this forcemeat and roasted in a preheated, moderate oven (375°) for 25 minutes or until done, being basted occasionally with some of the melted butter. When ready, the quail are served on a hot platter; a sauce is made in the pan in which they are cooked by adding a little melted butter and lemon juice.

ROBERT JOFFREY

CHICKEN MARINADA
(Marinated Chicken)

SERVES 4

A 2½-pound frying chicken, cut into serving pieces

MARINADE
½ cup salad oil or olive oil
2 teaspoons salt
¼ teaspoon pepper

¼ teaspoon oregano
⅛ teaspoon garlic powder
⅛ teaspoon cayenne

FOR COATING THE CHICKEN
½ cup flour
1 teaspoon paprika

Wash the chicken pieces, pat dry, place in a large bowl, and pour on the marinade, toss to coat the chicken. Cover, place in the refrigerator, and marinate at least 4 hours. Toss three or four times during this period.

Preheat oven to 425°.

Drain the chicken and save the marinade. Mix the flour and paprika, place in large flat dish. Dredge each piece of chicken in the flour mixture, and lightly dip all sides in leftover marinade. Place the chicken in a single layer, skin side up, in an ungreased shallow baking pan. Pour the remaining marinade over the top. Bake 55 to 60 minutes or until tender.

"Vogue's Own Menus," April 1963

DUCK IN ORANGE ASPIC
SERVES 12

3 5-pound ducks
3 teaspoons salt

½ teaspoon pepper

STUFFING
3 half oranges
3 onions, sliced

3 ribs celery, cut up

FOR THE PAN
1 onion, sliced
3 ribs celery, cut up

1 bay leaf
2 sprigs thyme

Preheat oven to 450°.

Wipe the ducks inside and out. Prick the legs, back, and lower back with a fork. Rub inside and outside with the salt and pepper. Stuff each with a half orange, 1 sliced onion, and 1 cut up rib of celery. Place the ducks in a roasting pan with the seasoning vegetables and herbs. Roast 30 minutes. Lower heat to 350° and roast for about 1 hour 20 minutes more, removing the fat from the pan and turning the ducks occasionally. Cool them. Set aside the pan with any remaining drippings.

Glaze cooled ducks with Orange Aspic:

ORANGE ASPIC

Rind of 4 navel oranges cut into
    fine julienne
1 cup tawny port wine

3 cups beef consommé
2 envelopes unflavored gelatin
½ cup water

GARNISH

1 bunch watercress
1 small jar preserved kumquats

Simmer the orange rind in the port 15 minutes. Remove all fat from the roasting pan; deglaze over a stove burner with the beef consommé; strain into the orange and wine mixture, simmer 10 minutes.

Meanwhile, soak the gelatin in the cold water until soft, then melt it in the simmering broth. Cool; remove any fat left (*see Note* below). Glaze the ducks by spooning over them the half-set aspic several times, letting each layer set before adding the next. Chill the remaining aspic, break it up with a fork, place it around the ducks on a serving platter. Decorate with tufts of watercress and preserved kumquats.

NOTE   The best way to remove fat from pan juices is to pour them into a stainless-steel bowl and put in freezer about 30 minutes and then remove all fat from the surface of the gravy. To make the ducks more attractive to serve, you may want to cut them into serving pieces *before* glazing.

FRANCESCO SCAVULLO

CHICKEN SCAVULLO   SERVES 4

1 chicken, 3½ to 4 pounds
1 onion, peeled and chopped
1 apple, peeled, cored, and
    chopped
Rind of 1 orange, in strips
Juice of 1 orange

1 teaspoon tamari sauce
1 tablespoon plain (unroasted)
    sesame oil
2 tablespoons grated fresh ginger
½ cup apple juice

2 zucchini   2 carrots
1 onion, peeled   ¼ cup halved unsalted almonds

BROWN RICE

¾ cup brown rice   sesame oil
1½ cups water   Salt to taste
1 teaspoon plain (unroasted)

Preheat oven to 350°.

Fill the cavity of the chicken with the onion, apple, and orange rind, place in a baking pan. Pour the orange juice over the chicken, mix the tamari sauce and sesame oil, and pour over the chicken. Sprinkle the ginger over the top. Pour over the apple juice, which keeps the chicken moist. Bake in oven 1 to 1½ hours. Meanwhile, for the gravy, boil the necks and gizzards with a peeled onion without salt or pepper; add this stock to the pan juices, at the table.

TO PREPARE THE VEGETABLES: Slice the zucchini, onion, and carrots fairly thin. (The zucchini and carrots should be scrubbed with a Japanese vegetable brush, not peeled or scraped.) Put into a deep saucepan with a tight-fitting lid, add a little water and the almonds, simmer until the vegetables are just cooked: crisp, not soggy.

Wash the brown rice well in a sieve, put into a very thick iron saucepan with tight-fitting lid. Add the water, oil, and salt, bring to a boil, and boil uncovered for 5 minutes. Cover, lower heat, and simmer very gently, covered, for 55 minutes.

MARY MCFADDEN

STRASBOURG CHICKEN ROLL   SERVES 8

1 medium-sized roasting chicken,   4 ribs celery, trimmed and cut
    about 3½ pounds   into small dice
2 tablespoons butter   ½ cup diced fresh string beans
2 carrots, scraped and cut into   1½ cups thick Béchamel Sauce,☆
    small dice   cooled
2 leeks, cleaned, green tops   2 eggs, lightly beaten
    removed, and white parts cut   1 tablespoon chopped parsley
    into small squares   Salt and pepper to taste
¼ pound shelled fresh tiny peas

Any favorite mushroom sauce,
    flavored with a little port wine

Remove the skin from chicken carefully, keeping it in one piece. Debone the chicken and grind the meat. Set aside. Melt the butter in a saucepan, add the carrots, leeks, peas, celery, and string beans. Cook gently for 20 minutes; let cool. Mix the ground chicken into the cooled Béchamel, add the vegetables and mix. Mix in the lightly beaten eggs, add the parsley, salt and pepper to taste.

Preheat oven to 350°.

Spread out the chicken skin, flesh side up, and spread the filling over it. Roll it up, tucking the ends in neatly and skewering, sewing, or tying it into a cylinder. Put the roll on a rack in a roasting pan, bake about 45 minutes or until golden brown. Serve the roll hot, thinly sliced and accompanied by the hot mushroom sauce.

Meat

KENNETH BATTELLE

STEAK DIANE

SERVES 4

"It's most important to this recipe to have all the ingredients ready, as the process is fast—it takes only 5 or 6 minutes. Also the platter must be hot, and it is, of course, important to have a very good cut of boneless sirloin steak.

"With this dinner I would probably serve a salad of romaine lettuce and sliced oranges with an oil and vinegar dressing. A red Bordeaux wine would go straight through dinner."

4 tablespoons cognac
4 individual boneless steaks, each
    weighing about ½ pound
1¼ sticks butter
4 tablespoons chopped chives
4 tablespoons chopped parsley

Salt and pepper to taste
½ cup dry sherry blended with 1
    teaspoon cornstarch
½ cup beef bouillon
Juice of 1 large lemon
1 teaspoon dry mustard

Pour the cognac into a small saucepan; set aside. Trim the meat of any fat and pound each steak thin (about ½ inch).

Cream together 1 stick of the butter, the chives, parsley, salt and pepper to taste; set this herb butter aside. Melt the remaining 2 tablespoons of butter in a large chafing dish or skillet, well heated. Quickly cook the steaks on each side until seared (no more than 2 minutes per side, less for rare), then remove to a hot platter. Warm the cognac, pour it into the hot skillet, and flame. Add the sherry-cornstarch mixture, herb butter, bouillon, lemon juice, and mustard, stir, heating this sauce well. Turn off the heat. Put the steaks in the sauce and ladle sauce over them, return to a freshly heated platter, and pour more hot sauce over them; serve without delay.

FIRST LADY ROSALYNN CARTER

BROILED MARINATED FLANK STEAK

SERVES 4

A White House recipe.

A flank steak, 1 to 1½ pounds, trimmed
¼ cup soy sauce

¼ cup dry red or white wine
Salt to taste

After trimming the steak, combine the soy sauce and wine in a shallow dish. Marinate the meat for at least an hour in the mixture, turning it occasionally. Drain well, keeping the marinade. For medium-rare steak, broil steak 5 minutes on each side in a preheated broiler, basting each side once with some of the marinade. Let the steak rest for a couple of minutes before slicing it thinly *across* the grain. Always salt steak *after* it is cooked to avoid toughening.

LOTTE LENYA
WEILL-DETWILLER

LENYA'S MEAT LOAF

SERVES 3 TO 4

"It's delicious, easy to make—nothing fancy and does not cost much. The recipe can be doubled, tripled, multiplied—depends on how many unexpected guests drop in."

1 pound chopped sirloin
Salt and pepper to taste
1 egg
½ cup good-quality packaged
    poultry stuffing

1 small can vegetable cocktail juice
1 small can button mushrooms
2 to 3 tablespoons sherry, or to
    taste

Preheat oven to 375°.

    Mix the meat, salt, pepper, egg, stuffing, and half of the juice together and form a loaf. Place in a greased loaf pan and bake for 1 hour. About 5 minutes before the loaf is ready, pour into a small saucepan the other half of the vegetable cocktail, the mushrooms, and the sherry. Heat, then pour over the loaf. Serve with noodles, rice, kasha, pilaf, or any other starchy accompaniment you like.

MADAME CHOURA DANILOVA

BEEF OLIVES

SERVES 4

2 cups water
1 cup kasha (buckwheat groats)
1 egg
Eye round of beef for roasting
    (about 1¼ pounds), sliced
    very thin
2 sticks butter
2 medium onions, chopped fine

Salt and pepper to taste
Herbs to taste (chopped parsley,
    crumbled dried thyme or
    oregano, for example)
Olive oil, about ¼ cup, or as
    needed
1 cup hot water
2 beef bouillon cubes

Bring the water to a boil in a heavy saucepan. Meanwhile put the kasha in a dry skillet, add the raw egg, and mix well. Toast over a stove burner, stirring and shaking all the time, until the kasha is golden brown. Then pour in the boiling water very slowly, bring to a boil, reduce the heat, and cook, covered, until the kasha resembles cooked brown rice, about half an hour. Cool a little.

    Meanwhile, place the beef slices on a board and beat with a rolling pin until as thin as possible. Cook the onions in part of the butter until soft and golden. Add them with the remaining butter, salt, pepper, and herbs to the cooked kasha. Place a spoonful of kasha on each piece of beef and roll the slice up, tucking in the sides slightly, tying it with string or fastening it with one or more toothpicks. Set aside the remaining kasha. Heat the olive oil in a skillet, brown the beef rolls on all sides, remove them from the skillet. Add the 1 cup of hot water, dissolve the bouillon cubes in it. Place the beef rolls in the skillet, cover, and let cook over low heat for a half hour to 1 hour or until tender. Serve with the remaining kasha, reheated, on the side.

COUNTESS LONGER
DE LA GUÈRONNIÉRE

FILET DE BOEUF POIVRADE
(Filet of Beef, Sauce Poivrade)

SERVES 6

Filet of beef, trimmed for roasting
Pork fat for larding beef
Salt
1 cup red Burgundy
½ cup tarragon vinegar
3 tablespoons Calvados

¼ teaspoon dried tarragon
Pinch of dried thyme
Pinch of powdered bay leaves
Pinch of ground nutmeg
Pinch of ground cloves
1 onion, thinly sliced

SAUCE POIVRADE
½ cup chopped carrots
½ cup chopped onions
Bouquet garni (thyme, bay leaf, and parsley, tied together)
¼ cup olive oil
¼ cup tarragon vinegar

1½ cups brown sauce (or canned beef gravy)
6 peppercorns, crushed
Salt to taste
1½ tablespoons butter

Lard the filet with narrow strips of pork fat. Place in an earthenware baking dish and sprinkle with a very little salt. Pour over it the Burgundy, vinegar, Calvados, tarragon, thyme, powdered bay leaves, nutmeg, and cloves; add the sliced onion. Cover loosely and marinate in refrigerator for 3 days, turning the meat three or four times a day.

Preheat oven to 350°.

Drain and dry the filet, reserving the marinade for use in making the sauce, and roast it for 20 minutes per pound (for medium rare), basting frequently.

Meanwhile, make the *sauce poivrade:* Cook the carrots, onions, and the *bouquet garni* in the olive oil until the vegetables begin to take on color, stirring frequently. Drain off the oil. Moisten the mixture with tarragon vinegar and the strained marinade from the filet. Reduce the mixture over high flame to two thirds of its original volume, stirring constantly. Add brown sauce or beef gravy and simmer gently for 30 minutes. Add the crushed peppercorns and simmer for 10 minutes longer. Strain through a very fine sieve, return to the fire, bring to a boil, and add salt to taste. When ready to serve, stir in the butter, cut into bits.

Arrange the roasted filet on a heated platter. Slice and reshape it, pour part of the *sauce poivrade* over it, and serve the rest in a sauceboat.

CHESSY AND BILL RAYNER

BOILED BEEF WITH MUSTARD SAUCE

SERVES 6

No well-bred guest alive,
Ever opts to be first to arrive.
Which no doubt explains the reason
Dinners grow later every season.

The hostess who announces "We'll dine at nine"
Might reasonably expect her guests on time.
But lo, our research will clearly state
That one out of eight is gonna be late.

Thus we offer two repasts
Which can be held for those half-castes
Who arrive an hour after being asked.

3 pounds short plate, round, or
    brisket of beef
2 tablespoons salt

4 quarts water
3 pounds beef bones

BOUQUET GARNI
1 sprig parsley
2 bay leaves
10 peppercorns
1 carrot, sliced

¼ yellow onion, sliced
A 3- by 6-inch piece of
    cheesecloth

MUSTARD SAUCE FOR THE BEEF
2 tablespoons butter
2 tablespoons flour
½ cup heavy cream

1 tablespoon dry mustard, prefer-
    ably English

Ask your butcher for high-quality meat and approximately 3 pounds of beef bones. Heat the salted 4 quarts of water to boiling in a large pot. Meanwhile prepare the *bouquet garni* by loosely wrapping the parsley, bay leaves, peppercorns, carrot, and onion in the cheesecloth. Tie with a piece of string.

Put the beef into the boiling water, bring to a boil again, and skim. Add the *bouquet garni* and beef bones. Cover and cook very gently for 2 to 3 hours, until the beef is tender.

Meanwhile, prepare the mustard sauce by melting the butter in a saucepan, blending in the flour with a wooden spoon, and gradually adding the heavy cream. Combine the dry mustard with enough cold water to make a thin paste, stir into the sauce. Season to taste and serve hot with the boiled beef.

JOE PASTERNAK

HUNGARIAN PAPRIKA STEAK   SERVES 8

8 thin rib steaks, trimmed
Salt and pepper to taste
2 tablespoons vegetable oil
1 medium onion, chopped fine
1 small clove garlic, crushed
1 sweet green pepper, stemmed, seeded, and chopped fine
1 beefsteak tomato, peeled,

seeded, and chopped
½ tablespoon paprika, or to taste
2 cups water
3 medium russet (baking) potatoes, peeled and quartered
1 sweet green pepper, cut into rings, as garnish

Pound the steaks on both sides with a wooden mallet and sprinkle them with salt and pepper. Cook them in a skillet with the oil, browning them to your taste. When they are brown, add the onion, garlic, chopped green pepper and tomato, cook until the onion and pepper are limp. Take the skillet from the heat, mix in the paprika, and pour in 1 cup of the water. Cover the skillet and cook the meat until fork-tender (add more water if needed). Remove the meat, place the potatoes in the skillet, replace the meat slices carefully on top, pour in 1 cup water or a little more if needed, cover the skillet, and cook until the potatoes are tender. Taste for seasoning and doneness. Serve on a meat platter, the potatoes on one side and the meat slices, overlapping, on the other. Decorate with green pepper rings and serve very hot.

TOURNEDOS ALEXANDRA
(Filet Steaks Alexandra)

SERVES 4

The final assembling and saucing of this dish are done at the table in a chafing dish.

4 *tournedos* of beef (slices of filet
    of beef), each weighing about
    4 ounces
4 thin slices of pork fat or
    unsmoked fat bacon, as wide
    as *tournedos* are thick
5 tablespoons butter
Salt and pepper to taste
2 bouillon cubes dissolved in 1
    cup boiling water
1 tablespoon tomato paste
½ cup canned brown gravy

1 tablespoon Madeira or dark,
    sweet sherry
1 large truffle (optional)
4 tablespoons Armagnac
½ stick butter
4 slices wheat bread, crusts
    removed and edges rounded,
    fried in butter or toasted
2 shallots or 1 small onion,
    chopped
1 tablespoon chopped parsley

Wrap each of the *tournedos* ringwise with a slice of fat pork, tie in place. Let them come to room temperature. Melt 3 to 4 tablespoons of the butter in a heavy iron skillet and get it very hot. Cook the *tournedos* at high heat for 3 to 4 minutes on each side. Season with salt and freshly ground pepper. Keep warm, covered with foil, on the platter on which they will be served. Pour off the fat in the skillet and deglaze the pan with ½ cup of the bouillon. Add the tomato paste, gravy, and wine, simmer a minute or two, stirring. Pour into a small pitcher or serving bowl. Dot with some of the remaining butter to prevent a crust from forming. Slice the truffle, if desired, adding the liquor from it to the sauce in the pitcher. Put the sliced truffle in a serving dish.

Assemble all ingredients around the chafing dish: Warm the Armagnac and pour into a small pitcher. Put the ½ stick of butter on a plate. Have ready the platter of steaks, fried toast rounds, shallots or onion, parsley, the pitcher of sauce, salt, the pepper grinder, the remaining ½ cup of bouillon, and very hot plates.

Melt half of the ½ stick of butter in the blazer pan over the chafing-dish flame. Simmer the minced shallots or onion until slightly golden; add the seared *tournedos* and heat quickly on both sides, adding a little more butter if needed. Pour the Armagnac into a large spoon. Hold in the chafing dish so the spoon heats up. Pour over the beef and light. When the flames have subsided, add the pitcher of sauce, with a little of the bouillon if it is too thick. Let simmer a minute, adding any juices from the meat platter. Turn off the heat, add the remainder of the butter, swirl it around, and sprinkle with parsley. Place each *tournedos* on a round of fried toast and pour some of the sauce over. Decorate each with a slice of truffle.

GORDON TEVIS, 1948

OX TONGUE BURGUNDY

SERVES 6

This is a recipe from Gordon Tevis's mother.

Fresh ox tongue weighing about 3 pounds
1 cup tarragon vinegar
3 or 4 peppercorns
2 bay leaves
1 teaspoon dried thyme, crumbled
1 tablespoon flour

1 teaspoon ground cloves
1 teaspoon dry mustard, preferably English
1 teaspoon brown sugar
½ cup red currant jelly
2 cups Burgundy wine
3 to 4 cups freshly boiled rice

Boil the tongue slowly in the following broth until it is tender (allow 2 to 3 hours): Put the tarragon vinegar in a pot with enough water to cover the tongue; add the peppercorns, bay leaves, and thyme. When the tongue is tender, peel it carefully and trim it so that there is no fat or gristle at the base, and fix it so that it will stand up. Then dust it with the mixed flour, cloves, mustard, and brown sugar. Place in a roasting pan.

Preheat oven to 425°.

Put the currant jelly in lumps on top of the tongue. Pour the wine into the pan. Roast the tongue for 30 minutes, basting it frequently. When you serve it, make a bed of piping hot rice on a platter and place the tongue on it. Then pour over the juice left in the pan.

EMILE DE ANTONIO

ROAST LEG OF LAMB AND FIREPLACE VEGETABLES
SERVES 6

"I cook this on Long Island in September, October, and November. It's terribly simple, very good, very few things to clean up, and no grease. I reheat the garlic cloves and eat them nut-brown with another dinner. The fat and juice from the lamb can be used in curry the next day."

A 6-pound leg of lamb
Salt to taste

30 cloves of garlic, peeled

VEGETABLES, SELECTED FROM THE FOLLOWING

6 onions, peeled
6 medium carrots, quartered, plus a few pinches minced parsley
6 medium zucchini, quartered, plus a few pinches fresh tarragon and a little pepper
6 medium yellow squash, quartered, plus a few pinches of thyme, fresh or dried
6 leeks; salt and pepper to taste

1 pound fresh mushrooms; lemon juice
3 whole peppers, green or red; salt
1 large eggplant, sliced thickly, plus a good quantity of chopped parsley
Local corn seasoned with lime juice and coarse salt

Cut 4 peeled cloves of garlic into slivers and insert into the leg of lamb; rub the meat with salt. Just before wrapping the lamb with three layers of heavy-duty aluminum foil, add 24 peeled cloves of garlic to the bottom of the package. Cook on a grill in a hot open fireplace, red coals, for 30 minutes. Remove the foil carefully. Pour out and save the juices and cooked garlic. Put the lamb on a grill over the open fire for 12 minutes, turning frequently so that it becomes charred but not too black. Put it aside for juices to flow back. Cook a selection of vegetables, each kind wrapped twice in double foil. (Which ones you cook should depend on what is best in the market.) Some—carrots, for instance—may have to begin before the lamb is removed from the grill.

All vegetables, packaged in doubled foil, are put directly onto the coals. No butter or oil is used for any of the vegetables. They cook very quickly:

ONIONS Outer layers should be charred, next layers brown, center crisp and white but cooked.

CARROTS Add fresh parsley; result should be crisp with brownish (not black) charred areas.

ZUCCHINI   Quarter; season with fresh tarragon and pepper.

YELLOW SQUASH   Quarter; season with thyme.

LEEKS   Trim off tops; split to base; season with salt and pepper if you like.

MUSHROOMS   A handful for each person; add a little lemon juice.

PEPPERS   Stem and core; cut into halves or quarters; salt.

EGGPLANT   Slice thickly or cut into wedges; season with plenty of fresh parsley.

PRINCE SERGE OBOLENSKY

SHASHLIK CAUCASIAN   SERVES 4 TO 6

Leg of young lamb

MARINADE

2 onions, peeled and cut up

2 green peppers, stemmed, seeded, and cut up

2 tablespoons minced parsley

Juice of 2 lemons

½ cup olive oil

Salt and pepper to taste

Take a leg of very young lamb and cut off all the fat. The meat should be cut from the bone in little pieces, about 28 pieces to a leg. Mix the onions, green peppers, parsley, lemon juice, olive oil, a bit of salt, and a few grains of pepper. All these are mixed together with the pieces of lamb and put in a cold place for 3 to 4 days. Fifteen minutes before you wish to serve, put the pieces of lamb on skewers and broil over hot charcoal. With this *shashlik* you serve rice, lemon, and a sauce called Diable, which is similar to Escoffier Sauce, or serve a steak sauce (A.1. sauce or a similar kind).

NADA PATCÉVITCH, 1942

TUNISIAN LAMB STEW   SERVES 4 TO 6

3 pounds shoulder of lamb, cut into 3-inch pieces

Olive oil

4 medium onions, peeled and sliced

2 tablespoons butter

2 tablespoons flour

Pinch of Spanish saffron

Salt and pepper to taste

2 dozen prunes, soaked overnight in water

Preheat the oven to 350°.

Brown the pieces of meat in olive oil in a large skillet, taking the pieces out as they are browned and putting them into an ovenproof glass or earthenware casserole. When they are all browned, half cover with water. Meanwhile cook the sliced onions in the butter over medium heat. When they begin to get golden, sprinkle in the flour, then cook the onions until they are nice and brown. Add the onions to the meat, cover the casserole tightly, put it in the oven, and bring the contents to a boil. Then add a good pinch of saffron, pepper, and salt. Lower the oven setting to 325° and simmer 1½ hours. Add the prunes and cook for about another hour or until the meat is done. Serve stew with hot boiled rice or, if you prefer, mashed potatoes.

CLINTON WILDER

BAKED LAMB WITH BEANS   SERVES 8

"This is one of my favorite recipes. It is for a cold winter's dinner or for big eaters or hungry people . . . and there are no hungrier people in all the world than actors after a rehearsal or show and dancers after a performance."

¾ pound dried white beans
1 quart water
1 teaspoon salt
6 carrots, scraped
2 medium turnips, peeled

2 medium onions, peeled and
 sliced
A 3- to 7-pound leg of lamb
Drippings, or combined butter
 and olive oil, as needed

SAUCE
1 cup white wine
¾ cup canned tomato sauce or 2
 tablespoons tomato paste
3 cloves garlic, pressed
1 teaspoon crushed dried thyme
½ teaspoon crushed dried
 oregano
½ teaspoon sugar

¼ teaspoon freshly ground black
 pepper
½ teaspoon salt
½ cup chopped parsley
½ cup beef stock
Additional wine and beef stock if
 needed

GARNISH
Chopped parsley

Soak the beans for an hour in water to cover. Pick out the "floaters" and damaged ones. Drain. Drop the beans into the quart of boiling water with the salt. When the water has regained its boil, turn the heat down to moderate and cook with the lid partially on for 20 minutes. Skim the foam at least once. Drain the beans in a colander. While they are cooking, cut the carrots into inch-long pieces. Cut the turnips into 8 pieces each. Drop the carrots into boiling water, boil for 1 minute. Add the turnips, continue boiling for another minute. Add the onions and continue boiling the three vegetables for 1 minute more; drain in a colander; set aside.

Trim excess fat from the leg of lamb. Holding the leg by the shank bone, brown it somewhat on all sides in a large heavy iron pan containing at least a tablespoon of drippings from some former roast, or a combination of butter and olive oil. Place the lamb in a deep roasting pan with a lid. Mix the beans and vegetables together in a large bowl.

Now in a medium-sized bowl mix all the sauce ingredients, pour over the vegetables, and give them a turn or two with a wooden spoon so that the sauce reaches all the vegetables. Now turn them into the roaster with the lamb. Bake covered for 30 minutes, then uncovered for 20 minutes for pink lamb. (Time would be 30 minutes if you like your lamb better done, but why spoil it?) If during the cooking the vegetables become too dry, add a little more wine and beef stock. The dish should end by being a little soupy, or at least moist. Let the meat rest out of the oven but in its roaster for 20 minutes before carving. Then carve it in the roasting vessel so that all the juices join. Sprinkle with lots of parsley and let everyone serve themselves.

BARBARA POSES KAFKA

RIS DE VEAU GRILLES, CHÂTELAINE
(Grilled Sweetbreads Châtelaine) SERVES 4

1 large bakery brioche or 4 small
    brioches (can be the frozen
    kind)
1 large pair sweetbreads
Water to cover sweetbreads dur-
    ing soaking, plus 2 table-
    spoons vinegar
½ pound mushrooms, both caps
    and stems, quartered
5 tablespoons butter
1¼ cups veal or chicken stock

Water for cooking sweetbreads,
    plus 1 tablespoon vinegar
2 egg yolks
Salt and pepper to taste
Pinch of nutmeg
½ pound cold boiled ham, diced
1 small can *foie gras*
1 small can truffles, drained and
    slivered
½ teaspoon lemon juice, or to
    taste

If you use frozen brioches, bake them according to package instructions. Soak the sweetbreads twice in cold water (acidulated each time with 1 tablespoon vinegar) for 2 hours, changing the water once. Cook the mushrooms 10 minutes in 2 tablespoons of the butter. Strain off the liquid and reserve; set the mushrooms aside. Make a Velouté Sauce,☆ using 1 cup of the veal or chicken stock; set aside.

Boil enough water to cover the sweetbreads, add 1 tablespoon vinegar, boil them 3 to 4 minutes. Remove; drain; trim off the inedible parts, but do not try to peel off the thin over-all membrane. Put them between two plates and place a heavy weight on top.

Preheat broiler.

In the top of a double boiler, not over heat, beat together the egg yolks and the remaining ¼ cup stock. Add the cooking liquid from the mushrooms and the *velouté* sauce, season with salt, pepper, and nutmeg. Place over hot water and cook, beating with a whisk, until the sauce clings to a spoon. Remove from the heat but keep over hot water.

If using 4 small brioches, remove the round knobby top and the soft center from each brioche, leaving a quarter-inch shell. If you use one large brioche, hollow it similarly but leave a thicker wall. Cut the sweetbreads into 4 equal portions. Brush with 2 tablespoons of the butter, melted. Place the sweetbreads under the broiler and brown quickly, turning as needed. Add the ham, the *foie gras* (shaped into small rounds), and the truffles to the pan with the mushrooms, heat together for 2 minutes. Slowly add the reserved hot sauce, the lemon juice, and the remaining tablespoon of butter. Place this mixture in the large brioche or divide it among the 4 small brioches. Use a slotted spoon to make sure any excess liquid remains in the pan.

Place the browned sweetbreads on top of the filling and replace the knobby top of the brioche or brioches. Surround with any leftover filling, then trickle over the top any liquid remaining in the pan.

BETTY WASON

ESCALOPE ZINGARA
(Veal Scallops Zingara), from Los Corales, Seville
SERVES 6

12 veal scallops (scaloppine)	minced
¼ cup flour	¼ cup minced ham
¾ teaspoon salt	¼ pound mushrooms, minced
2 tablespoons butter	¼ cup sherry·
2 tablespoons olive oil	1 cup water
2 tablespoons chopped onion	1 teaspoon cornstarch
Half of a sweet green pepper,	Salt to taste

Preheat oven to 325°.

    Pound the scallops with the mixed flour and salt until worked in thoroughly, using a mallet or the edge of a plate. Heat the butter and oil in a skillet until the butter is melted; cook the meat quickly over medium-high heat until lightly browned, remove to a shallow casserole or baking dish. Put the onion, green pepper, ham, and mushrooms in the same skillet, cook until tender and lightly browned. Place a mound of vegetable mixture on each scallop.

    Pour the sherry into the skillet, increase the heat until the sherry boils, then add the water, stirring to loosen all browned bits from the bottom of the pan. Simmer until the sauce is reduced. Make a thin paste of cornstarch and some of the sauce, add to the sauce, simmer until slightly thickened. Pour this over the scallops. Add salt if needed. Complete cooking the dish in the oven 30 minutes.

CHARLES ADDAMS

HOG'S JOWL

"This is my very favorite recipe—not simple but worth the revulsion . . . You will be rewarded by a superb gastronomic adventure well worth the loss of a few friends." [The smoked jowls can be simmered in water to cover, with or without seasoning vegetables, and served as a kind of boiled bacon.]

The snout being cut off, the brains removed, and the head cleft but not cut apart on the upper side—rub well with salt. Next day remove the brine and salt the head again. The following day cover the head with a mixture of ½ ounce of saltpeter, 20 ounces of bay salt, and 4 ounces of common sugar. Let the head be often turned. After 12 days smoke it for a week like bacon.

LILY AUCHINCLOSS

MARINATED LOIN OF PORK   SERVES 6

Center cut of pork loin, boned,
    weighing about 3½ pounds

½ cup imported soy sauce
½ cup Bourbon
4 tablespoons brown sugar

1 teaspoon powdered ginger, or a
few slices fresh ginger root
1 clove garlic, sliced thin

Mix the marinade and pour it over the meat in a flat dish. Marinate for at least 3 hours, turning the meat from time to time.

Preheat oven to 350°.

Transfer the pork to a baking dish, reserving the marinade. Bake 1 hour, basting occasionally with the marinade. Slice in thin slices. Serve with applesauce and mashed potatoes, and have sharp English mustard on the table. For a salad, tomato slices, zucchini slices, onion rings, and green pepper slivers, mixed with a sharp vinaigrette; you might serve a salad of watercress or arugula, dressed simply with salt and a little olive oil.

MONIQUE EASTMAN

POTÉE LORRAINE
(Pork and Vegetables in the Style of Lorraine)   SERVES 10 TO 12

2 cups white pea or navy beans,
    soaked several hours in cold
    water
15 white peppercorns
½ teaspoon dried thyme
4 bay leaves
2 medium onions, peeled, each
    stuck with 2 or 3 cloves
3 pounds smoked pork shoulder
    or smoked pork tenderloin

½ pound cured bacon in one
    piece
2 pounds garlic sausage
4 small white turnips, peeled
6 carrots, peeled and split
    lengthwise
1 young, small white cabbage,
    quartered
Cornichons (tiny sour pickles) and
    Dijon mustard to accompany

Drain the beans and put into an 8- to 10-quart lidded *cocotte* or other large pot. Tie together in cheesecloth the peppercorns, thyme, and bay leaves, add to the beans. Add the onions, smoked pork, and bacon, cover with cold water, and bring to a boil. Skim off all scum. Reduce heat and simmer 2 hours. With a fork, puncture the sausage in several places and add to the *cocotte* with the turnips and carrots. Simmer another 30 minutes. In a separate kettle of salted water, cook the cabbage, uncovered, for 20 minutes.

When the *potée* is done, arrange the elements on a deep platter: The three meats, carved, are surrounded by the vegetables and some of the broth. Serve in soup plates, with knives, forks, and large spoons; serve the *cornichons* and Dijon mustard on the side.

CHOUCROUTE GARNIE
(Sauerkraut with Mixed Meat)

SERVES 8

2 pounds fresh sauerkraut

6 thin slices smoked salt pork or bacon

2 to 3 cups inexpensive white wine

1 large or 2 medium onions, chopped very fine

1 bay leaf, crushed

½ teaspoon dill seed

Pepper (but no salt until the dish is finished)

2 cloves garlic, chopped fine

6 to 8 well-smoked pork chops or (compromise) 6 fresh pork chops

1 kielbasa (about ¾ pound)

8 bratwurst or knockwurst

8 weisswurst

Wash the sauerkraut, changing the water twice, and drain. Line a large casserole, which you will bring to the table, with the salt pork. (If the casserole is fireproof, put it on a stove-top burner; if it is not, do the cooking in the oven.) Add the sauerkraut, wine, enough water to cover the sauerkraut, and all the seasonings, let the mixture come to a boil, then reduce the heat and simmer, covered, for about an hour.

Add the smoked or fresh pork chops and the kielbasa (cut into 3-inch pieces) cook for another hour very slowly. (At this point you might need a little more wine and water.) Add the bratwurst or knockwurst, each cut in half, and cook for another 15 to 20 minutes. Add the weisswurst to the top of the dish and cook for another 15 minutes. Arrange the sauerkraut in a mound on a platter, with the meats encircling it.

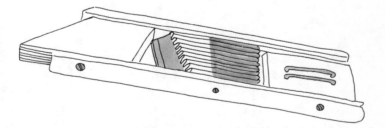

Vegetable Accompaniments

"Vogue's Own Menu," 1963

BRAISED LETTUCE

SERVES 6

6 heads Boston lettuce
4 tablespoons butter
1 medium onion, chopped
1 carrot, sliced thinly

¼ teaspoon nutmeg
Salt and pepper to taste
1 cup beef bouillon
½ cup heavy cream

Preheat oven to 400°.

Remove any bruised outer leaves from the lettuce. Do not remove the core, but scrape its base clean; then wash the heads well. Plunge the lettuce into a large pot of rapidly boiling, salted water, blanch for 8 minutes. Cool immediately in cold running water. Drain well, pressing out all the water. If the heads are large, cut in two lengthwise.

Melt the butter in a fireproof dish on top of the stove. Cook the onion and carrot gently in it 10 minutes. Arrange the lettuce neatly over them. Sprinkle with nutmeg, pepper, and a little salt if needed (if the bouillon is canned, it is already salted). Pour the bouillon over the lettuce. Bake 40 minutes or until nearly all the juice is gone. Turn the lettuce once halfway through the cooking. Remove the casserole from the oven to the stove top. Add the cream and heat to dissolve all the glaze in the pan. Bring just to a boil and serve immediately in the same dish.

MICA ERTEGUN

IMAM BAYILDI
(Eggplant Casserole)   SERVES 4 TO 6

1 good-sized eggplant, preferably
   long and thin
½ cup olive oil
1 large tomato, seeded and cut
   into thin slices
1 medium onion, cut into thin
   slices

One quarter of a green pepper,
   cut into thin slices
1 clove garlic, minced
Salt to taste
Chopped parsley and dill as
   garnish

Trim the eggplant and peel lengthwise, leaving some of the purple skin on. Quarter lengthwise or, if the eggplant is on the large side, cut into 6 to 8 pieces lengthwise. Heat the oil in a heavy pan or fireproof casserole and fry the eggplant over medium heat until light brown on all sides. Arrange the eggplant skin side down, add the tomato, onion, green pepper, and garlic, arranging decoratively. Salt to taste. At this stage you can cover the pan and cook over low heat for about an hour (on top of stove), or you can put the pan (if ovenproof) or the casserole in the oven, preheated to 350°, and bake it, covered, for about the same length of time.

Before serving, garnish with parsley and fresh dill. This dish can be eaten at room temperature. It is also very good when it is served after refrigeration. Yogurt may be served on the side, although this is not the custom.

NOTE   Usually when eggplant is cooked over low heat, the vegetable provides enough water for cooking; however, if you wish, you can add ¼ cup of water to the pot. The success of this dish depends entirely upon the eggplant you purchase. With too many seeds it tends to be bitter.

GERALDINE FITZGERALD

CABBAGE AND POTATO HASH   SERVES 6

"This dish is a variation of an old one, colcannon, a name that sounds Gaelic to me. The onion in it is optional and (for cholesterol watchers) the hash would probably stick together without the egg yolk. The butter could certainly be replaced by margarine."

1 head green cabbage, parboiled
    until tender
1 medium purple onion, par-
    boiled until tender
5 winter potatoes, peeled and

boiled
1 egg yolk, lightly beaten
Pepper and salt to taste
Butter for frying

Chop the cooked cabbage and onion. Combine with the cooked potatoes and mash them together. Bind with the egg yolk and season with salt and pepper. Form into patties or a single shape and fry in hot butter in a skillet. When the patties are brown and crisp on both sides, they are done.

SHEILA HIBBEN, 1950

SPINACH AND TOMATOES   SERVES 4 TO 6

6 medium tomatoes, peeled,
    seeded, and chopped
2 tablespoons butter
Salt and pepper to taste
½ teaspoon sugar

1 pouch frozen creamed spinach,
    defrosted and heated accord-
    ing to package directions
⅓ cup heavy cream
⅓ cup grated Parmesan cheese

Stew the tomatoes over medium heat with the butter, salt, pepper, and sugar until almost no juice is left. Combine the spinach, cream, and cheese, cook until the cheese is melted. Taste and add more salt and pepper if necessary.

BARBARA POSES KAFKA

SWEET-AND-SOUR LENTILS   SERVES 4 TO 6

1½ cups uncooked lentils, rinsed and drained
1 quart veal, chicken, or any other light stock
2 tablespoons chicken fat or butter
1 onion, diced

½ teaspoon salt, or to taste
¼ teaspoon coarsely ground black pepper
Juice of 1 lemon
2 tablespoons sugar
½ teaspoon paprika

Boil up and then simmer the lentils in the stock for 45 minutes or until tender. Drain, put the liquid back into the pot, and boil to reduce by about one half.

Preheat oven to 375°.

Heat the fat or butter in a fireproof casserole on top of the stove, add the remaining ingredients except for the paprika. Cook for a minute, then add ½ cup of the reduced stock from the lentils. Cook for a few minutes, then add the lentils. Put in the oven and bake, uncovered, for 15 minutes. Sprinkle with the paprika and serve. This dish can be made in advance except for the baking, and then reheated in the oven for 20 minutes.

NORMAN MAILER

STUFFED MUSHROOMS   SERVES 6

"I have a dish I like of stuffed mushrooms, adapted from the Larousse Gastrono- mique *. . ."*

2 pounds fresh large mushrooms
3 medium onions
1 bunch scallions
2 cloves garlic
2 sticks sweet butter, or amount needed
Salt and pepper to taste

A good pinch of thyme
1 whole nutmeg
1 cup bread crumbs
Dry mustard to taste
Pinch of ground cinnamon
½ teaspoon grated lemon rind

Separate the stems from the mushroom caps. Wipe the caps clean and set aside. Chop the stems fine and squeeze out the moisture. Chop the onions and scallions fine. Crush the garlic in a press. Cook the chopped vegetables in as much sweet butter as necessary without browning them. Toward the end (after 4 to 5 minutes), when the liquid has cooked away, add salt, pepper, thyme, and grate a whole nutmeg over the pan. Remove, cool, cover, and chill this *duxelles,* as the French call it.

Preheat the broiler, then broil the tops of the mushroom caps for 5 minutes. Reset oven control to 500°. Stuff the caps with the chilled *duxelles* and sprinkle on the bread crumbs, mixed with the dry mustard, cinnamon, and lemon rind. Arrange them in a buttered baking dish and bake 5 minutes, or until they are heated through and the topping is brown.

SOYER'S POTATO

This comes from an article on French chef Alexis Soyer by Robert Price, published in 1948.

Cut out a round core lengthwise from one end of a potato to the other. Fill with well-spiced sausage meat, plug up the hole with a piece of potato, and bake with the cut side uppermost. [NOTE: It is easy to remove a "plug" of potato lengthwise with a cylindrical apple corer. The sausage meat can then be inserted and the hole closed by part of the plug that was removed by the corer.] A stiff cream sauce, highly spiced and seasoned with herbs, is a good alternative to the meat. This method can also be used on peeled, parboiled potatoes that are afterward roasted in lard or with a roast of meat or fowl.

DIANA VREELAND

POMMES SICILIENNE
(A Sicilian Potato Recipe)   SERVES 6

6 medium potatoes, boiled   Butter
Cream as needed   2 shallots, chopped fine
1 small orange   Salt and pepper to taste

Preheat oven to 425°.

    Rice the potatoes, add cream to make a good purée. Take a small orange, cut it into slices (using the rind as well), remove the pips, dry each slice in a cloth, and fry them for a few minutes in butter. Chop the oranges into little pieces. Fry in butter one or two finely chopped shallots and add them to the orange. Mix the orange and shallots into the potato purée, add salt and pepper, and form the mixture into little balls. Put them into a buttered shallow fireproof dish, place on the upper shelf of a quick oven (425° is suggested) for a few minutes, until the potato balls are nicely browned.

BABE PALEY

CANDIED TOMATOES   SERVES 8

6 tomatoes, unpeeled, sliced ½   ½ cup brown sugar
   inch thick   Salt to taste
3 tablespoons flour   ½ cup heavy cream
6 tablespoons butter

Dredge the tomato slices in flour. Heat the butter in a skillet, add the tomato slices with about a teaspoon of brown sugar sprinkled on top of each slice, plus a bit of salt. When lightly browned, turn the slices and sprinkle with brown sugar and salt again. Remove them to a hot serving dish before they get too soft and untidy. They are very good as is, but even better if you pour cream into the pan with the remainder of the butter and sugar, stir to thicken slightly, and pour over the tomatoes.

JOANNA STEICHEN

MUSHROOMS NADEZHDA
VORFLAMEYAVNA

SERVES 4 TO 6

1 stick butter
3 shallots or 2 onions, finely
    chopped
1 pound mushrooms, sliced

3 tablespoons chopped parsley
1 cup dairy sour cream
¾ cup boiled rice

Melt the butter in a skillet, add the shallots or onions, and cook until tender, without browning. Then add the mushrooms, parsley, and sour cream. Stir well over heat but do not boil. Add the rice, then heat thoroughly before serving. Good with plain roasted or broiled meat.

SUE VERDEREY

SUMMER SQUASH FROM PROVENCE

SERVES 6

12 small whole yellow squash or
    12 small whole zucchini
3 small onions, peeled and sliced
    thin
3 medium tomatoes, peeled and
    sliced thin

1 green pepper, stemmed,
    seeded, and cut into strips
4 medium mushrooms, sliced
Olive oil
Crumbled dried thyme
Salt and pepper to taste

Preheat oven to 350°.

Scrub the squash or zucchini and dry thoroughly. Cut the tip off the larger ends and trim off stems. Make 5 or 6 lengthwise incisions about a quarter-inch deep in each. Insert into the incisions, in any order you like, slices of onion, tomato, green pepper, and mushroom. Grease a large baking dish with olive oil. Brush each squash or zucchini with olive oil, sprinkle with thyme, salt, and pepper, arrange in the dish. Bake approximately 1 hour. Near the end cover with foil to prevent browning. The vegetables should be firm and not lose their shape.

Pasta

CRISTINA FORD

SPAGHETTI ALLA CARBONARA   SERVES 4

4 egg yolks
¼ pound freshly grated Parmesan
     cheese, or amount needed
1 pound bacon (thickly sliced if
     possible), cut into squares

½ stick butter
1 pound thin spaghetti
Salt
¼ teaspoon pepper, or to taste
Additional Parmesan for the table

Mix the egg yolks lightly and add the Parmesan—as much as the egg yolks
will absorb. There will be a very thick paste. Set aside. Fry the bacon
squares in a skillet until golden, remove most of the bacon fat. Add the
butter to the bacon and melt, keep hot. Cook the thin spaghetti in a big
pot of salted water until *al dente*, approximately 6 minutes. Drain, reserving a little of the water the spaghetti was cooked in (approximately ¾ cup).
Add this water to the egg and cheese mixture until it is the consistency of
thick cream; season with pepper. Put the spaghetti into a warmed large
serving bowl or platter. Add the bacon and butter and the egg-cheese mixture, and more pepper if you like. Toss and serve immediately, piping hot.
Serve more grated Parmesan if desired.

LIZA MINNELLI

FETTUCCINE CIGLI BELLI DE LA MINNELLI   SERVES 4

1 pound fettuccine
5 egg yolks
1 cup light cream
Salt and freshly ground black
     pepper to taste

½ cup black olives, pitted, sliced
     into thin strips
½ pound freshly grated Parmesan
     cheese
Additional Parmesan for the table

Cook the fettuccine in a lot of salted water until *al dente*. Drain and return
to the cooking pot or a heated casserole. Beat together the egg yolks and
cream, season with salt and pepper, and heat gently in a saucepan. Toss

the fettuccine alternately with the cream and egg mixture and the olives. Then add the cheese, allowing the pasta to heat thoroughly and absorb the sauce over very low heat with an asbestos pad under the pot. The cheese needs a little time to melt; the reheating takes about 5 minutes. Serve very hot, with extra grated Parmesan on the side.

ELEANOR LAMBERT

SPAGHETTI EN CROÛTE
(Spaghetti in a Pastry Case)

SERVES 8 TO 10

A 10- or 12-inch *vol-au-vent* pastry
    case
4 tablespoons melted butter
1 pound spaghetti
1 to 1½ pints heavy cream,
    whipped
⅔ cup good brandy
¼ pound cooked crab meat,
    flaked and free of shell, mari-
    nated in juice of 2 lemons
½ cup finely chopped celery
¼ clove garlic, minced
½ cup shaved, blanched almonds
    or pine nuts
1 scant cup finely chopped parsley
½ teaspoon chopped fresh dill
½ teaspoon chopped sweet basil
½ teaspoon celery seed
2 to 3 leaves fresh mint, chopped
Sea salt and freshly ground black
    pepper to taste

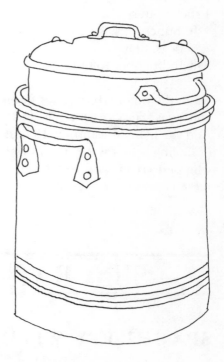

Heat the large *vol-au-vent* on a baking sheet or a heatproof platter in a moderate oven. (I order these cases at a good bakery in New York). Brush the inside of the shell and lid with the melted butter. Let stand at the back of the stove to keep warm. Break the spaghetti in 6-inch lengths, cook in ample boiling salted water until *al dente,* just before needed for table. Have the other ingredients ready. Drain and rinse the spaghetti; pour into a heated large mixing bowl. With wooden fork and spoon toss the pasta with alternate additions of whipped cream and brandy, allowing the spaghetti to absorb them gradually. Then toss with the crab meat, celery, garlic, nuts, and herbs, season with sea salt and pepper. Do this on the stove if possible to keep warm, but not over heat. Pile into the *vol-au-vent,* replace the pastry lid, and serve.

BENI MONTRESOR

GREEN-ON-GREEN PASTA À LA MONTRESOR
SERVES 6

1 onion, chopped
¼ cup olive oil
1 stick butter
1 10-ounce package frozen tiny
    peas, thawed
Salt and pepper to taste

½ pound ham, finely diced
1 pound spinach tagliatelle
½ pint heavy cream, lightly
    whipped
Freshly grated Parmesan cheese

Sauté the onion 10 minutes in olive oil without browning. Add the butter and peas. Season with salt and pepper. Cover and simmer 15 minutes. Add the ham and simmer 10 minutes longer. Cook the pasta in a large pot of boiling salted water until done to your taste. Drain. Pour in the lightly whipped cream and toss briefly. Add the sauce and freshly grated Parmesan cheese to each serving.

SUNI RATAZZI-AGNELLI

SPAGHETTI WITH LIVER SAUCE
SERVES 6

4 medium slices calf's liver, about
    ¾ pound
4 tablespoons butter
Salt and pepper to taste
3 juniper berries, crushed
1 tablespoon mixed Provençal
    herbs

1 can beef consommé
Other herbs (thyme, rosemary,
    basil) to taste
1 pound imported Italian
    spaghetti
Olive oil

TO MAKE THE LIVER SAUCE: Cook the slices of liver in the butter with salt, pepper, a few juniper berries, and the herbs, just until done. Purée the liver in a food processor, then process it with the consommé so that it becomes a liquid purée. Heat this sauce, add a few more herbs if necessary (thyme, rosemary, basil) and pour part of it over the just-cooked spaghetti. Serve immediately. Keep some sauce to serve on the side.

TO COOK GOOD SPAGHETTI: First buy Italian spaghetti, then use an enormous pot with lots of boiling, well-salted water (taste it), at least 7 quarts for a pound of pasta. Throw the spaghetti into the wildly boiling water (one pound for 6 Italian boys) and stir once in a while with a big fork. Try a strand often. As soon as the spaghetti is almost cooked but still firm on the inside, add a spoonful of olive oil to the water and then 5 to 6 cups of icy-cold water. Drain the spaghetti and serve at once with the sauce. Taste everything often; it is the only way you can make good food.

FERNANDO SARMI

RISOTTO

SERVES 8

1 stick sweet butter
1 medium onion, sliced very thin
2 chicken livers, trimmed,
    washed, and dried
2 chicken gizzards, washed, dried,
    and skinned
2 cups rice, preferably from Italy
Salt to taste
¼ cup Marsala or sherry
5 cups chicken broth

1 ounce imported Italian dried
    mushrooms, soaked 1 hour
    or more in water to cover
1 tablespoon cognac or good
    brandy
1 tablespoon sweet butter
4 tablespoons freshly grated Par-
    mesan cheese
Additional grated Parmesan to
    serve with the risotto

Put the stick of butter into a saucepan and melt. When it is hot add the onion and cook over low heat until golden. Cut the chicken livers and gizzards into small pieces, add to the butter and onion, stir and cook 1 to 2 minutes. Add the rice to the saucepan, stir, add salt to taste. Add the wine, cook for a moment to let the alcohol evaporate, then add the chicken broth, which must be boiling, and stir (always use a wooden spoon). Add the mushrooms, drained, and cut up. Cover the saucepan, lower the heat, and cook 20 minutes. The rice must be *al dente;* when it is almost at that point, stir in the cognac or brandy and let the alcohol evaporate from the uncovered pan. Cover again and continue to cook. When the rice is ready, add the 1 tablespoon of sweet butter and the Parmesan cheese. Serve with additional Parmesan cheese at the table.

Salads
and Salad Dressings

ALEXANDER SCHNEIDER

POTATO SALAD

Boil new potatoes in their jackets; don't let them get too soft, or the skins will be hard to remove. Skin the hot potatoes and put them into a serving bowl with a very good olive oil, preferably from Provence, on top. Mix them very gently and let them cool off. Then cut the potatoes into small pieces. Add wine vinegar and salt to your taste, along with some finely cut chives, and mix again. Excellent served with a hot sausage dish and, of course, a good wine.

ANGELO DONGHIA

FENNEL AND ENDIVE SALAD   SERVES 2

1 medium head of fennel
2 Belgian endives

Slice the fennel thinly to make rings. Separate the leaves of endives, leaving each leaf whole. Dress with Vinaigrette Sauce.✫

MAXIME DE LA FALAISE

RICE, PARSLEY, AND CARROT SALAD
SERVES 8 TO 10

2 cups cooked rice
2 cups cooked wild rice
4 cups grated carrots
½ cup salad oil

2 tablespoons lemon juice
1 tablespoon orange juice
1 cup finely chopped parsley
Pepper and salt to taste

Mix all ingredients together an hour or two before serving time. Serve at room temperature.

MARIAN MAEVE O'BRIEN, 1950

ORANGE, ONION, AND AVOCADO SALAD

SERVES 6

It is the long marinating period which brings about the delightful "marrying" of flavors here: the withdrawal of the oil of orange into the dressing transforms it completely, and the orange and onion flavors blend to make a most interesting combination with the avocado.

3 oranges, peeled and sliced
3 large sweet onions, peeled and
    sliced
⅔ cup Vinaigrette Sauce☆

1 avocado, peeled and sliced
Juice of 1 lemon
2 bunches watercress, rinsed and
    well drained

Arrange the orange and onion slices on a flat shallow dish. Pour over them the vinaigrette sauce. Cover and let stand in the refrigerator for at least 8 hours, turning once or twice so that every part of the slices comes in contact with the dressing. When ready to serve, drop the avocado slices into lemon juice for a moment, then arrange them with the onions and oranges on a bed of crisp watercress. Dress with the vinaigrette that was used as a marinade.

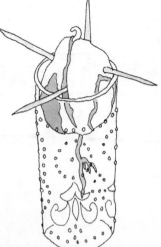

SANDRA WEIDENFELD

ARMAND SALAD

SERVES 8

½ pound white button mushrooms, sliced thin
Juice of 3 lemons
¼ cup finely chopped parsley
3 celery roots

Salt to taste
French Dressing☆
2 avocados
Pepper to taste

Marinate the mushrooms in the juice of 2 lemons, add the parsley. Blanch the whole celery roots for 2 minutes in boiling salted water. Cool quickly in cold water. Peel and slice into thin strips (this should be done at the last minute). Add salt, pepper, and the remaining lemon juice to the celery root to keep the color. Serve on a round platter, arranged in four wedge-shaped segments: 2 wedges of avocado slices, sprinkled with enough French dressing to prevent darkening, dividing one wedge each of mushrooms and celery root. Pass more dressing if you wish.

JULIAN TOMCHIN

SUPER SALAD

"In my life, unexpected dinner parties always seem to come on weekends, when all but the most ill-supplied neighborhood groceries are closed. And so I keep on hand the ingredients for my solution—a super salad."

FROM THE FREEZER, PACKAGES OF
French-cut green beans
Broccoli spears
Chinese pea pods

Asparagus
Green peas

FROM THE CUPBOARD
Red potatoes
Spanish and Bermuda onions
Cans of Spanish pinto beans, red
kidney beans, white beans,
and chick-peas (garbanzos)

Bottled pimientos
Canned tuna
Cans of anchovies
Cans or jars of olives

Eggs, hard-cooked

Cucumbers

Fresh lettuces (romaine, Boston,
and the other "bitter" types)

Tomatoes

Select any or all of these things:

Frozen vegetables should be blanched briefly and quickly drained and cooled. Boil potatoes, peel, cool, and cube or slice. Slice or dice onions. In general, cut everything into chunks. Toss with herb-flavored oil and vinegar dressing. This is usually served with corn bread made from a mix kept on the shelf. One dish only, heaped in a wooden bowl with lots of California Burgundy wine. Come . . . partake!

Desserts

ANGELO DONGHIA

STUFFED PEACHES

SERVES 8

4 large freestone peaches, not
   overripe
8 teaspoons sugar

Amaretti cookies, 2½-ounce box
4 pats of butter
A little brandy

Preheat oven to 375°.

    Halve the peaches, lift out the stones, do not peel. Enlarge the holes
left by the stones a little. Put all 8 halves into a buttered baking dish, hollow
sides up. Crush the *amaretti* into crumbs, fill the peach centers with them.
Put half a pat of butter (about 1 teaspoon), then 1 teaspoon of sugar over
the filling of each peach half. Bake 15 minutes. Remove from the oven,
add a few drops of brandy to each half, then bake 15 minutes more.

Remove from the baking dish immediately, put on a serving plate to cool, but do not refrigerate. They may be eaten as they are, or with whipped cream or *zabaglione*.

PEARS COOKED IN WINE   SERVES 6

6 large firm pears, preferably
    brown pears
4 cups dry red wine
1 scant cup tawny port wine

1 cup water
Juice of a half lemon
1 piece lemon rind
5 tablespoons sugar

Peel the pears, leaving the stems on. Cut off a slice at the bottom of each so they will stand up when placed in a saucepan just large enough to hold them so they will not tip over. Stand them in the container, add the red wine, port, water, lemon juice, lemon rind, and 4 tablespoons of the sugar. Cover the saucepan tightly, bring to a boil, lower the heat, and simmer for about 25 minutes, just long enough to cook the pears. Then leave them in the saucepan 10 to 15 minutes to cool, remove them, and stand them up on a serving dish. Place in the refrigerator. Remove the lemon rind from the pan, add to the juice the additional tablespoon of sugar, and cook again, reducing the liquid until it reaches the consistency of syrup. Pour this over the pears and put back in the refrigerator. Serve cold.

GEORGE BRADSHAW AND RUTH NORMAN

PEPPERMINT BAVARIAN CREAM
SERVES 4 TO 6

1 package unflavored gelatin
2 cups milk
½ teaspoon salt

¼ pound peppermint candy,
    crushed
½ pint heavy cream, whipped

Soak the gelatin in ¼ cup of the milk. Scald the rest, with the salt and the candy, in the top of a double boiler over boiling water. When the candy has melted, remove from the fire and stir in the gelatin. Cool. As the base begins to thicken, fold in the whipped cream. Pour into a chilled mold. The cream will take several hours, even overnight, to set. Unmold and serve with hot chocolate sauce on the side.

NAN KEMPNER

COLD LEMON SOUFFLÉ
SERVES 8 TO 10

2½ envelopes unflavored gelatin
½ cup cold water
10 eggs, separated
2 cups sugar

1 cup unstrained lemon juice, any seeds removed
½ teaspoon salt
2 teaspoons grated lemon rind

Sprinkle the gelatin over the water and let stand 5 minutes. Beat the egg yolks with 1½ cups of the sugar until very fluffy and pale colored. Put in the top of a double boiler, add the lemon juice and salt, and cook over simmering water, stirring, until the custard coats the spoon. Take off the heat, add the gelatin and lemon rind, and cool a little. Beat the egg whites until they are stiff, gradually adding the rest of the sugar toward the end. Fold into the slightly cooled custard. Have a soufflé dish prepared with an upstanding collar of several layers of waxed paper tied around it so that you can fill the dish about 2 inches above its rim. Chill in the refrigerator. Remove the paper collar and sprinkle with Praline (below) before serving.

PRALINE

¾ cup sugar
¼ cup water
¼ teaspoon cream of tartar

½ cup shredded blanched almonds

Bring the sugar and water to a boil, add the cream of tartar and almonds, cook without stirring until the syrup turns thick and pale gold. Turn onto a buttered slab to cool; when brittle, chop into small pieces. Store airtight.

BROOKE ASTOR, 1946

MARMALADE SOUFFLÉ WITH FOAMY SAUCE

SERVES 4 TO 6

3 egg whites
3 tablespoons sugar
2 tablespoons bitter-orange mar-

malade (Seville oranges)
¼ teaspoon orange extract
½ cup chopped toasted almonds

Beat the egg whites to a stiff foam. Gradually add the sugar and continue beating until the mixture forms peaks that bend slightly when the beater is lifted. Fold in the orange marmalade, orange extract, and almonds. Pour into the greased top of a double boiler, place over simmering water, cover, and cook 1 hour. Turn out onto warm serving plate and serve with Foamy Sauce (below).

FOAMY SAUCE

3 egg yolks
¾ cup confectioner's sugar
½ teaspoon vanilla

⅛ teaspoon salt
2 cups whipped heavy cream
¼ cup crushed toasted almonds

Beat together the egg yolks, sugar, vanilla, and salt in a double boiler until at least double in bulk and foamy. Cool a little. Fold in the whipped cream. Chill and sprinkle the top with the almonds just before serving.

SONIA RYKIEL

TARTE AUX RAISINS
(Grape Pie)

SERVES 6

PASTRY
1 tablespoon cinnamon
2 cups flour
½ cup sugar
⅛ teaspoon salt

1 stick butter
3 tablespoons oil
3 tablespoons hot water

2 cups white grapes, stemmed   1 cup milk
3 egg yolks   Half a vanilla bean
3 tablespoons sugar

CARAMEL TOPPING
25 sugar cubes   1 drop of vinegar
1 drop of water

Preheat oven to 375°.

THE PASTRY: Sprinkle the cinnamon over the flour, add the sugar and salt, mix. Make a well in the center, put in the butter, which you have softened, and the oil. Blend, mixing the flour into the butter and oil, until the dough is compact. Add, at that moment, the hot water. Form into a big ball. Take a quiche pan (9- or 10-inch size), dust it with flour, and spread the dough in it with the palm of your hand. (If the dough is successful, you should not be able to do it any other way.) Prick a few little holes in it with a fork, but don't go all the way through. Bake for about 20 minutes, but watch over it—the pastry must be golden, not burned. Remove from the oven. Leave the crust all alone in a corner.

THE FILLING: Seed the white grapes or use seedless grapes. Leave them in a sieve. Beat the egg yolks with the sugar until creamy. Pour in cold milk, add half of a vanilla bean, and set on the fire, stirring constantly until about to boil. Stir on low heat until thick; don't boil. Remove the vanilla bean. When you decide to eat the pie, spread the grapes in the pastry shell and cover with the custard filling.

THE TOPPING: In a small saucepan make a caramel by melting the 25 sugar cubes and one drop of H_2O. When it is dark brown, pour into it a drop of vinegar. It makes a noise like a volcano, but it's good for the caramel. Pour it over the pie. Eat it at once. It's fantastic because you have the sensation of swallowing an entire vineyard. If you are in love, *naturellement!*

LADY BIRD JOHNSON

PEACH ICE CREAM
MAKES 1 GALLON

"Our little Valley of the Pedernales is good 'peach tree country'—the ripening and harvesting time is a high point in the year—and we always serve this Peach Ice Cream, which is most delicious, many times during those weeks of summer."

1 quart heavy cream
1 pint milk
3 eggs, lightly beaten

1 cup sugar
2 quarts mashed and sweetened
   ripe peaches, peeled

Make a boiled custard of the cream, milk, eggs, and sugar, cooking just until it will coat a spoon. To this, when cool, add the soft peaches, mashed and well sweetened. Chill, then freeze in a manual or electric freezer.

JAN MITCHELL

COLD RASPBERRY PUDDING   SERVES 6 TO 8

4 packages frozen raspberries,
   thawed
⅔ cup sugar
2 pieces lemon rind about 1 inch

   long
1 pint red wine
2 cups water
½ cup quick-cooking tapioca

TOPPING
1 cup heavy cream
¼ cup confectioner's sugar

In one or more batches, process the raspberries in a blender until puréed. Strain, discard the seeds. Place the purée in an enameled kettle; sprinkle with the sugar. Add the lemon rind, wine, and water, bring to a boil, and simmer 10 minutes. Let cool, strain through a fine sieve. Reheat the raspberry mixture. Add the tapioca and cook, stirring continually, until clear— about 5 minutes. Pour into glass dessert dishes; chill thoroughly. Whip the cream, gradually adding sugar as it thickens, and decorate the top of each dessert dish just before serving.

THE ORMSBY-GORE FAMILY

SUMMER PUDDING   SERVES 6 TO 8

This excellent dessert comes from Woodhill, the Shropshire country house of the Ormsby-Gore family; this recipe was given to me in New York.

8 to 10 slices firm white bread
(preferably homemade)
1 pound berries (a soft kind—
blueberries, raspberries,
blackberries), plus currants if
available
1½ cups sliced peeled apples
Sugar as needed
Light cream for sauce

Line a bowl with the bread, cutting a circle for the bottom and wedges to fit around it. Simmer the berries and apples in a heavy saucepan with a little water and sugar to taste (we like this on the tart side) for about 5 minutes, until the fruit yields some of its juice but is not stewed. Spoon the fruit into the bread-lined bowl. Fit a plate just inside the rim of the bowl and place a weight on top, let stand in a cool place overnight, or for 3 hours in the refrigerator. To serve, turn pudding out onto a platter and serve with fresh light cream.

BETSY BLOOMINGDALE

FRESH COCONUT PUDDING WITH CARAMEL SAUCE
SERVES 8 TO 10

"One of my treasured recipes, and I've never parted with it before. One coconut will do the whole thing—the pudding as well as the final decoration."

2 cups heavy cream
2 envelopes unflavored gelatin,
soaked in 3 tablespoons water
1 cup sugar
1 teaspoon almond extract
2 cups grated fresh coconut
3 cups heavy cream, whipped
½ cup additional grated coconut
for garnish

Let the 2 cups of cream come just to a boil, add the soaked gelatin and the sugar, and stir until dissolved, cool. Add the almond extract and coconut; fold in the whipped cream. Pour into a 2-quart mold and chill until firm. Remove from the mold, garnish with the additional coconut, and serve with Caramel Sauce (below).

CARAMEL SAUCE

1 tablespoon butter
1 pound light brown sugar
2 egg yolks, beaten
1 cup heavy cream
⅛ teaspoon salt
1 teaspoon vanilla

Combine the butter, sugar, egg yolks, cream, and salt in the top of a double boiler, cook over simmering water, stirring, until smooth and creamy. Cool and add the vanilla.

MARY WHITEHOUSE

GLORIOUS FLOATING ISLAND SERVES 6 TO 8

CUSTARD
8 egg yolks
½ cup sugar

4 cups milk
1 teaspoon vanilla

CARAMEL SAUCE
2 tablespoons water
½ cup sugar

MERINGUE
8 egg whites
8 tablespoons sugar

½ teaspoon cream of tartar

GARNISH
Slivers of toasted almonds

Preheat oven to 350°.

CUSTARD: Beat the egg yolks well. Beat in the sugar, then the milk, and cook in the top of a double boiler over simmering water, stirring, until the mixture coats a spoon. Then add the vanilla and set aside to cool completely.

CARAMEL SAUCE: Put the water in a small saucepan, add the sugar, and cook over medium-high heat until you have a thick golden syrup. Pour into a Bundt pan.

MERINGUE: Beat the egg whites until foamy, then continue to beat, adding a tablespoon of sugar at a time until all has been added. Beat in the cream of tartar; whip the whites until they form stiff peaks. Pour into the Bundt pan over the caramel sauce. Set the pan in a larger pan containing hot (not boiling) water. Bake 30 to 45 minutes or until the meringue is firm. Remove from the water bath and let cool 30 minutes. Put the custard into a glass serving bowl large enough to hold the meringue mold. Then turn the meringue onto the custard and garnish with toasted almonds. This may be chilled for up to 2 or 3 hours before serving, or served at room temperature.

OKLAHOMA FUDGE CAKE   SERVES 10 TO 12

"When I became Music Director of the Tulsa Philharmonic Orchestra, I grew very fond of Oklahoma cooking. I am also a chocolate fancier, so this recipe is one of my very favorites. The cake is quite rich—almost like a candy—and is it good!"

2 sticks butter or margarine
2 cups sugar
4 eggs
1½ cups flour
½ teaspoon salt
⅓ cup cocoa
1 teaspoon vanilla
Miniature marshmallows

ICING
1 stick butter or margarine
⅓ cup cocoa, sifted
⅓ cup evaporated milk
1 pound confectioner's sugar,
    sifted
Pinch of salt
1 teaspoon vanilla
1 cup broken pecans
1 can flaked coconut

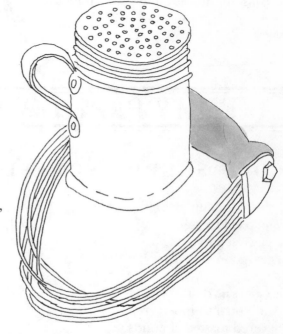

Preheat oven to 350°.

    Cream the butter or margarine and the sugar. Beat in the eggs. Sift together and add the flour, salt, and cocoa. Add vanilla, beat well. Pour into a greased and floured 8- by 12-inch baking pan, bake 25 to 30 minutes or until done. Cover the top of the cake with miniature marshmallows and return to the oven; barely let them melt—be sure to let them get brown.

    TO MAKE THE ICING: Melt the butter or margarine. Stir in the cocoa, milk, and half the sugar, beat well, stirring. Pour this hot mixture over the remaining sugar in the bowl of an electric mixer, beat well. Add the salt and vanilla. Stir in the pecans and coconut and spread over the marshmallow topping. Let the cake rest, covered, 12 hours before serving.

SOPHIE GIMBEL

COFFEE SAUCE FOR COFFEE ICE CREAM
SERVES 6 TO 8

2 cups strong brewed coffee
1 cup sugar

½ cup coffee liqueur

Boil the coffee and sugar until they begin to thicken into a syrup. Then at the last minute add the coffee liqueur. Serve hot over coffee ice cream.

EMILY BIGELOW STAEMFLI

COLD SHERRY SOUFFLÉ
SERVES 8 TO 10

2 envelopes unflavored gelatin
½ cup cold water
8 eggs, separated
1 teaspoon salt

1½ cups good sherry
2 cups granulated sugar
2 cups heavy cream

GARNISH (OPTIONAL)
Additional whipped cream
Slivered toasted almonds

On the day you want to serve this soufflé, start several hours before dessert time. Fold a 30-inch piece of aluminum foil in half lengthwise, tie around the outside of a 1½-quart soufflé dish as a collar rising well above the edge.

Sprinkle the gelatin over the cold water and let soften. In the top of a double-boiler combine the egg yolks, salt, sherry, and 1 cup of the sugar. Cook over boiling water, stirring constantly, until slightly thickened and custardy. Then stir in the gelatin. Turn into a 3-quart bowl; cool.

Beat the egg whites until they hold a soft peak, then gradually beat in the second cup of sugar, continue to beat until the mixture will hold a stiff peak. Whip the cream until stiff. Pile the stiffly beaten egg whites and whipped cream on top of the sherry mixture, gently fold the mixtures together. Pour into the soufflé dish; refrigerate at least 3 hours or until firm but spongy. Remove the foil at serving time. If desired, garnish with whipped cream and toasted slivered almonds.

GEORGE NELSON

ALMOND AND WALNUT ICEBOX CAKE

SERVES 10 TO 12

"A favorite concoction, not recommended for anyone on a diet!"

1 cup butter
1 cup sugar
2 eggs, separated
4 to 6 ounces chopped blanched
　　almonds

4 to 6 ounces chopped walnuts
Kirsch and water, 1 part kirsch to
　　3 parts water, lightly
　　sweetened
30 to 40 ladyfingers

ICING
Confectioner's sugar
1 egg white

Lemon juice
Kirsch

In a lukewarm bowl cream the butter and sugar until frothy and free of lumps. Add the 2 egg yolks and stir until completely incorporated. Then stir in the almonds and walnuts. Beat the egg whites until firm and fold them in. Pour just enough kirsch and water mixture over the ladyfingers so that they are moist but not soaked. Line the bottom of a mold with ladyfingers, then add a layer of the nut mixture; repeat until everything has been used, finishing with the nut mixture. Put into the refrigerator, covered, for 3 days, then unmold. Ice it with a smooth, fairly thin mixture of confectioner's sugar, egg white, lemon juice, and kirsch.

LUCY MONROE

BREAD PUDDING GRAND MARNIER

SERVES 6 TO 8

"This sophisticated version of bread pudding may be cooked the day before and refrigerated, but it is best served at room temperature. The recipe came from Henri Soulé."

½ cup seedless raisins
¼ cup Grand Marnier
Butter as needed
16 thin slices French bread
5 eggs

4 egg yolks
1 quart milk
1 cup heavy cream
1 cup sugar
1 teaspoon vanilla

Preheat oven to 375°.

    Cover the raisins with boiling water; after 5 minutes drain them. Soak them in the Grand Marnier. Butter a 2-quart baking dish. Butter one side of each slice of bread, spreading generously. Arrange the bread, butter side up, and raisins in the baking dish. Whisk the eggs and egg yolks together in a large mixing bowl until light. Combine the milk and cream in a large saucepan, bring just to a boil, stir in the sugar. Beat into the eggs. Add the vanilla. Strain this custard over the bread and raisins in the baking dish, place it in a larger pan of hot water, bake until set, about 45 minutes. Serve at room temperature.

ROSE KENNEDY

BOSTON CREAM PIE
MAKES A 9-INCH CAKE

"The favorite of the Kennedy family as the children were growing up."

1 cup pastry (cake) flour
1¼ teaspoons baking powder
Few grains of salt
4 eggs, separated

1 cup sugar
1½ tablespoons cold water
1½ tablespoons lemon juice
1 teaspoon vanilla

FILLING

3 tablespoons cornstarch
⅔ cup sugar
Few grains of salt
3 egg yolks

1½ cups milk, scalded
2 tablespoons butter
1 teaspoon vanilla

TOPPING
Confectioner's sugar

Preheat oven to 325°.

    Sift the flour three times with the baking powder and salt. Beat the egg whites until stiff but not dry. Beat in ½ cup of the sugar gradually.

Beat the egg yolks, water, and lemon juice together until very thick and pale yellow. Beat in the remaining ½ cup sugar. Combine the yolks and whites, folding until blended. Add the vanilla, fold in the flour mixture. Pour into a buttered 9-inch layer-cake pan, bake 1 hour or until a cake tester emerges clean and dry from the center. Cool on a rack, turning out of the pan after 10 minutes. Wrap and keep this *cake* for 24 hours, then split it horizontally into 2 layers.

TO MAKE THE FILLING: Mix the cornstarch, sugar, and salt. Beat the egg yolks until thick, combine with the cornstarch mixture, beating until perfectly smooth. Pour in the hot milk gradually. Add the butter and vanilla. Cook in the top of a double boiler over boiling water until thick, stirring all the time to prevent scorching. Cool this filling, then spread it thickly on one layer of the cake, cut side up. Place the other half, cut side down, over the filling. Dust the top generously with confectioner's sugar, shaking through a smaller sieve or sifter.

DIANE VON FURSTENBERG

MY MOTHER'S CHOCOLATE CAKE

MAKES A 10-INCH CAKE

6 ounces unsweetened chocolate	1 teaspoon vanilla
1½ sticks butter	1 cup sugar
3 eggs	1 cup flour

Preheat oven to 400°.

Melt the chocolate and butter together over low heat, mix, and set aside. Beat the eggs well in the large bowl of an electric mixer. Add the vanilla, then add the sugar slowly in small amounts, beating well after each amount. Add the flour gradually, again beating well after each amount. When the mixture is thoroughly blended, add the melted chocolate and butter, mix again. Grease the bottom of a 10-inch springform pan, pour in the batter. Bake approximately 25 minutes or until the sides shrink very slightly and the center is no longer soft to the touch. Let the cake cool entirely in its pan, set on a rack. Then unmold it and serve with fresh cream or ice cream.

MITZI NEWHOUSE

CHAMPAGNE MOUSSE
SERVES 8 TO 10

3 eggs
5 egg yolks
1 cup sugar
2 cups champagne
2 envelopes unflavored gelatin

¼ cup cold water
5 egg whites
1 cup heavy cream, whipped
¼ cup sliced blanched almonds

Beat the eggs and the egg yolks together thoroughly; add the sugar, beating until thick and light. Gradually add the champagne. Place in the top of a double boiler over hot water and cook, stirring constantly, until thick and custardy. Soak the gelatin in the water 5 minutes, then add to the champagne custard, stirring until dissolved. Cool for 10 minutes. Beat the egg whites until stiff but not dry; fold in the whipped cream. Combine with the champagne mixture, folding very gently. Pour into a 2- to 3-quart mold or soufflé dish, chill for at least 4 hours. Sprinkle with almonds and serve.

JOAN MONDALE

BURNT CREAM, OR EASY CRÈME BRÛLÉE
SERVES 6

1½ cups heavy cream
1¼ cups milk
One 3¾-ounce package of instant

vanilla pudding mix
½ cup brown sugar, *not* packed
    down

Pour the cream and milk into a bowl, add the pudding mix, and beat with a rotary or electric beater (at low speed) for 2 minutes. Pour into an oven-proof dish, refrigerate it for 30 minutes or until it has set.
  Preheat the broiler.
  Sprinkle the pudding with the brown sugar, set it 3 to 4 inches below the broiler heat. Then cook the top until the sugar melts, 6 to 8 minutes; watch carefully so the top does not burn. Refrigerate the burnt cream again and serve cold, with fruit if desired.

WHOLE-TREE ICE CREAM SERVES 6 TO 8

4 egg yolks, lightly beaten
2 squares (2 ounces) bitter choco-
    late, grated
1 level teaspoon fresh, strong cof-
    fee powder dissolved in 1
    tablespoon boiling water
1 ounce blanched almonds, lightly
    toasted, then ground
1 tablespoon maple syrup
1 tablespoon honey
¼ teaspoon ground cinnamon
¼ teaspoon sugar
Dash of dark Jamaica rum
2 cups heavy cream

Mix all ingredients except the cream. Whip the cream until stiff and fold
in. Pour into a loaf pan or two ice-cube trays, place in the freezing com-
partment of the refrigerator (or deep freeze) to freeze.

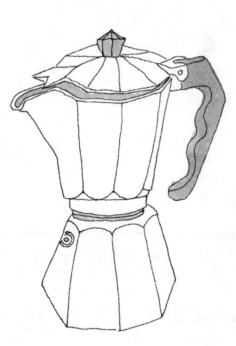

Sauces

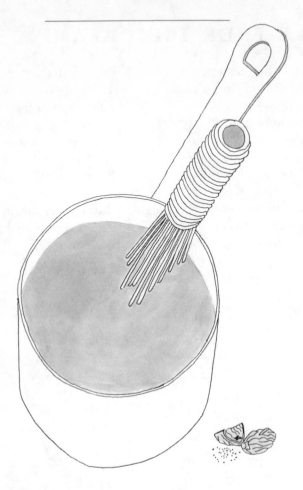

MARION W. FLEXNER, 1946

BEN BUCKNER'S SAUCE FOR STEAK

SERVES 6

1 cup meat gravy
¼ cup tomato ketchup
2 teaspoons flour
1 teaspoon brown sugar
Salt

Red (cayenne) and black pepper
    to taste
⅛ teaspoon allspice
¼ cup red currant jelly
½ cup claret

Into a small skillet or saucepan pour the gravy, ketchup, flour, sugar, salt, cayenne, black pepper, and allspice, stir well and set over low heat. When the sauce comes to a boil, add the currant jelly and claret, heat once more, stirring until the jelly dissolves. Serve hot.

PETER BEARD

MUSTARD SAUCE FOR COLD CUTS

1 cup powdered mustard, prefer-
    ably English
½ cup sugar

¼ cup red wine vinegar
1 teaspoon salt

Mix all the ingredients well, let stand a short time before serving. This is a good way to prepare one version of English mustard.

MISS MOLLY MALONEY, 1963

CHUTNEY SAUCE FOR COLD CUTS

SERVES 4 TO 6

1 cup chutney
½ cup sherry

½ cup currant jelly
1 tablespoon Worcestershire sauce

Blend all the ingredients well, serve in a sauce bowl.

JOE PASTERNAK

HORSERADISH SAUCE

MAKES ABOUT 2 CUPS

2 teaspoons prepared horseradish, drained
1 tablespoon prepared mustard
½ teaspoon sugar
⅛ teaspoon cayenne

¼ teaspoon white pepper
Few drops of lemon juice to taste
⅛ teaspoon salt, or to taste
1 cup heavy cream, whipped

Mix the horseradish mustard, sugar, cayenne, pepper, lemon juice, and salt, fold lightly into the whipped cream, and serve promptly.

DENISE BOUCHÉ

TURNER SAUCE

"Here is a sauce that is as soft and light as a Turner landscape," says Mrs. René Bouché, who recommends it for white fish, veal, and hot or cold vegetables.

1 cup heavy cream
2 egg yolks, lightly beaten
1 teaspoon prepared French mustard (Dijon type)

1 tablespoon white vinegar
1 tablespoon lemon juice
1 to 1½ teaspoons sugar

Whip the cream until stiff. Fold in the egg yolks. Mix together the mustard, vinegar, lemon juice, and sugar, fold into the cream mixture.

Sauces for Poached Fish

"Two pounds of any mild game fish (walleyed pike, bass, sauger, lake trout, and landlocked salmon, salmon, and so on can be poached and drained and served with any of the following sauces":

OLIVE AND PARSLEY SAUCE
SERVES 6

Blend a cup of strained fish broth or court bouillon with 2 tablespoons flour. Pour into the top of a double boiler, add 2 tablespoons melted butter, stir over boiling water until thickened. Add 2 tablespoons chopped parsley and 4 tablespoons stuffed green olives, sliced into rings. Taste for seasoning, adding salt, pepper, and lemon juice as needed.

CAPER SAUCE
SERVES 6

Brown 5 tablespoons butter in a skillet. Add 1 tablespoon chopped capers, 1 tablespoon vinegar from the capers, and ½ teaspoon anchovy paste. Let simmer until well blended (about 1 minute), pour over poached fish, and serve.

DILL AND FENNEL SAUCE
SERVES 6

Melt ½ cup butter in a skillet but do not brown. Add 2 teaspoons chopped fresh dill or fennel (or 1 teaspoon of either of the dried herbs). Pour over poached fish.

TARRAGON SAUCE
SERVES 6

To 1 cup butter, heated in a skillet until a medium brown, add 3 tablespoons tarragon vinegar and a dash of hot pepper sauce. If fresh tarragon is available, use 2 tablespoons of the vinegar and 1 teaspoon freshly minced tarragon.

OLD ENGLISH FISH SAUCE

MAKES ABOUT 2 CUPS

"Here's a very old fish sauce I found in an early-nineteenth-century book. I added more sherry than the recipe called for, but perhaps my 'sack' was not as potent as that sold a hundred years ago."

1 rounded tablespoon flour
½ cup milk
½ cup heavy cream
½ stick butter
2 tablespoons anchovy paste
Pinch of cayenne
⅛ teaspoon freshly grated nutmeg

2 teaspoons vinegar
1 tablespoon Worcestershire sauce
1 tablespoon sherry or more to taste
Salt and pepper if needed
Pinch of sugar if needed

Blend the flour, milk, and cream to a paste, pour into the top of a double boiler. Add the butter and anchovy paste, blended. Add the cayenne, nutmeg, vinegar, Worcestershire, and sherry. Taste for seasoning, adding salt, pepper, and sugar if necessary. Stir over boiling water until the sauce is the consistency of thick cream. Serve hot.

DIONE LUCAS, 1948

FRENCH DRESSING (A Vinaigrette Sauce)

MAKES 3 TO 3½ CUPS

"It is good to make a large quantity, as, contrary to most beliefs, this keeps very well."

3 teaspoons salt
1 teaspoon onion salt
2 teaspoons black and white peppercorns, freshly crushed
½ teaspoon sugar
1 teaspoon dry mustard, preferably imported

½ teaspoon Worcestershire sauce
1 teaspoon lemon juice
¾ cup tarragon vinegar
2⅔ cups oil (best is a mixture of 2½ cups vegetable oil and ¼ cup olive oil)

Put all ingredients into a quart Mason jar and shake well before using. If garlic is to be added to the salad, the best way of introducing it is to take the end of a fresh loaf of French bread and spread it well with crushed garlic. Toss it in your salad with the dressing just before serving.

VINAIGRETTE SAUCE

MAKES ¾ TO 1 CUP

3 tablespoons wine vinegar (or the kind you prefer)
1½ teaspoons salt
A little freshly ground pepper

1½ teaspoons either dry or prepared mustard
½ to ¾ cup oil, olive or vegetable

Blend to a paste the vinegar, salt, pepper, and mustard; stir in the oil. (This can also be made in a blender: process for 1 second at lowest speed.) This is enough dressing for a salad for 6 to 10 people; it is easily doubled. Leftover sauce will keep if refrigerated.

MAYONNAISE

MAKES ABOUT 2 CUPS

1 egg yolk
Heaping tablespoon Dijon mustard
1½ to 2 cups olive or vegetable oil

Juice of 1 lemon, strained
Salt and pepper to taste
Pinch of cayenne to taste

In a deep, narrow bowl (such as a large mortar) put the egg yolk and mustard, beat together with a wooden spoon until blended. (This will stop the mayonnaise from "turning" later.) Add the oil in a very thin steady flow, beating with the spoon. Stop pouring each time the oil seems to settle on top, beat vigorously until the mayonnaise is again smooth before adding more oil. As it thickens, add a little lemon juice from time to time—this will soften and whiten the sauce. Continue this method until all the oil and lemon juice have been worked in. Add salt, pepper, and cayenne.

This process should be carried out in a fairly cool room. If for any reason the mayonnaise falls apart into curds, you can: 1) add a little warm water and rebeat; 2) put a fresh egg yolk in a clean, dry bowl and slowly beat in the curdled mayonnaise, which will regain its original creamy texture.

AIOLI (GARLIC MAYONNAISE)

MAKES 1 TO 2 CUPS

This is a mayonnaise based on crushed garlic—a lot of garlic for *aioli*-lovers, less for the uninitiated. Serve with fish, boiled beef, or assorted cooked vegetables.

Make as for Mayonnaise☆ (above) but begin with 2 to 4 cloves of peeled garlic crushed to a smooth pulp in your mortar. Add one peeled, crushed boiled potato (optional) and a pinch of powdered saffron. Beat in 2 egg yolks instead of 1, blend well with the garlic before beginning the slow addition of 1 to 2 cups olive oil. Omit the mustard. Gradually add lemon juice to taste—perhaps as little as 1 tablespoon—after the sauce thickens. Add salt to taste.

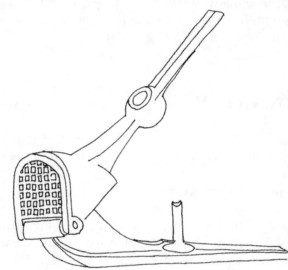

SHEILA HIBBEN, 1950

HERBED MAYONNAISE

MAKES ABOUT 2 CUPS

1 cup Mayonnaise☆
1 bunch watercress, coarse stems
    removed, leaves coarsely
    chopped

1 teaspoon finely chopped chives
2 teaspoons finely chopped fresh
    tarragon

To highly seasoned homemade mayonnaise (having more salt, pepper, mustard, and lemon juice) add the watercress, chives, and tarragon. If fresh tarragon is not to be had, the sort put up in vinegar will do very well.

TARTAR SAUCE

MAKES ABOUT 1½ CUPS

For fish, shellfish, vegetables, and cold meats.

1 cup Mayonnaise☆
1 teaspoon (or more, to taste)
    Dijon mustard
1 teaspoon minced shallots or 2
    teaspoons snipped chives
2 tablespoons minced parsley, or a
    combination of parsley, tarra-
    gon, and other herbs of your
    choice

1½ tablespoons capers, drained
1½ tablespoons chopped sour
    pickle, drained
1 hard-cooked egg, cooled and
    finely chopped
Salt and pepper to taste
A squeeze of lemon juice if
    needed

Mix all the ingredients except the salt, pepper, and lemon juice, then taste, adjusting the seasoning.

RUSSIAN DRESSING

MAKES ABOUT ¾ CUP

2½ teaspoons bottled chili sauce
1 tablespoon chutney
½ cup Mayonnaise☆
8 stuffed green olives, sliced
1 tablespoon minced green

    pepper
½ teaspoon minced onion
⅛ teaspoon cayenne
2 drops hot pepper sauce

Stir the chili sauce and chutney into the mayonnaise. Add the olives, green pepper, onion, cayenne, and the hot pepper sauce, stir until thoroughly blended.

FRUIT SALAD DRESSING BRUXELLES

MAKES ABOUT 1⅓ CUPS

A dressing much used by Belgian cooks.

1 teaspoon salt
1 teaspoon celery seed
1 teaspoon dry mustard, prefera-
    bly imported
½ cup sugar

1 teaspoon lemon juice
1 teaspoon onion juice
3 tablespoons white wine vinegar
1 cup olive oil

Blend all of the dry ingredients in the small bowl of an electric mixer, rubbing them together well with a pestle or the back of a tablespoon. Set the bowl in place on the mixer and start the beaters at low speed. Add the juices and vinegar all at once, beat until well blended. Continuing beating, add the oil, a tablespoonful at a time, allowing each to be absorbed thoroughly before the next is put in, just as with mayonnaise. Beat at least 10 minutes, when the mixture will become light and transparent. It should be of the consistency of honey when finished. Serve over fruit salad. A drop or two of red food coloring in the dressing, if canned fruits are used or if the fruits are to be served from one large bowl, will add interest and color to the whole.

EUNICE GARDNER

BEET DRESSING FOR GREEN SALADS

3 medium-sized beets, cooked and
    peeled
1 teaspoon honey

1 teaspoon lemon juice
½ cup plain yogurt

Place all the ingredients in a blender, and process until smooth.

MAXIME DE LA FALAISE

WHITE SAUCE OR "ROUX," AND SOME ELABORATIONS   MAKES ABOUT 1½ CUPS

This is the base for many sauces and often acts as a binder for varied ingredients such as croquettes. When it is made even thicker, it becomes a soufflé base.

1 to 1½ tablespoons butter
1 to 1½ tablespoons flour (less for
    thin sauce)

Hot milk, about 1 cup
Salt and white pepper to taste

Melt the butter in a saucepan. Add the flour and blend well over medium heat. Add the hot milk gradually while stirring until thickened; cook for 2 to 3 minutes more, stirring. Season with salt and pepper. (This sauce with meat or fish stock replacing the milk becomes *velouté* sauce. For a rich *velouté* sauce add heavy cream just before serving.)

If time permits, use double the amount of liquid for the final thickness you want and simmer sauce over low heat until it is reduced by half. Stir often, preferably with a whisk, during reduction.

BÉCHAMEL SAUCE OR VELOUTÉ SAUCE

Make a thin, medium, or thick White Sauce☆ as described in the recipe above, using milk for *Béchamel* and veal or chicken stock for *velouté*. For a richer sauce, for each 2 cups of liquid used in the basic sauce, prepare:

2 egg yolks, beaten
1 teaspoon lemon juice

2 tablespoons butter, cut up, or 2 to 3 tablespoons cream

When the white sauce has been prepared, add a spoonful to the beaten egg yolks, mix quickly, and return to the sauce in the pan. Whisk over low heat until thickened further, just a minute or two. Remove from the heat, stir in the lemon juice, then add the butter or cream, blend in by shaking the pan gently with a circular motion, which thickens the sauce better than stirring.

MORNAY SAUCE (Creamy Cheese Sauce)

Make a White Sauce☆ as described above, adding a little freshly grated nutmeg to the seasonings. For every cup of liquid in the basic sauce, enrich the mixture with 2 tablespoons grated Gruyère cheese and 1½ tablespoons grated Parmesan cheese. When the cheeses have melted over low heat, add 2 tablespoons heavy cream per cup of milk in the base.

From "My Cook Is Hungarian," 1935

HUNGARIAN SAUCE FOR VEGETABLES
MAKES ABOUT 2 CUPS

Peas, wax beans, carrots—in fact most vegetables—are served in Budapest with this *rantas,* that is, in a little of their own liquor, to which butter, flour, salt, and a soupçon of vinegar and sugar have been added.

2 tablespoons butter
2 tablespoons flour
⅓ cup lemon juice or vinegar

½ teaspoon sugar
1⅔ cups liquid in which vegetables were cooked

Melt the butter in a saucepan, stir in the flour, and cook 1 minute on a low flame. Add the lemon juice (or vinegar) and sugar, stirring slowly. Add the cooking liquid from the vegetables, stirring and cooking until the sauce is creamy.

HOLLANDAISE SAUCE

MAKES ABOUT 1 CUP

2 sticks butter, cut into very small pieces, softened at room temperature
3 egg yolks at room temperature

1 tablespoon water
Salt and white pepper to taste
1 tablespoon lemon juice

Whip together the butter, egg yolks, and water in the top of a double boiler over hot but not boiling water; whisk until fluffy. The butter bits should be added one third at a time, and the sauce briskly whipped until each addition has melted; then the sauce should be whipped until slightly thickened. The top pan may be lifted out of the bottom one from time to time to avoid any chance of curdling. The sauce should thicken more with each addition of butter. Remove from the heat and season with salt, pepper, and a squeeze of lemon juice. If too thick, the sauce can be thinned with a little hot water, whipped in. This sauce should never be warmer than tepid when served.

BLENDER HOLLANDAISE SAUCE

MAKES ABOUT ¾ CUP

1 stick butter
4 egg yolks
⅛ teaspoon cayenne, or to taste

1 to 2 tablespoons lemon juice
Salt to taste

Melt the butter in a small saucepan until it bubbles but doesn't brown, and keep it warm. Place the egg yolks, cayenne, and lemon juice in a processor, run at high speed for about a minute or until the yolks begin to thicken. With the blender on, pour in the butter in a steady stream, stop when the sauce has thickened. If necessary, correct the seasoning by adding more lemon juice and salt. Serve immediately or keep warm in a double boiler over very warm but not boiling water.

MOUSSELINE SAUCE

Make Hollandaise Sauce as given above, but whip ¼ cup of heavy cream and fold in just before serving.

BÉARNAISE SAUCE

1 teaspoon dried tarragon, or 3 sprigs fresh tarragon
1 teaspoon minced fresh chervil (optional)
¼ cup tarragon vinegar
¼ cup white wine
3 egg yolks
1 tablespoon water

2 sticks butter, cut into small bits, at room temperature
Salt and white pepper to taste
⅛ teaspoon cayenne
1 tablespoon lemon juice
Chopped fresh tarragon and chervil (optional)

Boil the tarragon and chervil in the tarragon vinegar and white wine, cooking fast until the liquid is reduced to about 2 tablespoons. Strain into the top of a double boiler, place over the bottom half, containing hot but not boiling water. Add the egg yolks, lightly beaten with the water, and whisk until fluffy. Once the sauce has warmed through, this can be done partly off the heat (remove the top saucepan from the base) to avoid any risk of the eggs curdling. Return to low heat. Add the butter, a few very small pieces at a time, while whisking vigorously. Again, the upper saucepan may be removed several times from the heat of the base to avoid curdling. Season with salt, pepper, cayenne, and lemon juice. Add a spoonful of some chopped fresh tarragon and chervil just before serving.

MINT BEARNAISE FOR LAMB

In the preceding recipe for Béarnaise Sauce, use mint instead of tarragon and chervil. Use ¼ cup cider vinegar and 1 teaspoon brown sugar instead of the tarragon vinegar and white wine. Chopped fresh mint should be added just before serving.

PART IV

SUPPER

Sometimes it is more fun to take friends home after the theatre, an opera, or a ballet . . . restaurants at this hour can be crowded, noisy, and expensive. The essentials for a gay midnight supper:

To maintain the evening's feeling of excitement and interest, one must get the new show on the road at once. Chilled wine opened and food on a festive, prearranged table in a flash. To keep the tempo up, cook in front of your friends, but neatly and fast, with ingredients chopped and ready ahead of time. Or have a dish cooking gently in the oven with the aroma coming out to greet your hungry friends at the door. Have things ready to nibble . . . cheese, crackers, salami, raw vegetable strips. Finish with a glorious bang by flaming a dish at the table with brandy, Cointreau, or Grand Marnier.

GEORGE BRADSHAW AND RUTH NORMAN

BAKED CRAB

SERVES 4 TO 6

3 tablespoons butter
3 tablespoons flour
1 cup heavy cream
Salt and pepper to taste
1 pound crab meat, picked over, and 1 or 2 (depending on size) cleaned and empty large

crab shells
4 hard-cooked eggs, chopped
1 tablespoon lemon juice
1 teaspoon onion juice
Dash of hot pepper sauce
½ cup grated sharp cheese

Heat the butter in a saucepan and stir in the flour, cook 1 minute, then gradually add the cream. Cook, stirring, until thickened. Season with salt and pepper. Add the remaining ingredients except the cheese. Pile the mixture into crab shells (or a casserole) and cover with cheese. Bake in a preheated 375° oven until the cheese melts and begins to brown. You may prepare this dish well ahead and refrigerate it until ready to heat.

BROOKE ASTOR, 1946

CHICKEN HASH OCTOBER

SERVES 6

"This is called Chicken Hash October because October is my cooking month. The maids come to town and we stay in the country and do all our own cooking."

1 small roasting chicken (3½ pounds)
Salt and pepper to taste
1 bay leaf

2 sprigs of thyme
2 sprigs of sweet basil
Heavy cream as needed—about ½ cup

GARNISH
Crisply cooked bacon
Parsley sprigs

Simmer the chicken in salted water to cover, together with the herbs tied in a small cheesecloth bag; cook until tender. Cut the meat from the bones (discard the skin), put through a grinder or chop it. Put the chicken in the top of a double boiler *over* boiling water, add slowly the richest cream you can get—just enough to keep the chicken from becoming dry. As you stir, add salt and pepper. When heated through, pour onto squares of crisp toast, garnish with bacon curls and parsley, serve at once.

GEORGE BRADSHAW AND RUTH NORMAN

SMITHFIELD HAM WITH CUMBERLAND SAUCE

SERVES 6 TO 8

"The ham should be the best Smithfield you can buy, already baked (by the purveyor or yourself) and cooled, then carved into tissue-thin slices at the table. A casserole of candied yams to which a half cup of crushed peanuts has been added is good with the ham and this sauce."

CUMBERLAND SAUCE

½ cup currant jelly
1 tablespoon orange juice
2 tablespoons lemon juice
Pinch of cayenne

1 teaspoon dry mustard, preferably imported
1 teaspoon ground ginger
2 tablespoons grated orange rind

Mix all the ingredients in the upper part of a double boiler and cook over hot water until the jelly melts. Serve with slices of cold ham.

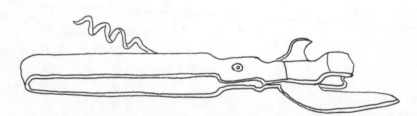

FERNANDO SARMI

TORTINO DI PATATE
(Casserole of Potatoes, Mozzarella, and Prosciutto)

SERVES 6

2½ pounds potatoes
1 stick butter
2 tablespoons grated Parmesan
   cheese
¼ cup light cream or milk
Pinch of salt
2 eggs, beaten
¼ pound mozzarella cheese, thinly

sliced
4 tablespoons bread crumbs
¼ pound prosciutto, sliced, preferably imported
2 hard-cooked eggs, sliced
2 tablespoons additional butter,
   cut up

Boil the potatoes in their skins, peel them, and mash them. While they are still hot, add most of the stick of butter, leaving enough to grease a 1½-quart casserole. Mix the Parmesan cheese, cream, and salt, add the beaten eggs, and mix vigorously. Spread the butter you saved in the casserole, both bottom and sides; cover the butter with bread crumbs, invert the casserole, and shake to remove superfluous bread crumbs (save them).

Spread in the casserole a layer of the potato mixture and cover, in order, with slices of mozzarella, prosciutto, and hard-cooked egg; repeat with a second layer of potatoes, mozzarella, prosciutto, and egg. Cover with a last layer of potatoes and top with bread crumbs. Dot with 2 tablespoons butter. (The *tortino* can be prepared ahead up to this point.)

Preheat the oven to 375°.

Bake the casserole for about 30 minutes or until the top becomes golden brown. Serve immediately.

FROM VOGUE'S "GREAT PAELLA PERIOD"

A HOT SPANISH SANDWICH

SERVES 4

"This is something decidedly novel to American palates . . ."

8 slices day-old bread
4 generous slices boiled ham
½ cup sherry

4 eggs, lightly beaten
Butter for frying

Trim the crusts off the bread, place a slice of ham between each two. Press each sandwich well, dip it quickly into sherry and then into the beaten eggs. Fry in butter until a delicate brown, serve at once.

JON STROUP

COLD EGG ROLLS WITH HAM MOUSSE

SERVES 8

EGG ROLLS

10 eggs
¼ cup finely chopped parsley
Salt and pepper to taste

2 tablespoons olive oil, or amount needed to cook the *frittate*

FILLING

3 shallots, finely chopped
⅓ cup dry white wine
1 tablespoon butter
1 tablespoon flour
½ cup milk

3 cups finely ground cooked ham
½ cup chopped dill pickle
Tomato paste as needed
Dijon-type mustard as needed
½ cup heavy cream, whipped

THE EGG ROLLS: Make 2 *frittate* (well-cooked omelettes), using for each 5 eggs beaten with 2 tablespoons of chopped parsley, salt, and pepper. Fry each one in olive oil in a 10-inch pan, turning it to cook both sides. Let them cool.

FILLING: Put the shallots and wine in a saucepan, reduce over low heat until the wine is almost gone. Add the butter, stir in the flour, and then the milk to make a smooth sauce. Add the ham and dill pickle. Add the tomato paste and mustard a little at a time until you obtain a good, zesty flavor. Fold in the whipped cream. Spread half of this coarse mousse on each of the *frittate*, roll them up, and chill them well. Slice to serve.

SALAD CORONADO

SERVES 8

6 tablespoons garlic oil (see directions below)
3 to 4 heads of lettuce, washed, dried, and kept wrapped in refrigerator until ready to use
¼ cup olive oil
Salt and coarsely ground pepper to taste

6 heaping tablespoons Romanello cheese or a similar cheese, put through a meat grinder or grated
Toasted croutons, about ¾ cup
1 egg
Juice of 3 lemons
1 tablespoon Worcestershire sauce

Use a pint jar to make a supply of garlic oil. Chop or mash enough garlic to cover the bottom of the jar an inch deep. Fill with olive (or plain salad) oil. Keep at kitchen temperature. To use, pour off the oil, leaving the garlic behind. This mixture will keep indefinitely.

Put the lettuce leaves in a large wooden bowl, leaving the small ones whole and tearing the larger into bite sizes. Pour on the garlic oil and olive oil; add salt and pepper. Sprinkle on the grated cheese and croutons. Break the raw egg onto the salad, pour the lemon juice and Worcestershire on top of the egg. Toss the salad from top to bottom, using a wooden fork and spoon. Serve at once.

TRUMAN CAPOTE

MY FAVORITE SUPPER FOR TWO

"This always makes a success and leads to interesting things."

4 baking potatoes
1 pint dairy sour cream

1 pound fresh caviar
2 bottles champagne

Bake the spuds, split them, and mash them about a bit with gobs of sour cream. Stuff the whole mess with masses of caviar, and devour between gulps of *freezing* champagne.

SALMIS OF CHICKEN

SERVES 4 TO 6

2 small frying chickens, about 2
    pounds each
1 stick plus 2 tablespoons butter,
    softened at room
    temperature
1 Bermuda onion, finely chopped
2 small carrots, finely chopped
2 cloves garlic, minced
1 cup good red wine
1 rounded tablespoon flour
1½ cups chicken stock

2 sprigs thyme or ½ teaspoon
    dried thyme
1 bay leaf
Salt and pepper to taste
½ pound button mushrooms,
    sliced
Juice of a half lemon
12 bread triangles, crusts
    removed, fried until crisp in
    additional butter
2 tablespoons minced parsley

Several hours before serving, clean and truss the chickens. Spread each with a little of the softened butter, and roast in a preheated 375° oven until almost cooked. Cut into serving pieces and reserve, together with pan juice.

Sauté the onion, carrots, and garlic in 4 tablespoons of the butter until golden. Pour in ¾ cup of the red wine, simmer, stirring constantly, until the wine reduces a little. Add the flour, mixed until smooth with the remaining wine, and stir vigorously until the sauce thickens. Add the chicken stock, pan juices from the birds, the thyme, bay leaf, and freshly ground black pepper. Cover the pan and simmer gently for 1 hour. Strain the sauce and keep hot.

AT THE TABLE: Sauté until tender the sliced button mushrooms in 2 tablespoons of butter in a chafing dish, adding lemon juice after the first few minutes. Add the chicken pieces and enough of the sauce to cover them, simmer 5 to 10 minutes or until the chicken is heated through and the flavor of the sauce has permeated the birds. Place 6 of the fried bread triangles on a heated serving dish; cover them with the salmis; sprinkle with finely chopped parsley, and garnish with the remaining pieces of fried bread and remaining sauce.

SECTION III

VOGUE TWISTS

CULINARY TIPS FOR THE BUSY COOK AND HOSTESS

These are quick ideas, last-minute inventions in the kitchen, solutions for times when unexpected guests appear and the meager contents of the icebox must be gussied up. All these Why-don't-I's went into a sort of kitchen diary, successful notions were quickly scribbled down before I could forget them. They were printed from time to time in *Vogue* as "Vogue Twists," twists of the tongue, if you like!

Our grandmothers' era was rich with household notebooks of this sort: family methods for starching collars, preserving plums, for making cosmetics or treating small wounds or toothache. Some of their suggestions are still smart and ingenious, such as using the inside membrane of a raw egg to protect and heal a small burn or scald. It works like a dream.

People nowadays could well keep these notebooks and hand them on to younger members of the family. This is how what the French call *la petite histoire*, the little history, of a country is told and remembered.

LARDING NEEDLE, CHOP, CHOP

To lard beef for *boeuf à la mode*—sensational jellied in the summer—any ordinary tapered wooden chopstick is easier to find and use than a special larding needle. Poke holes through the length of the beef, nudge strips of fat through.

Vogue Twists, September 1970

DOING THE ICE-CREAM THING

America has a dazzling number of good ice creams. Get a quart of ice cream or sherbet and take it from there. Here, ideas for enchanting favorite flavors. Soften ice-cream enough to blend in additives, then refreeze

Lime Ice Cream   Mix with peeled wedges of 4 limes; splash with 2 tablespoons of heated light rum.

Coffee Ice Cream   Stir in chopped rind of 2 oranges and 1 cup chocolate kisses.

Pineapple Sherbet   Jolt it with 1 cup minced candied ginger.

Chocolate Ice Cream   Stick helpings with skewers of candied orange peel; splash with a little Cointreau or Triple Sec.

Lemon Sherbet   Frame each serving with canned tangerine sections; douse with the fruit syrup, reduced by half and with a tot of Bourbon added.

Peach Ice Cream   Add crunch with $2/3$ cup ground almonds, first damped with 2 tablespoons apricot brandy.

Vogue Twists, November 1972

HOT-SOUP SPEEDER

SERVES 4

Prepare a package of dehydrated mushroom soup as directed, add 3 to 4 fresh mushrooms, finely chopped, and 2 tablespoons chopped fresh dill; simmer 2 minutes more.

Revive other soups made from dried bases by the same method, mincing the fresh ingredients for fast cooking.

Vogue Twists, November 1972

COLD-SOUP MIXER

SERVES 6 TO 8

Combine 1 can each of green pea soup and beef bouillon (dilute if the label directs); put into a blender with 1 cup spinach leaves and blend; chill. Before serving, add cold chopped fresh mushrooms, sliced avocado, diced green pepper, and one chili pepper, minced. Top with sour cream.

Vogue Twists, November 1972

For buffet suppers Mrs. Zachary Scott uses a boldly printed bed sheet as a cloth on her large dining room table . . . Mince parsley no more than 15 minutes before using; this herb loses its aroma fast, once chopped.

Vogue Twists, December 1972

Throw a handful of raisins into the pan when cooking sliced carrots in butter; add a little chicken stock. The raisins should be puffed and juicy when the carrots are done.

Vogue Twists, December 1972

Silver salt cellars can be used on the dinner table as tiny flower vases, one for each guest.

Vogue Twists, December 1972

New salad allies, diced or sliced: boned pickled herring, dill pickles, black olives, boiled potatoes, hard-cooked eggs. The dressing: sour cream seasoned with salt, pepper, and Dijon mustard.

Medieval gold: Add a pinch of saffron when cooking applesauce, or reheat bottled applesauce with saffron. Flavor—subtle. Color—radiant.

Flower-up the dining room, not the table, with big, long-lasting orchid plants; let decanters provide the eye appeal on the tabletop.

From the Paris of the Twenties, a variation of *pommes de terre Anna* by Maxim's restaurant: In a buttered pan, layer potatoes with artichoke bottoms, both cut in matchsticks; add butter, salt, and pepper. Cook, covered, over a low flame or in the oven. When fork-tender, turn out and brown (if necessary) under the broiler.

Buy a really long platter—two and a half feet is not impossible—so that you can serve two whole chickens, or a vast roast with two vegetables.

POWER-SAVING DO'S AND DON'TS

Do buy a pressure cooker. Learn to use it as versatilely as a Hammond organ. Pressure cookers rarely explode: the safety valve pops up and releases steam if pressure is too high. This pressure can be reduced instantly by putting the cooker under the cold-water tap. (Follow the manufacturer's instructions on when to do this.) Quick pressure reduction means that vegetables can be added later than meat and in the right order of cooking time. *Coq au vin* is better made this way, a French chef once whispered to me.

Don't open the refrigerator door unnecessarily. Cold escapes, needs power to build up again.

Do learn to use canned foods, adding fresh raw vegetables and herbs to enhance them.

Do remember that uncooked food is colorful. Think color.

Do cook enough for two meals in one operation—the surplus to reheat quickly or to eat cold. When selecting recipes, DO think, "Will this taste good cold?"

Do use polyunsaturated oils, not butter, for cooking foods to be served cold—better looks, better taste.

Do buy a large round plaque of heavy metal to place over one gas burner. It will conduct the heat sufficiently to heat food in several saucepans placed upon it.

Do use your hands, your wrists, your body: Whip cream by hand . . . squeeze oranges by hand . . . mash and grind foods in a mortar by hand.

Don't use the dishwasher until it's really full, then run it on short cycle.

Don't keep food warming in the oven; cook and eat, or cover and put over the pilot light, which produces quite a sneaky amount of heat. Keep soup warm in vacuum flasks.

Do learn to cook in the fireplace.

Do become a fish addict: Fish takes so little time to cook.

Vogue Twists, March 1974

"EGG TIPS"

Boiled eggs taste better when water is salted . . . the flavor goes through the shell.

Furious boiling toughens the whites of boiled eggs—simmer instead.

Egg whites beat faster and stiffer if done one at a time in a vessel barely wider than the beater.

A raw egg that floats in water is not fresh.

For the face: Apply a raw yolk stirred with a little lemon juice. Allow to dry, then cover with the lightly beaten white. Remove in 30 minutes.

For the hair: Egg yolks beaten with champagne (or beer) make a great shampoo.

Moonshine eggs were so called because the moon is said to be made of cheese—they are a dish of lightly baked eggs, with grated cheese above and below.

For sunny-side-uppers whose eggs are always fried, some variants:

On thick slices of fried eggplant: garlic. Why not?
On a half grilled tomato stuffed with finely chopped mushrooms.
On a bed of puréed spinach mixed with snips of anchovy fillets.
In a baked potato whose insides have been scooped out, mashed with butter, cream, salt, pepper, and nutmeg, then replaced around the egg.

Soufflés

For lighthearted, light-fingered soufflé makers, here are some fillings. You fill in the basics . . .

Purée of raw shrimp, whole poached oysters (can be canned), sliced mushrooms.

Chopped cooked spinach, grated Parmesan, finely minced anchony fillets.

Puréed cooked kippers or finnan haddie, flavored with curry powder.

Chopped braised lettuce (use the outside leaves for this).

Puréed leftovers of fish . . . add a pinch of saffron or fennel.

And for sweet fillings, try these . . .

Apricots (can be canned, fresh are even better) cooked in syrup until just caramelizing, flavored with kirsch.

Vanilla cream, crushed macaroons, slivered almonds, flavored with rum.

Black cherries (canned or frozen), their juice reduced to syrup with some sugar or honey; flavored with cherry brandy.

Applesauce (cooked to evaporate excess liquid), grated lemon rind.

Tea (jasmine is divine!) infused in the milk used for the soufflé base.

SECTION IV

MENU IDEAS

In France the composition of a menu used to be as rigorous as the rules of grammar and syntax. Break these rules and one was no longer in the league of *haute cuisine*.

The Do's and Don'ts are in fact simple, and they make for a more agreeable meal as well as for a well-balanced diet. It is important, when creating a menu, not to include more than one farinaceous element in each course. Few cooks would serve potatoes and rice at the same sitting, but rice and lima beans would be an equal error. Care should also be taken to avoid repeating the elements of one course in another. Obviously carrots should not accompany the entree if it is to be preceded by carrot soup, and a starter that contains pastry or brioche cancels out pastry pies for dessert.

The subtlety of a delicately flavored dish should not be overwhelmed by pungence in a preceding dish.

It's fun to make attractive colors for each course so that the composition of each course balances, visually, like a total work of art. The way food smells is so important: the seductive fragrances of wine, herbs, and spices, like a woman's perfume, should be light and subtle. To be banished from the kitchen are odors of hot grease, burned meats and fats.

Plates for hot dishes, especially for those with egg and butter sauces that coagulate quickly, should be warmed: chilled plates are an extra luxury for iced and jellied dishes.

I have invented some rules of my own and defined an imaginary topography of "Northern" and "Southern" produce that induces Northern or Southern recipes. I find that each group works best with its own kind and that by selecting the ingredients of a dish from one group or another, rather than mixing them, I get far better results.

My Northern group includes dairy produce: cream, butter, and cow cheese (rather than goat cheese): herbs such as dill, tarragon, chervil, and chives: vegetables such as onions, shallots, beets, cauliflower, cabbages, most of the root vegetables, green salads, and endives. I include the tenderest meat good for grilling and roasting, firm-fleshed fish from icy waters.

For my Southern group I choose olive oil, herbs such as thyme, basil, marjoram, the savories, and oregano: the taste of anise, fennel, garlic, and saffron. I choose tomato, squash, fennel, eggplant, and artichoke. I list the stringier meats (as though the animals had been reared on dryer soil than in the North) that make tasty stews and ragouts. For fish I think of the softer-fleshed varieties and the rock fish that come from warmer seas. The smoky taste they get from a rich underwater diet makes them ideal for fish stews and soups.

Depending on what is in season and at what price, I cook Northern or Southern. Sure of the compatibility of my ingredients, I toss them into the pan or pot in greater or lesser degrees depending on my mood and the temperaments of my guests.

I also love to invent menus to suit my guests, rather the same way a designer creates an outfit with a certain woman in mind. I like to prepare food that will especially please certain people, accentuate a good mood, alleviate a bad one.

A menu should have a focus, should express the feelings and personality of its chef, and never be just a shuffling together of food. Light and rich ingredients should be blended with skill, throughout a menu, so that one can eat with gusto without desperately counting calories, without leaving the table with a groan of repletion. Finally, one must consider the total cost of a menu; sometimes it is best to go for broke on one glorious item and deck it out with inexpensive trappings. Sometimes it is best to view a week's menus together, figuring on cleverly used leftovers to fill the gaps in the budget caused by generous hospitality. Also, one should remember that "Time is Money" and count one's own time, or one's housekeeper's, as part of the expense of a meal. Although a fish like salmon is expensive, if one is to serve it at one meal, it is expedient to buy a large enough piece that, once cooked, can be adapted to other easy recipes such as kedgeree and *rissoles*.

Menu planning is easiest when the individual recipes are kept in file cards. This way the meal can be laid out in front of one and the cards interchanged until the perfect meal for the occasion is selected.

All Menu Recipes Are Presented in the Index

SUMMERY LUNCHES

Menu One

Verdura Pasta
Seafood Salad
Pineapple Sherbet

Menu Two

Tomatoes Vinaigrette (with fresh basil)
Chicken Suzanne
Russian Dressing
Granita di Limone

Menu Three

Potted Shrimp
Hot Chicken and Rice in Melon
Green Salad with Diced Celery and Fennel, with French Dressing
Blueberry Kissel

Menu Four

Poached Egg Soufflé
Seviche
Raw Spinach with Raw Sliced Mushrooms, with Vinaigrette Sauce
Tarte aux Pommes

Menu Five

Andalusian Gazpacho
Grilled Chicken on Watercress Salad
Grated Zucchini
Devil Kisses

Menu Six

Crab Meat Soufflé
Boeuf-à-la-Mode
Cucumber Mousse
Porto Fruit Jelly

WINTRY LUNCHES

Menu One

Oyster Stew
Orange, Onion, Avocado Salad
Cheese, Crackers, Winter Pears

Menu Two

Black-Gold Linguine
Super Salad
Fresh Coconut Pudding, Caramel Sauce

Menu Three

Cucumber and Carrot Soup
Three-Pepper Chicken
Fennel and Endive Salad
Ginger Loaf, Lemon Sauce

Menu Four

Blue Cheese Charlotte
Brandy-Wine Scallops
Raw Spinach and Grated Carrot Salad with Beet Dressing for Green
Salads
Vanilla Ice Cream with Coffee Sauce

Menu Five

Consommé, Oeufs Pochés
Marion's Fish Dish
Bread Pudding Grand Marnier

Menu Six

Consommé with Okra New Orleans
Veal-Stuffed Lemon
Chocolate Ice-Cream

SUMMERY DINNERS

Menu One

Eggs Considine
Cold Salmon with Dill Mayonnaise
Cold Sherry Soufflé

Menu Two

Chilled Avocado Soup
Duck in Orange Aspic
Peppermint Bavarian Cream

Menu Three

Pernod Soup
Roast Quail Henriette
Braised Lettuce
Cold Lemon Soufflé

Menu Four

Hot Stuffed Artichokes
Marinated Loin of Pork
Marmalade Tart

Menu Five

Herring Salad
Tunisian Lamb Stew
Summer Squash from Provence
Raspberry Tart

Menu Six

Lemon Caviar
Dominican Crabmeat Pie
Boiled Potatoes or Plain Boiled Rice
Celery Root Rémoulade
Glorious Floating Island

WINTRY DINNERS

Menu One

Mussel Soup
Butcher's Tenderloin, Sauce Bordelaise
Potatoes à la Couvrey
Hot Fruit Salad

Menu Two

Chicken Giblet Soup with Pickles
Striped Bass
Oriental Salad
Marmalade Soufflé with Foamy Sauce

Menu Three

Raw Spinach Soup
Lotte Lenya's Meat Loaf
René Verdon's Gratinéed Spinach
Whole-Tree Ice Cream

Menu Four

Salted Fresh Salmon
Choucroute Garnie
Apples and Potatoes
Cold Sherry Soufflé

Menu Five

Fonds d'Artichauts Pauline Trigère
Chicken Marinada
Panache
Pears in Wine

Menu Six

Rissoles of Foie Gras
Cold Salmon with Dill Mayonnaise
Zucchini Salad
Soufflé de Pamplemousse

FAST FOOD

Starters

Tomatoes Vinaigrette
Lemon Caviar
Sardines in Vine Leaves
Seviche of Bay Scallops
Grated Zucchini
Chilled Avocado Soup
Claret Consommé
Hot Soup Speeder
Cold Soup Mixer
Green Bean Soup

Eggs

Oeufs Mollets Carême
Oeufs Mollets Niçoise
Oeufs Mollets with Seafood

Fish

Fried Bass Fillets
Bay Scallops in Cream
Fillets of Sole

Poultry

Eleven-Minute Chicken Breast Sauté
Grilled Chicken Legs and Wings
Chicken Paillarde

Meat

Butcher's Tenderloin, Bordelaise Sauce
Overnight Steak
Scaloppine di Vitello al Marsala

Vegetables, Salads

Grated Zucchini
Candied Tomatoes
Fennel and Endive Salad
Sautéed Mushrooms and Snow Peas

Desserts

Strawberries in Orange Juice
Orange and Mint Salad
Easy Blender Ice Cream
Doing the Ice-Cream Thing

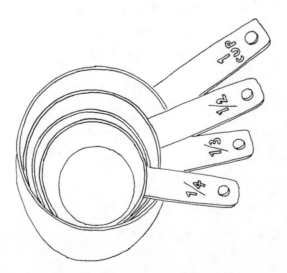

COLD BUFFET SELECTIONS

Cucumber Mousse
Cold Egg Rolls with Ham Mousse
Egg Mousse
Vegetable Salad
Potato Salad
Rice, Parsley, and Carrot Salad
Armand Salad
Salad Coronado
Zucchini Salad
Oriental Salad
Seafood Salad
Bulgur Salad
Salted Fresh Salmon
Jellied Whitefish or Salmon
Cold Salmon with Dill Mayonnaise
Barquettes de Homard Froid Matignon
Cold Curried Chicken and Melon in Melon Shell
Duck in Orange Aspic
Vitello Tonnato
Veal and Ham Pâté
Cold Green Meat Loaf
Corned Mutton Ham, Cold
Boeuf à la Mode

HOT BUFFET SELECTIONS

Green Chili and Cheese Flan
Lasagne Verde for Sixty
Dominican Crab Meat Pie
Clam Pie
Fish Stew
Creole Gumbo
Poulet à l'Estragon
Chicken Scavullo
Strasbourg Chicken Roll
Hot Chicken with Rice in Melon
Pollo à la Chilindrón
Grilled Chicken Legs and Wings
Pastel de Choclo
Beef Stew
Pot Roast
Flemish Beer Stew
Meat Loaf
Potée Lorraine
Lamb and Green Chili Stew
Tunisian Lamb Stew

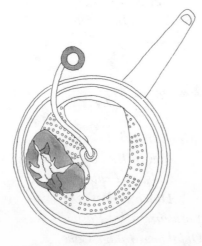

BUFFET DESSERT SELECTIONS

Marron Icebox Cake
Toffee Flan
Raspberry Tart
Marmalade Tart
Rich Chocolate Cake
My Mother's Chocolate Cake
Cold Lemon Soufflé
Oklahoma Fudge Cake
Almond and Walnut Icebox Cake
Boston Cream Pie
Bob Hope's Favorite Lemon Pie
New York State Flat Apple Pie

PICNIC FARE AND FINGER FOODS

To Serve in Bowls with Toast or Crackers

Potted Shrimp
Honey-Nut Butter
Veal and Ham Pâté

Bakery Suggestions

Mexican Fried Cakes
Indian Bread
Cranberry Fritters
Dutch Babies
Yorkshire Mint Pasties
Oklahoma Fudge Cake
"I Make-It-Every-Weekend" Cake

Spread for Sandwiches

Savory Butters

To Pack or Serve with Toothpicks

Sardines in Vine Leaves
Tomatoes and Feta Cheese
Asparagus Tips with Prosciutto
Stuffed Grape Leaves
Potato Salad
Cold Roast Chicken
Cold Green Meat Loaf
Corned Mutton-Ham
Boeuf-à-la-Mode

And to Drink

Wine Cup

A MEAL FOR HUNGRY KIDS

Cream of Potato Soup
Turkey with Apricots
Stuffed Mushrooms
Burnt Cream or Easy Crème Brûlée

A SEXY MIDNIGHT SUPPER
FOR TWO

Caviar Pie
Breasts of Partridge Sauté
Lettuce and Endive Salad with Beet Dressing
Champagne Mousse

BARBECUE SELECTIONS

Broiled Squabs
Barbecued Squab or Chicken
Smoke-Roasted Chicken
Grilled Chicken Legs and Wings
Charcoal Steak and Corn on the Cob
Broiled Marinated Flank Steak
Ben Buckner's Sauce for Steak
Roast Leg of Lamb and Fireplace Vegetables
Shashlik Caucasian
Gigot à la Ficelle
Barbecued Fish
Grilled Pig's Feet

A French Menu

Oeufs Mollets with Seafood
Poulet à l'Estragon
Soyer's Potatoes
Braised Lettuce
Tarte aux Raisins

A Spanish Menu

Sardines in White Wine
Langosta con Pollo Catalana
Strawberries in Orange Juice

A Moroccan Menu

Tomatoes Vinaigrette
Moroccan Pigeon Pie
Moroccan Marmalade with Rose Water

An Italian Menu

Green-on-Green Pasta à la Montresor
Striped Bass, Pesto Sauce
Pommes Siciliennes
Zucchini in Lemon
Stuffed Peaches

An English Menu

Oyster Soup
Potted Shrimp with Toast
Cumberland Chicken
Baked Onions
Cabbage and Potato Hash
Summer Pudding

INDEX

Beard, Peter, 251
Béarnaise Sauce, 267
　Mint, for Lamb, 267
Béchamel Sauce (Besciamella), 56–57,
　　265
Beef
　Boeuf à la Mode, 105–6
　Boiled, with Mustard Sauce, 212–13
　and Chicken, Corn Pie with (Pastel de
　　　Choclo), 200
　Cooked on a String, 33–34
　Filet of, Sauce Poivrade (Filet de
　　　Boeuf Poivrade), 211–12
　Olives, 210–11
　Roast with Anchovies, 75
　Sliced, and Mayonnaise, 131
　Stew, Carmen's, 59
　See also Meat main courses; names of
　　　cuts of beef
Beene, Geoffrey, 141, 189
Beer Stew, Flemish, 76
Beet Dressing for Green Salad, 264
Bellissimo Bellini, 7
Ben Buckner's Sauce for Steak, 256–57
Bergé, Pierre, 87–88
Berra, Yogi, 157
Besciamella (Béchamel Sauce), 56–57,
　　265
Birnbaum, Glen, 148–49
Biscuits, Leftover, 101
Black Bread, Eggs with, 117
Black-Gold Linguine, 54–55
Black Radishes, 18
Blass, Bill, 162
Blender Hollandaise Sauce, 266
Blini with Smoked Salmon, 117–18
Bloomingdale, Betsy, 247–48
Blueberry
　Ice-Cream Pie, 168–69
　Kissel, 11
Blue Cheese Charlottes, 182
Bluefish, Nantucket, 32
Boar, Sweet-and-Sour, 45
　Sauce for, 46
Bob Hope's Favorite Lemon Pie, 171
Boeuf à la Ficelle (Beef Cooked on a
　　　String), 33–34
Boeuf à la Mode, 105–6
　culinary tip for, 279
Boiled Beef with Mustard Sauce, 212–13
Bordelaise Sauce, for Rib Steaks, 20–21
Boston Cream Pie, 252–53
Bouché, Denise, 67, 258
Bouché, René, 67
Boxer, Lady Arabella, 49

Bradshaw, George, 122, 144, 242–43,
　　271, 272
Braised Endives, 95
Braised Lettuce, 224–25
Braised Loin of Veal with Kidneys
　　　(Rognonnade de Veau), 29
Brandy
　Sauce, 15
　-Wine Scallops, 127–28
Bread
　Black, Eggs with, 117
　Indian, 66
　Irish Buttermilk, 99–100
　Leftover, 101
　Saffron, 98–99
Bread Pudding with Grand Marnier,
　　251–52
Breakfast/Brunch recipes, 115–23
　Basque Omelette, 120–21
　Blini with Smoked Salmon, 117–18
　Crab Meat in a Skillet, 122
　Dried Fruits Olympus, 123
　Eggs with Black Bread, 117
　Kedgeree, 119
　Mocha Brunch Drink, 118
　Off-with-a-Bang, 29
　Potato Knishes without Dough, 121
　Sour-Cream Coffeecake, 120
　for Two, 121–22
　Yogurt, 119
Breasts of Partridge Sauté, 201–2
Broiled Marinated Flank Steak, 209
Broiled Squabs on Toast, 202
Broth, Chicken
　Basic, 135
　Double, 135
Brown, Helen Gurley, 177–78
Brown-Butter Sauce, Salmon Cutlets
　　　with, 142–43
Bruce, Evangeline, 162–63
Buckley, Pat, 133–34
Buffet menu ideas
　cold, 296
　dessert, 298
　hot, 297
Bulgur Salad, 86
Buñuelos (Mexican Fritters), 16
Burden, Amanda, 149, 161, 186
Burgundy, Ox Tongue with, 215
Burnett, Carol, 154
Burnt Cream, or Easy Crème Brûlée, 254
Butter
　Anchovy, Crab Meat, or Lobster, 71
　Brown-Butter Sauce, Salmon Cutlets
　　　with, 142–43

East Hampton Fish Stew, 59
East India Salad, 25
Eastman, Monique, 222
Easy Blender Ice Cream—a Diet
        Dessert, 171–72
Edge, David, 21
Egg(s), 107–10
    Basque Omelette, 120–21
    with Black Bread, 117
    Cold Picnic Omelette, 132
    Considine, 179
    culinary tips for, 282–83
    Hide-and-Seek, 108–9
    Leftover Whites, 101
    Lucchese, 109
    Mousse, 43–44
    Normandy, 108
    Oeufs Mollets Carême, 110
    Oeufs Mollets Niçoise, 110
    Oeufs Mollets with Seafood, 110
    Poached, Chilled Consommé with
        (Consommé Oeufs Pochés), 188–
        89
    Poached, with Sauce Verte, 180–81
    Poached, in Soufflé, 24–25OPotted,
        and Sardines, 110
    Salad with Asparagus, 110
Eggplant
    Casserole (Imam Bayildi), 225–26
    and Green Bean Casserole, 161
    Stuffed with Anchovies, 97–98
Egg Rolls, Cold, with Ham Mousse, 274
Eisenhower, Mrs. Dwight D., 149–50
Elderberry-Blossom Pancakes, 8
Eleven-Minute Chicken Breast Sauté,
        152
Emmerich, André, 118
Endive(s)
    Braised, 95
    and Fennel Salad, 237
    Leeks, and Celery, 18
    and Onions, Three-Pepper Chicken
        with, 89
Erté (artist-designer), 64
Ertegun, Mica, 225–26
Escalope Zingara (Veal Scallops
        Zingara), 220–21

Face Cream, Giorgio's Grandmother's, 83
Fast food menu ideas, 294–95
Felici, Argia, 56
Fennel
    and Dill Sauce, 259
    and Endive Salad, 237
Feta Cheese, Tomatoes with, 73

Fettuccine
    Cigli Belli de la Minnelli, 232–33
    Portable, 69–70
Fig Dessert, 84
Filet of Beef, Sauce Poivrade (Filet de
        Boeuf Poivrade), 211–12
Filet Steaks Alexandra (Tournedos
        Alexandra), 214–15
Fillets of Haddock Francesco, 146
Fillets of Sole, see Sole
Finger foods menu ideas, 298–99
Fish main courses, 140–46, 190–97
    Baked Striped Bass, 192
    Barquettes de Homard Froid
        Matignon (Salad of Zucchini
        Stuffed with Lobster), 194–95
    Bay Scallops in Cream, 193–94
    Chowder, New England, 139
    Clam Pie, 144
    Cold Salmon with Dill Mayonnaise,
        190–91
    Côtelettes de Saumon Pojarski (Salmon
        Cutlets with Brown-Butter
        Sauce), 142–43
    Crab Meat Kiev, 145
    Crab Meat Soufflé, 141
    Darnes de Poisson à la Crème,
        Katharine (Fish Steaks Simmered
        with Cream and Mushrooms),
        141–42
    Dominican Crab Meat Pie, 192–93
    East Hampton Stew, 59
    Fillets of Haddock Francesco, 146
    Fried Bass Fillets, 143–44
    Langosta con Pollo Catalana (Lobster
        and Chicken Catalana), 195–96
    Marion's Fish Dish, 143
    Old English Sauce for, 260
    Poached, Sauces for, 259–60
    Red Snapper Ring, 145–46
    Salt-Air, 32
    Scallops for Lester Persky, 196–97
    Soup, 103
    Stock, 14
    Very Easy Dish, A, 196
    See also names of fish
Fitzgerald, Geraldine, 226
Flageolets and Caviar, 182
Flank Steak, Broiled Marinated, 209
Flans
    Green Chili and Cheese, 163–64
    Toffee, 44
Flemish Beer Stew, 76
Flexner, Marion W., 138, 143–44, 170,
        256–57, 259–60

Rognonnade de Veau (Braised Loin of
Veal with Kidneys), 29
Rosemary Butter, Chicken Paillarde
with, 148–49
Rosenberg, Harold, 132
Rose Water, Moroccan Marmalade with, 5
Rousseau, Theodore, 195–96
Russian Dressing, 263
Ryan, Mrs. John Barry, III, 31
Rykiel, Sonia, 244–45

Saffron
Apples with Almond Cream, 97
Bread, 98–99
Saint, Clara, 88
Saint Laurent, Yves, 87, 88, 89
Salad dressings, *see* Sauces; names of
dressings
Salads, 236–40
Armand, 239
Bulgur, 86
Citrus, for a Picnic, 33
Coronado, 275
Cucumber, 63–64
Curried Rice, 85–86
Green, Beet Dressing for, 264
East India, 25
Egg with Asparagus, 110
Fennel and Endive, 237
Fruit, Dressing Bruxelles for, 263–64
Green, 41
Hot Fruit, 41
Lily's Oriental, 61
Orange and Mint, 37–38
Orange, Onion, and Avocado, 238
Potato, 237
Rice, Parsley, and Carrot, 237–38
Seafood, 78
Super, 239–40
Tomato, 38
Watercress, Grilled Chicken on, 50
of Zucchini Stuffed with Lobster
(Barquettes de Homard Froid
Matignon), 194–95
Salmis of Chicken, 276
Salmon
Cold, with Dill Mayonnaise, 190–91
Cornucopias, 181
Cutlets with Brown-Butter Sauce,
142–43
Jellied, 184
Marinated, 85
Salted Fresh, 178
Smoked, Blini with, 117–18
Salt-Air Fish, 32

Salted Fresh Salmon, 178
Sandwiches
Hot Spanish, 273–74
Resandwich, 35
Spreads for a Picnic, 71
San Faustino, Genevieve di, 186–87
Sant'Angelo, Giorgio, 80–81, 83
Sardines
and Eggs, Potted, 110
in Vine Leaves, 70
in White Wine, 79
Sargent, John Singer, 43
Sarmi, Fernando, 235, 273
Sarris, Andrew, 73–74
Sassoon, Vidal, 119
Sauces, 256–65
Aioli (Garlic Mayonnaise), 262
Béarnaise, 267
Béchamel, 56–57, 265
Beet Dressing for Green Salads, 264
Blender Hollandaise, 266
Bordelaise, for Rib Steaks, 20–21
Brown-Butter, Salmon Cutlets with,
142–43
Caper, 259
Caramel, Fresh Coconut Pudding
with, 247–48
Chutney, for Cold Cuts, 257
Coffee, for Coffee Ice Cream, 250
Cranberry Cumberland, 48
Cumberland, Smithfield Ham with,
272
Curry, Cold Chicken with Melon in,
42
Dill and Fennel, 259
Drambuie or Brandy, 15
Foamy, Marmalade Soufflé with, 244
French Dressing (A Vinaigrette
Sauce), 260
Fruit Salad Dressing Bruxelles, 263–
64
Herbed Mayonnaise, 262
Hollandaise, 266
Horseradish, 258
Hungarian, for Vegetables, 265–66
Lemon, 10
Liver, Spaghetti with, 234–35
Madeira, 199
Marchand de Vin, 21
Mayonnaise, 261
Mint Béarnaise for Lamb, 267
Mornay (Creamy Cheese Sauce), 265
Mousseline, 267
Mustard, Boiled Beef with, 212–13
Mustard, for Cold Cuts, 257